ASTROLOGICAL ASPECTS

Photo: Tony Milner

ASTROLOGICAL ASPECTS

A Process-Oriented Approach

Leyla Rael
Dane Rudhyar

Artwork by Tony Milner

AURORA PRESS

P.O. Box 573   Santa Fe, N.M. 87504

Aurora Press, Inc.
P.O. Box 573
Santa Fe, N.M. 87504
Printed in the United States of America

Library of Congress Cataloging in Publication Data

Rael, Leyla, 1948-
   Astrological aspects.

   Bibliography: p.
   Includes index.
   1. Astrology.   I. Rudhyar, Dane, 1895-
II. Title.
BF1708.1.R33   133.5   80-18617
ISBN 0-943358-00-0

To Barbara Somerfield
and Henry Weingarten
in warm appreciation
and friendship

LR and DR

by Dane Rudhyar

Philosophy and Literature:

Beyond Individualism
Culture, Crisis and Creativity
Directives for New Life
Fire Out of the Stone
Occult Preparations for a New Age
Of Vibrancy and Peace
Paths to the Fire
* The Planetarization of Consciousness
Rania
Rebirth of Hindu Music
Return from No Return
The Rhythm of Human Fulfillment
We Can Begin Again—Together
White Thunder

Astrology and Psychology:

The Astrological Houses
* Astrological Insights Into the Spiritual Life
An Astrological Mandala
Astrological Signs
An Astrological Study of Psychological Complexes
Astrological Timing
* An Astrological Triptych
Astrology and the Modern Psyche
The Astrology of America's Destiny
The Astrology of Personality
Astrology of Transformation
From Humanistic to Transpersonal Astrology
* Galactic Dimension of Astrology
The Lunation Cycle
New Mansions for New Men
* Person-Centered Astrology
The Practice of Astrology

* Indicates a title published by AURORA

Contents

Preface
by Dane Rudhyar

After the publication in 1946 of the first version of the book now known in its expanded form as *The Lunation Cycle*, I had intended to write a book on astrological aspects. I had already outlined the sequence of the chapters when Marc Jones, who was then editor of the books on astrology published by McKay in Philadelphia, advised me that the publisher had decided to stop dealing with occultism and astrology and was disposing of his stock on hand. As, at that time, I could not find any American or English publisher interested in my writings, I gave up the project I had in mind. I nevertheless wrote series of articles dealing with aspects in a couple of astrological magazines.

Recently, having filed and indexed most of the many articles I had written since 1933—when I began to write for Paul Clancy's new magazine American Astrology—Leyla mentioned to me some of these old articles on aspects. As she herself had successfully developed in a class she had just given in San Franciso, an approach to the subject which I had only barely suggested, she thought that her teachings, which had aroused a warm response in her students, could be significantly combined with my old articles, and this might produce a valuable book for people eager to have a practical basis for the interpretation of interplanetary aspects.

I have always taken the approach that no aspect between two celestial bodies moving at different speeds—as they all do—could be truly understood unless it was considered a particular phase of the cyclic process established by successive conjunctions of the two bodies. The prototype of such *cycles of relationship* is the lunation cycle extending from new moon to new moon; but any two planets considered as a pair produce such a kind of cycle. The actual meaning of the cyclic series of aspects, from conjunction to conjunction, depends on the character of the two related planets, but the *basic pattern* of all such cycles has the same abstract, or rather 'archetypal', character. If we understand the archetypal pattern of *the* cycle—that is, of any cycle of relationship between two interacting entities—we have in mind an instrument of universal validity. It can be applied at any level of existence and consciousness. It provides a remarkably useful tool for the understanding of the life-processes whose development is the warp and woof of all series of events. We may think these events unrelated, as mere happenings, yet they are in fact outer symptoms of the manner in which a cyclic series of phases unfolds within a process that has a definite beginning, culmination and end. Any phase of that process can significantly be referred to the original impulse that started the process. It can also be understood in the light of the manner in which the process culminates, and of the way in which it is drawn to an inevitable end, out of which a new beginning may once more occur.

What I have just outlined in an abstract way will be found expressed in a multiplicity of concrete details in this book. By far the major portion of it has been actually written by Leyla who inspired the particular sequence of developments in a few chapters. My main contributions have been the chapters on the less familiar aspects and rectangular and triangular configurations in horoscopes, though evidently the basic approach is always in line with the type of astrological thinking I have used during the last 45 or more years. This is assuredly not the only legitimate way of *thinking astrologically;* and the strictly empirical and event-oriented approach remains valid for those who can only operate in terms of external occurrences and/or neatly classified psychological characteristics and types. But today, especially among the searching and restless youth wary of fashionable solutions and especially of traditional recipes, the demand for a deeper kind of understanding is still constantly increasing in intensity.

I feel that this book will fill an important place in the spectrum of astrological thinking and its study should amply repay the reader. Leyla has given to it much time and has, I believe, carefully and effectively nurtured its development, which is consistent and thorough. I trust it will be read in the same attitude of concentrated attention and openness to ever expanding mental vistas.

Leyla and I wish to thank our friend and assistant, Sandra Maitri, for going over the manuscript and offering valuable editorial suggestions. The example birth-charts found in Appendix I have been calculated with Campanus house cusps, and we also thank Nicki Michaels for assuring their accuracy by calculating them on her computer. We also extend our thanks to Tony Milner who has artfully calligraphed these example horoscopes.

D. R.
Palo Alto
March 23, 1979

1.

A Process-Oriented Approach to Astrology, Chart Interpretation, and Aspects

Astrology as it is taught and practiced today has by and large lost its sense of process. It deals primarily with traditionally established definitions and descriptions, keywords and categories. A birth-chart is drawn on paper, framed perhaps, and looked at as an objective thing, set once and for all with an essentially static character. Whatever changes occur over the span of a person's life are referred back to various, separately and statically defined factors in his or her horoscope.

Yet astrology is based on celestial *motion*, and the human experience of the sky is one of unceasing *change*. Every celestial entity is in a state of perpetual motion, and celestial motions are also regular and periodical. Astrology should therefore deal with the dynamism of existence. Because of the regularity of the changes it records and interprets, it should be considered a study of the *processes* of existence.

A process is nothing more nor less than an ordered sequence of changes. It starts at some more or less well-defined beginning, unfolds in time through a series of changes, steps or phases, eventually reaching some kind of conclusion on the basis of which a new process proceeds. The alternation of days and nights, the seasonal cycle of the year, the slow shifting of the Earth's polar axis in relation to the 'fixed' stars: all are processes deeply affecting human existence—which is itself a process operating individually in the chronological unfoldment of the human life-span (with all its implications of biological and psychological growth) and collectively in terms of long-range cultural and historical developments. Astrology merely broadens, conceptualizes, generalizes and codifies into principles applicable to human development, the experience of such processes as seasonal changes and the periodic change from light to dark, which are facts of common human experience. It also extends this concept of process to the periodic relationships between moving planets—indeed between everything in the sky and everything else.

Because this sense of process is essentially missing from astrological thinking today, the aim of this book is to reawaken in astrologers' minds the realization that astrology does indeed deal with constant and rhythmic, dynamic celestial motions rather than with merely static factors and categories. Therefore, when interpreting birth-charts and applying astrology to matters of human development and concern, a sense of process and of the structure of celestial cycles must underlie the astrologer's efforts.

It is true that astrologers study and interpret what are called progressions and transits. When such notions as dynamic process, ordered change and unfoldment in time are mentioned, most astrologers immediately think of these two techniques. Yet progressions and transits deal with time, motion and change only in an overt, obvious way. Even they, however, are not interpreted by most astrologers in terms of continuing processes, i.e., in terms of real, existential motions or changes—human or celestial—and thus not in terms of their fundamental, holistic nature and meaning.

Nevertheless, basic in astrological thinking and interpretation should be the feeling that every factor and technique used in astrology—zodiacal signs, houses, planets, aspects as well as progressions and transits—can only be fully understood in terms of whole processes of change. The application of the rhythms of celestial motion to corresponding developments in the lives of human beings can never be fully significant and revealing if the astrologer does not realize that human experience acquires its essential meaning when studied in terms of personal and collective unfoldment. Process is at the very root of human experience and development, because human life is primarily the working out of a complex set of relation-ships between the components of the total personality and between a person and all other persons or objects and events encountered as the life process which began at birth unfolds its potentialities.

To speak of relationship is also to speak of what in astrology are called *aspects*. This book is primarily about astrological aspects. It is also a book about chart interpretation. And it is also a book about *life*-interpretation, that is, how to use birth-charts and astrological thinking to see and understand the unfoldment of dynamic, pur-poseful processes in people's lives, or rather, how to see people's lives *as* the unfoldment of dynamic, purposeful processes—*their* pro-cesses, their *dharma*, destiny or truth-of-being. Dharma, however, does not refer merely to a state to be achieved, but to a process to be lived, step by step.

This process, which must be lived and acted out step by step over the span of a person's life, is nevertheless *implied* in the spatial organization of the birth-chart, in the aspects and aspect-patterns linking the planets—themselves representing dynamic centers or principles of activities and functions. Aspects in astrological charts should be understood as injunctions—*instructions* telling us how the activities or functions represented by two planets should be related to one another in order to fulfill what is needed at a particular phase of the whole cycle during which the two planets relate to one an-other in all possible ways. In other words, aspects tell us what to do with what is represented by two planets relating to one another in an especially significant way; the particular significance of the aspect or interplanetary relationship derives from the place this phase-relationship occupies in the two planets' overall cycle with one another.

Conversely, if we are experiencing in our life a certain situation which we can identify as being symbolized by two planets, the natal aspect or relationship between those two planets can help us under-stand why—for what productive purpose—we must deal with such circumstances. Implied also is the best way for us to meet them. Even if what we face is not immediately apparent in our birth-chart, if we understand the principles of process underlying aspects, we will be better able to understand situations as parts or phases of our lives as wholes, and we will be better able to deal with them (or realize how we might have dealt with them) in conscious, creative ways.

It is to be hoped that a practical, specific understanding of astrological aspects will become clear in concrete ways as we proceed with the more or less didactic material which will make up the bulk of this book. This book, which talks a great deal about process, is itself a process. It needs to unfold gradually in the reader's mind, step by step, as any ordered process of growth or development. How could a book about principles of process do otherwise than to itself unfold step by step, each step building upon the preceding ones? Please do read it that way.

But now, back to the matter at hand. We have made a rather serious allegation: Astrology has lost its sense of process. Perhaps we should first inquire as to how and why before suggesting how we believe it should be restored and reincorporated into astrological thinking to meet the needs of modern men and women.

HOW ASTROLOGY LOST ITS SENSE OF PROCESS

When cycles in time became circles in space, astrologers became so involved with the circles that they forgot about the cycles of which the circles were merely representations or symbols.

Any experience of time is difficult to measure or to define accurately. Space (although philosophically just as 'abstract') is much easier to deal with in a practical or conceptual way, especially when one is dealing with a relatively small and manageable space such as one can 'trap' on a clay tablet or piece of paper—space that stands still and doesn't squirm around when one puts a ruler or compass to it in order to divide it up into even more manageable segments.

Time and especially time-measurements, which are all derived from celestial motions, are not as well-behaved and manageable as that. Everything in the heavens is in constant motion, moving in relation to everything else. Even the so-called 'fixed stars' are not actually fixed—they merely appear to remain in the same patterns with reference to one another. They also move, quite slowly but significantly, in relation to the vernal equinox point and the seasonal cycle between the Sun and the Earth. Moreover, although celestial motions map out many cycles—various orders of time, let us say, such as the year or the day—and others like the sidereal cycle of the Moon, the synodic cycle between the Sun and Moon—the sidereal cycles of the planets, synodic cycles between planets, etc.—none of these time-measurements can be precisely expressed in terms of any of the others. There is always some ungraceful, inelegant shortfall or leftover whenever we try to equate some number of one kind of celestial cycle with exactly another, longer cycle. For example, 365¼, rather than exactly 365 days make up a year. There is therefore always some time 'unaccounted for', as it were, and as smaller cycles go into but never exactly make up larger cycles, shortfall or leftover time piles up. It intrudes itself in a spiralic, unmanageable way. In order to make time less squirmy and more manageable, calendars—and astrology per se—were devised.

Calendars actually 'trap' time in space to handle it more easily. They project time onto spaces which can then be more easily measured, divided up and meted out to appropriate activities than the time-experience when not projected onto a particular space. Clocks (especially the now old-fashioned kind with face and hands more than the new-fangled electronic, digital ones) are a similar, although later and more ambitious because mechanical, projection of time onto space.

Long before the kind of clocks and calendars we have now, astrology was born as a means to provide a spatial method of measuring time—an objective method. The creative, change- and growth-producing flow of time was referred by astrologers and early calendar makers to the ordered motions of celestial dots and discs of light. The first astrologies were the first calendars and vice versa. They spatialized time for appropriate tribal use just as later time was recorded and standardized for every person's individual use by means of clocks and calendars which are synchronized to celestial motions. To interpret and make time-experience concrete by space-patterns became the function of astrology, in the same way in which to interpret and make concrete the properties of numbers was the function of geometry—and even today geometrical models are made to make intricate algebraic functions more concretely intelligible.

A whole of time-experience—a complete cycle such as a year or a day, a lunar or planetary sidereal cycle or a synodic cycle between two celestial bodies—thus came to be projected into space, and it took the form of a circumference: the serpent swallowing its own tail of archaic symbolism, less exaltedly but more ubiquitously, the circle. The circle came to stand as the symbol for wholeness—wholeness in space as a projection of less-easily-defined and worked with wholeness in time. The advantage of working with a circle was that the circle could be visually grasped as a whole in one glance; a cycle unfolded at its own rate over time and could neither be experienced all at once nor speeded up or slowed down. Circles could also be divided into any number of segments or arcs. And while actual cycles—both natural cycles on Earth and celestial cycles—are also divided into phases, they are divided into more or less set numbers of phases.

In any cyclic experience there are particularly significant moments or turning points. These mark out the phases whereby cycles develop. It seems quite evident that the concepts of the signs of the zodiac, the houses of the horoscope and astrological aspects as divisions or segments of a whole circle originated in the recognition of such especially important moments when something always seemed to happen that would give a vital direction to the sequence of events developing throughout the complete cycle being considered. Quite obviously, the beginning of vegetation in the spring and the fall of leaves following the harvest stood out in the agricultural civilizations of Mesopotamia and other temperate regions as high-points in the basic seasonal cycle of the year. Likewise, sunrise, noon and sunset were selected as similarly basic moments in the full day-and-night cycle leading—together with a mysterious point opposite noon in the cycle of the day—to the basic quadrature of all astrological charts and concepts.

A similar and even more graphic or geometrical fourfold cyclic pattern was related to the phases of the Moon during the month. It seems quite plain to us that the observation and recording of lunar phases led to the rational and geometrical concepts of astrological aspects. The three basic aspects of archaic astrology are thus likely to have been the conjunctions (New Moon), opposition (Full Moon) and square (First and Last Quarters). These are aspects born of the experience of time, and, from what we know of archaic geometry even as late as Pythagoras, the figure of the square, which the four-fold time-experiences of day, year and synodic month all inferred when projected as space-patterns, must have been, together with the circle on which the square was projected, the basic measurements of space.

The astrological aspect called trine, however, does not seem to have come out of any primary sense of time-division. If we divide a circle into three arcs and inscribe the geometrical figure of a triangle in it by connecting the points defining the arcs, we would not be following a pattern suggested by the flow of natural processes in the biosphere. Neither can an essential threefoldness be inferred from observing any celestial cycles. If we think of dividing a cycle into three parts, we do so as a result of being able to separate the *concept* of a process from all our experiences of processes—our experiences of processes in nature displaying always an essentially two- or fourfold structure.

Herein lies the rub between circle and cycle, space-projection and time-experience, geometry and process. With the trine, the danger of astrology losing its sense of process arises. But so also comes into play the possibility of astrology becoming truly a key to understanding the mysteries of man and the universe!

When we speak about a trine, we are not specifically or exclusively referring to the astrological aspect we use today, but more generally to astrological notions of three-fold linking not based on time-experience and process, but on space-projection, geometry and concept. In other words, when triangulation appears in astrological thinking, it means that a shift in emphasis has occurred. The change is from emphasis on experience to emphasis on abstraction from experience, from cycle to circle.

We see the same nexus being reached in terms of the zodiac, when the time-experience of the seasons became embodied, as it were, in a geometrical design. In nature, unfoldment is paramount and the process of change is step by step, although some steps may be seemingly large or sudden. When the seasons unfold in time, what is important is the relationship of each sign (or solar 'month') to the signs preceding and succeeding it—thus, the 30° aspect semi-sextile, which, as we will see in the next chapter, forms the foundation for a time-approach to astrological aspects. But neither the 30° aspect nor the relationship of each zodiacal sign to its two adjacent ones is or has been for a long time as significant in astrology as, say, the relationship of opposite signs, signs at the four arms of crosses or squares, or signs at the three points of equilateral triangles inscribed in the zodiacal circle.

That the zodiac has come to be considered more of a circle than a cycle even though its very basis is time-experience should be obvious. Otherwise, how could we refer to something like 'Mars in Virgo'? In a very curious, Alice-in-Wonderland way from the time-experience point of view, such phrases make the same kind of sense as saying it is March, but my typewriter is in September. Astronomically, it is like saying something more to the effect of it is March, but Mars is where the Sun was last September and will be this coming September. But why should the particular section of the sky the Sun crosses in September carry September's qualities and somehow transfer them to or through Mars when the Sun is not there and it is in fact spring? We have always found it puzzling that astrologers have not considered the way the zodiac is used to be more mysterious, or at least have not generally asked deep and probing questions about it.

Such phrases as 'Mars in Virgo' and its attendant, above-mentioned conundrums make sense if we understand that as the human capacity for abstraction and conceptualization, and therefore astrology and the zodiac, developed, the cycle of the seasons was projected as a circle in space. This gave rise to the significance of the cardinal, fixed and mutable crosses, and the earth, air, fire and water triangles, which developed as significant symbols in their own right. However, as the 'timeward' flow of zodiacal signs was 'interrupted' and, as it were, reshuffled by geometric inscription and linking, the signs became increasingly thought of as separate entities, eventually becoming in most people's minds little more than twelve boxes or categories into which fall a variety of characterizations and personality traits—these often having little if anything to do with natural processes such as the unfoldment of the seasons or the span of a human life, but gaining far more of what are attributed as their meanings from geometric, particularly triangular, linking with other signs.[1]

Of course, it will be asserted that from a sidereal point of view the zodiac arose as a frame of reference associated with the constellations, which provided reference areas for celestial motions in the heavens where nothing else stood relatively still long enough to be used as such a framework. This may be so—at least in part and in some areas of the world—but it would also appear that even before the constellations were 'fixed' as definite celestial entities, the *process* of heliacal and achronycal rising and setting of certain brilliant stars, along with seasonal changes, played a significant role in astronomical understanding.[2] Moreover, whether the zodiac is considered in its tropical or sidereal aspect, it is always divided into 360 degrees, even though the Sun appears to move a little over 365 times around the Earth before returning to its starting point—be that the vernal equinox or a point in relation to fixed stars. The number 360 is thus a geometrical rationalization or conceptualization of the experience of change—i.e., of time.

In any case, an in-depth discussion of zodiacal development is beyond our intent here. Our main point at the moment is that whether one approaches the zodiac from a sidereal or seasonal point of view, the cycle/circle, experience/concept, time/space issues remain the same: what was for the earliest star-gazer/astrologers essentially the mystery of unfoldment of time and the experience of change and process became for later astrologer/geometers the fascinating possibilities of mathematically and intellectually manipulating a two-dimensional abstract diagram in space.

Why the fascination? Because Greek philosophers like Pythagoras and Plato believed geometry and mathematics held the keys to the mysteries of Man, God and the universe. To the evolving Western intellect, geometry and mathematics revealed a supersensible, 'perfect' or ideal pattern of order *behind*, but not actually *in*, what were considered the less-than-perfect manifestations of

---

[1]Cf. *Manilius Astronomica*, tr. G. P. Goold (Harvard University Press, Cambridge, Massachusetts: 1977) pp. xxxviii ff, text pp. 270 ff. *Ptolemy's Tetrabiblos*, tr. J.M. Ashmand (Health Research 1969 reprint of the 1917 English Edition), Chapters XVI, XVIII, XXI, pp. 36 ff.
[2]Rupert Gleadow, *The Origin of the Zodiac* (New York: 1969) pp. 176-7.

nature—human nature and the unruly periods of celestial motions included. Geometer/philosophers sought their world of archetypal perfection not in experience and existential reality, but in exact geometrical patterns and rational numerical sequences and ratios which could be handled by man's divine component, Reason, but which could never be encountered exactly in the real world of the senses. Plato, for example, encouraged young men destined for the responsibilities of public service to develop their minds by studying, among other things, astronomy. But he warned that they were not to trouble themselves too much about the actual heavenly bodies, but rather with the mathematics of motion of *ideal* heavenly bodies.[3]

It was not a very large step from the mathematics of the motions of ideal heavenly bodies to the mathematics of the *geometry inferred* from the motions of ideal heavenly bodies. Planetary rulerships—i.e., geometric, symmetrical schemata of relationships or 'affinities' between planets and zodiacal signs—fairly soon became more significant than the planets themselves or their motions, actual or ideal.[4] The zodiac, the perfect circle, first became more significant than the process it represented and the planets for which it served as a frame of reference,[5] then, the geometric relationships among its individual signs became more significant than the perfection, let alone the process, represented by the whole.[6]

Thus, in all fields of human endeavor, and not only in astrology, the chasm between the realm of static archetypes and the world of ever-changing phenomena, between intellect (in the Greek sense of the term) and experience widened. Experience—the realm of the senses and all natural processes—was consigned to a rung of the value-ladder quite below the rank of Reason, i.e., the realm of thought and rational processes. Nature had to be subdued by Reason, considered the ensouling principle of man, and human nature was at the head of the list. The body and its natural inclina-

---

[3]Bertrand Russell, *A History of Western Philosophy* (New York: 1945), p. 131.

[4]*Manilius, op. cit.*, pp. xiv ff, text pp. 433-452.
    Ptolemy, op. cit., Ch. XX-XXV, pp. 41-53.

[5]*Manilius, op. cit.*, p. xcviii

[6]*Manilius, loc. cit.*, (1)
    Ptolemy, loc. cit., (1)

tions, character and destiny as 'written in the stars' had to be forged into a fitting receptacle for the divine soul, Reason.

Hence, the purpose of an individual's horoscope became to enable him to 'rule his stars.' The horoscope was a conventionalized map of the places of the real heavenly bodies at the time of birth. It therefore referred to the realm of nature, human nature, to the part of the human being which had to be controlled or subdued by his reason. But if the wise man was to rule his stars, i.e., his natural inclinations and destiny, he had to know what they were and how to do combat with them. Astrology developed as an increasingly complex descriptive typology, from which every person could ascertain his or her strengths and weaknesses, wielding the former as weapons in order to conquer the latter.

While the horoscope was referred to nature, the *interpretation* of the horoscope was the province of the intellect. Since manifestations of nature are many and celestial factors describing them relatively few, the myriad relationships between factors in the horoscope became increasingly significant. The ruler of one sign in the house of another indicated one thing, which could be mitigated or tempered one way or another if something else, the ruler of such-and-so rose in conjunction with the ruler of still some other house or sign. This is not terribly different from what many astrological textbooks today present as a more sophisticated psychological approach: "If planet x is in sign or house y, the native tends to be.... At times he may do such-and-so, creating this or that type of problem. He will be most happy (or successful) if he...rather than....He should use extra caution when...and should try instead to cultivate...."

In terms of what we are developing here, we should first realize what a tremendous change this represents from the way in which ancient people reverenced the stars and planets and sought to attune themselves to the natural, seasonal processes and inevitable periodic changes over which they believed the heavenly discs and dots of light unquestionably held sway. To seek to attune oneself to natural processes is evidently quite different from trying to rule and bend them to one's will! And it matters only slightly whether the processes one interferes with are external, biospheric-natural ones or internal, psychological, human-natural ones.

We are beginning, quite uncomfortably, to realize where the 'conquer' mentality has led Western civilization, most obviously in terms of its particular brand of science and technology. And yet, humanity has evidently passed the point at which a more or less passive attunement to purely natural and biospheric rhythms is possible or even desirable. Can there not be a meeting ground between these two contrasting approaches to life? Can a sense of process and attunement rather than separation and manipulation be reincorporated, not only into astrology, but into human consciousness and actions as well?

What we must realize is, first, that the time/space, process/geometry, attune/rule dualities in astrology are representative of a whole range of similar conflicts in practically all areas of human enquiry and endeavor. Whether we say that the horns of the dilemma are represented by the right and left sides of the brain, or whether we rely on feeling and experience or on our intellects, a holistic world-view vs. an atomistic one, really makes little difference. These are all different ways of depicting the same crossroads. For, second, we must recognize that all such dualities essentially reflect the fact that human consciousness has passed through the first two stages of a developmental process which must now proceed to its third stage just as synthesis must follow thesis and antithesis. But synthesis, contrary to popular opinion, is not like running something willy-nilly through a Waring Blender; it is more than mere eclecticism. True synthesis is like the integration of Yin and Yang within the Chinese symbol Tai-Chi, the enfolding and encompassing, dynamic Tao. It is a harmonization of opposites within a more inclusive vision.

Astrologically, such a synthesis means bringing together the essence and unique contributions of both the archaic/attunement approach and the classical/archetypal approach. We must restore to astrological thinking and understanding a sense of process and of reverence for the wholeness, integrity and elegant necessity of life-processes, while retaining astrology's sophisticated, abstracted symbology, conceptual tools and geometric schema bringing into play the qualitative and archetypal aspects of number and form. The approach resulting from this type of synthesis should of course encompass qualities of each earlier approach, but it should also far surpass both in psychological sophistication and philosophical inclusiveness. Because human consciousness was able to formulate and use the two earlier approaches, it developed the capacity for a broader perspective through the experience and the process—even though the experience and process consisted largely of, first, denying the significance of experience and process in relation to a supersensible ideal, geometric realm and developing the powers of abstraction, rationalization and conceptualization; then, turning those very powers back on the material world, asserting that only what was physical *and* could be grasped and manipulated by the intellect could be considered 'real'!

We believe that the process-oriented approach we are developing in this book has the possibility of going far toward stimulating the needed synthesis in astrology. The reader should recognize, however, how different it is, especially from the purely descriptive approach he or she may be used to encountering in most textbooks. The process-oriented approach we are envisioning is an approach not only to chart interpretation *per se*, but also, we repeat, an astrological approach to *life interpretation*. It is an approach in which the motions of celestial bodies become symbols of how processes operate and unfold everywhere, and an approach in which a person's life is seen and understood as the polyphonic unfoldment of a variety of processes, all aimed at fulfilling some necessary evolutionary step or function. Such an approach, like the approach of archaic or indigenous peoples, seeks attunement rather than forcible mastery. But it is not an approach advocating passivity or resignation. It is an approach promoting understanding and meaningful living, and a transformative willingness to pass through whatever life brings in order to grow and develop and actualize the potentialities inherent in one's birth. It is an approach which ultimately flows from—and toward—the realization that every life-process, whether in nature, human nature in general, or in a particular person's life, is a phase of a larger process, a step in the step-by-step unfoldment of something essentially necessary for personal, collective or cosmic evolution.

A PROCESS-ORIENTED APPROACH TO THE BIRTH-CHART

From a process-oriented point of view, we can best understand the birth-chart—the map of the heavens drawn for the exact time and place of a person's first breath—if we picture it as a stop-motion snapshot of a moment in the flow of the life of the cosmos. It is, as it were, a slice of celestial space-time as seen from planet Earth. The whole past of celestial motion is behind and implied in the particular planetary, zodiacal, house and aspect pattern appearing at the moment of our birth. And implied in both its totality and each of its parts is dynamic momentum, that is, an inexorable continuation of motion toward a future unfoldment. A birth-chart is thus a celestial statement of where the universe 'is', and therefore *what it needs next*, at the moment of our birth.

This celestial situation symbolizes the existential, human one— or vice versa. In the history of the cosmos, or at least what we know of it, of *our* cosmos—the Earth, humanity, our society, family, etc. —certain things have been done, certain developmental and evolutionary steps have been taken; certain attitudes, values, institutions, patterns of behaving, thinking and feeling have been built, cycle upon cycle, process upon process, step by step. The newborn inherits, as it were, a world and a cosmos already in progress. Many things have been done, and they have been done well or badly. Some lines of development have produced beautiful accomplishments or valid and workable solutions to life's challenges. Other evolutionary attempts have failed partially or utterly, or left behind toxic by-products or decaying remains which must be neutralized or eliminated before the next constructive steps can be taken in a particular area. Some new developments may be just beginning and need to be nurtured to maturity; innovation may be drastically needed in other areas.

At all times, a host of cycles of development, terrestrial and celestial, is in process—and *the next steps need to be taken in all of them.* The birth-chart shows us that each one of us is the potential taker of some next step(s). It shows us not only *that* each of us is a potential taker of some step, it shows us *how*—by handling what types of energies and by meeting and passing through what types of challenges in what areas of life—we can endeavor to answer the need we were born to fulfill. What is implied as a 'next step' by the myriad of cycles frozen and focused into a birth-chart—each planet-to-planet relationship, each relation of planet to sign, planet to house, sign to house, etc.—has to be made actual, to be fulfilled in the world by a person born at that particular time and place. Past karma demands that this be so; the future, yet unborn but 'present' in seed, yearns for it as a foundation. If we believe that life is indeed ordered and meaningful, we can also trust that we will be 'given' to experience whatever situations we need, either through, or in spite of which we can best fulfill our function.

This may seem somewhat abstract, but we can perhaps make it more concrete by saying that, at least astrologically and archetypally, we can follow many developmental processes as they unfold by relating them to the phases—i.e., aspects—of symbolically appropriate celestial or planetary cycles: for example, long, universalizing cycles of the development of culture and civilization to the nearly 500-year-long Pluto/Neptune cycle; cycles of sociocultural formation and transformation to the Uranus/Saturn cycle; local political and social patterns to Jupiter and Saturn, and so on. From such a point of view, we can actually watch our birth-charts taking form over time, the natal positions and aspects 'clicking in', as it were, one after another, step by step.

Similarly, if we are process-oriented students of history, psychology and sociology, we can see the kinds of situations we face in our lives having been formed over time and through individual and collective cycles of development during the decades and years before our birth. We can actually see that the kinds of problems we face in life *become possible* through such a process. It may seem rather strange to speak of problems almost as if they were privileges, but in a sense—an evolutionary, process-oriented sense—this is indeed the case. Problems occur when traditions crystallize and become ineffective, when the pressures of past karma necessitate unprecedented solutions to equally unprecedented 'messes', or when new potentialities engendered by positive steps forward in human development require bold and enlightened innovation in order to be actualized.

From such a point of view, we should realize that as our birth-charts were once the 'transits' of a day in the life of the cosmos, so, too, are our lives phases in the process of human development. What we often fail to realize when we deal with what we call our personal problems is that they are actually particular or individual focalizations of the developmental challenges of our times. Changing values in interpersonal relationship, in social institutions such as marriage and the family, in the roles of men and women—problems with our children, their education, involvement with peer-group activities, drugs, TV or fashion—economic difficulties brought about by job-loss or the obsolescence of skills built over a life-time—situations of psycho-spiritual crisis or conflict encountered in an eager search for 'new realities,' modes of consciousness or levels of being: all these and more are reflections and personal manifestations of much larger patterns operating within our society and humanity as a whole at this time in history and evolution.

To say this, however, is not to minimize or take away from the gravity or importance of individuals' problems. Rather, it is to put the kinds of challenges facing each of us today into a proper, work-able and process-oriented perspective. On the one hand, we can endeavor to understand our birth-charts and lives from the point of view of a purely individual psychology, exploring and primarily try-ing to deal with the personal-psychological causes of our problems. We can even personally relate to the past antecedents of our lives in a historical way, seeing what we presently face as a continuation of a past having produced and passed on an impersonal type of karma (residua) and dharma (potentialities). Or we can consider our con-nectedness to the past in a reincarnational way—that is, in terms of having been associated in some way with actual personalities who lived and acted and participated in the past, creating and passing on a more personal kind of karma or need for a 'next step'. Reincarna-tion can, of course, also be thought of by postulating 'being' or 'hav-ing' a divine or immortal soul or monad which, having incarnated here or elsewhere in the past, returns to finish certain unfinished business or take the next step in some on-going process of develop-ment. The variations on such themes are practically endless.

On the other hand, it may be equally important to also recog-nize the reality of our interconnectedness with a larger whole, with collective processes of development and unfoldment, to recognize the fact that we as individuals with particular birth-charts face certain situations or problems in our relationships, families, jobs, psyches or checkbooks because the development of humanity as a whole, and particularly of the society of which we are a part, has reached a stage at which new approaches to the principles of human consciousness and activity underlying the forms of such situations are needed. In other words, certain kinds of problems, capabilities or challenges are indicated in individuals' lives and birth-charts because they represent—*both* for the individuals and the collectivity—the means whereby all can take the next steps in their respective, but interconnected evolutionary processes.

Even this, we realize, may sound rather abstract and far-removed from the experience and usual thinking of many people, astrologers and astrology students. But it is a conclusion to which a truly process-oriented approach to astrology inexorably points. Anyone who thinks he or she or his or her life is independent of larger processes of development, or not structured by the principles of cyclic unfoldment is not thinking realistically—*or astrologically*. For if we encounter a situation in someone's life which we can identify as having something to do with, say, Neptune in Libra or Venus square Saturn in their birth-chart, we would not avow that either of these are purely personal indications. While they may manifest in the personal life of an individual, they are nevertheless sybols of universal human functions and phases of development which must be lived through and actualized. . .for a purpose.

We perhaps more readily see and acknowledge this when we look at the birth-charts and lives of certain 'larger-than-life' personalities or public figures. Some of us do indeed wind up performing large, public roles in shaping values, disseminating information, inspiring great movements, etc. But we should first of all recognize that the function of such 'greatness' is not dependent *only* upon indications in birth-charts. Many people are born with similar planetary placements and aspects, and many people born with so-called 'promising' charts never seem to actualize much in the way of positive results in their lives at any level. On the other hand, just as important as the more obvious contributions of persons who gain some degree of renown or notoriety is the growth and development that is called for in each of our lives. Not only what we do, but also the quality of consciousness and spirit in which we do it, perpetuates itself and continues to evolve, refine or break down basic patterns of human behavior over millennia, whether we operate at the level of personal psychology or in terms of larger social or cultural patterns. Such a transmission is focused into the 'seed harvest' of our lives— which can refer to our children (biological level), life-work (socio-cultural level) and/or our contributions or 'input' to the one Mind of Humanity. As the occult saying goes, "No work is ever lost."

This is perhaps a good opportunity to mention why we will present examples of well-known contemporary and historical figures in connection with, especially, the less well-understood and used aspects we will be exploring. We present them because they fulfill two requirements of being good examples: (1) their charts contain the particular aspect or configuration we are discussing, *and* (2) the lives of these persons seem to have fulfilled or exemplified in some way the taking of the step represented by the particular aspect. This is not to say that a particular aspect indicates that such-and-so *will* manifest in a person's life or that it 'makes' a person or his or her life a certain way. No aspect or configuration presents a guarantee or a 'given'— for as we will see, even trines need to be actualized through a process of development and do not 'magically' manifest by themselves. It *is* to say that the particular example—chart and person and life—exemplifies for us the meeting of a challenge and the taking of some 'next step,' i.e., the at least partial fulfillment of the *need* the aspect symbolized.

Such examples notwithstanding, the questions still remain: When we are not dealing with persons whose lives have, at least to some extent, already been lived out and made manifest on a public level, how do we go about understanding what is represented by aspects in a client's (or in our own) chart? How do we know what particular 'need' or 'next step' in development is necessary and possible for that person to fulfill or take over the course of his or her life? Our answer: By familiarizing ourselves with the *principles* of planetary meanings, cyclic unfoldment and aspect formation, we allow the essential truths expressed through the principles to permeate, enlighten and transform our thinking. By so doing, we greatly expand our capacity to give meaning to life via astrological symbolism—for we evoke and develop *intuition*.

WHY PRINCIPLES?

In a complex and dynamic universe in which countless variables constantly interact, no one could possibly memorize enough definitions of particular situations to 'cover' everything he or she might encounter. Thinking in terms of broad, inclusive but flexible principles is the most effective, and ultimately the wisest 'way to go'. But for some people, principles are like scotch whiskey: a taste for them is not inherent and has to be acquired. Especially today, astrological principles are often stated quickly, then shunted aside in favor of more particular, memorizable statements or paragraphs neatly tabulated in textbooks attempting to provide a compendium of definitions for all possible combinations of factors under scrutiny.

It is, however, impossible to tabulate all possible combinations of astrological factors if we take into account more than two of them at a time. We can consider factor *a* in relation to twelve others, as when we deal with planets in signs, or planets in houses, or signs on cusps of houses. (The situation merely becomes more complicated if we take intercepted signs and signs spread over two houses into account.) We can easily tabulate planet *x* in six aspect-relations to each of the other planets. We can even turn this around and make all the various pairings via six relationships mutual. But we would certainly need a lot of paper and pencils to account for all the possible threefold combinations of ten planets and six aspects—such as Venus square Mars, with Venus also square Saturn (and Mars therefore opposition Saturn); Venus square Mars, with Venus also square Jupiter (and Mars therefore in opposition to Jupiter) . . . Venus square Mars, with Venus also sextile Saturn (and therefore Mars quincunx Saturn); Venus square Mars, with Venus sextile Jupiter (and Mars therefore quincunx Jupiter), etc.

Even if we managed to tabulate each of such manifold combinations of three planets and six-aspects with a computer, how would we deal with the definitions? Each two- or threefold combination would still find itself in the company and context of several other two- and threefold combinations, and we would not be very much better off than when we started, when separate definitions of twofold combinations were 'added' to one another. As many astrology students have discovered, this procedure provides a less-than-brilliant or even satisfactory overall interpretation—what is usually (and wrongly) called 'synthesis'. Actually, each combination of factors not only adds itself to the others, but *changes them by its very presence*. It is as true in astrology as elsewhere that the whole is always greater than the sum of its parts—and even greater than the sum of relationships between all its parts. The interpretation of a birth-chart must proceed from an intuitive grasp of the whole—and intuition is developed by understanding and using principles to the point that they transform the thinking of the one who thinks in terms of them.

What we have mainly considered so far in terms of tabulating complex, interrelated factors is just the astrological side of the matter. What about the human side? Human psychology being what it is, one can never account for and define in advance all possible constellations of factors interweaving in the life of a person. Even if by some stretch of the imagination it were possible to tabulate all possible horoscopic combinations of astrological configurations, one could never account for the variety of human beings having similar enough charts; nor could one account for the actual level of functioning at which persons live out what is symbolized in their birth-charts. Because of differences in race, culture, religion, class, circumstances of birth, etc., people differ widely as to the level at which they operate.* No reference book—astrological or psychological—could ever pinpoint what should be explored as significant and meaningful in a particular person's life or chart at a particular time. The only way an astrologer can rise to every occasion presented by a client's life and birth-chart at a particular time in the client's life is by becoming thoroughly versed in principles—astrological, psychological and philosophical principles giving a broad, inclusive and flexible overview of the entire human and astrological situation at hand.

It is often feared that principles, especially those associated with astrology, are too 'abstract.' But abstraction is *not* unreality, and the term should not scare anyone willing to exercise his or her power of thought. To 'abstract' means literally 'to draw out of'. To

---

*Cf. *Beyond Individualism: THe Psychology of Transformation* by Dane Rudhyar (Quest Books, Wheaton, Illinois: 1979) for a complete discussion of the psychology of levels of functioning.

abstract principles from experience means to penetrate the opacity of particularity and to perceive the workings of the universal in and through the existential, no matter how distorted or dense the material reality may be. It is to see the archetypal behind and in every actual manifestation, and in some cases, to infer the latter from the former. This is the true function of the humanistic, process-oriented astrologer *vis-a-vis* his or her client's chart and life.

In order to be able to truly work with principles—or rather to have archetypal principles work in us and operate through our thinking—we must become so thoroughly acquainted with them that we 'forget' about knowing them. Whatever we have to labor over in a (colloquially speaking) self-conscious way—like trying to fit keywords into cumbersome sentences, which often turn out to be grammatically perfect but don't really *say* anything—we really don't know well enough. It hasn't become part of us yet, and it therefore cannot work in and through us. True knowledge—which can come through the use and direct understanding of astrological symbols (as well as through a variety of other means, of course)—is always at the back of the mind, quietly and unobtrusively structuring the thinking, never in the forefront cluttering the conscious mind with a lot of memorized, half-assimilated definitions or confusing and inconsistent intellectual associations.

The back of the mind in terms of thinking is very much like the back of the neck in human anatomy, for neither are areas of which we are normally conscious. Nevertheless, they are both exceedingly sensitive. We may be unaware of the back of our neck for a long time if nothing particularly stimulates it. But when something comes along and tickles it or stings it, we know about it immediately, and we react spontaneously—and appropriately, depending on the state of our expectations and inner fantasy at the time, on what is doing the stimulating and the quality of it.

So too should basic astrological principles be so well assimilated that they are 'stored' at the 'back of the neck'. When a particular client and chart with no matter how complex a configuration or situation comes along and stimulates that area, we will react spontaneously and appropriately, intuitively grasping in one whole mental gesture the meaning of the situation confronting us.

This may come as a new idea for many students laboring to 'put it all together,' although it no doubt comes as no surprise to seasoned, experienced hands used to the spontaneous working of what we would rather call 'active intuition' than synthesis. Regardless of the term one uses, the way in which one becomes able to respond at that level should be explored from several angles and is perhaps prematurely discussed here; we'll return to the matter in the last chapter of this book. For the moment, a general idea of where working with principles could lead serves as a foundation for discussing significant principles underlying astrological aspects and configurations from a process-oriented point of view.

WHAT PRINCIPLES?

The principles we have to work with regarding aspects in astrology are neither many nor complex. Most are based on commonly experienced phenomena such as the changing of the seasons and the phases of the Moon, or on everyday sorts of arithmetic procedures such as simple addition, subtraction, multiplication and division. Most of all, what we have to try to do is to approach the situation consistently, trying to follow to its conclusion one line of reasoning and development at a time, all the while staying in touch with and building upon the foundation provided by the basic facts of celestial motions.

Very simply stated, certain principles structure all cycles. A basic twofoldness is evident in all natural processes, whether we speak of the alternation of light and dark in the day/night cycle, the waxing and waning of the Moon in the lunation cycle, the 'waxing' and 'waning' of warmth and cold, fertility and barrenness, the relative lengths of days and nights in the cycle of the seasonal year. It really doesn't matter which phenomena we look at, for evident underlying all of them is a basic distinction between the two halves of cyclic process. The two hemicycles of a cycle refer to two realms of activity, two directions of energy-flow, each of which predominates during one half of a cyclic process.

Whether we think of spring, summer, fall and winter—sunrise, noon, sunset and midnight—or New Moon, First Quarter, Full

Moon, Last Quarter—doesn't matter either, for a basic quadrature or fourfold structure is also apparent within twofoldness in natural cycles. Because the two halves of a cycle refer to different realms or levels of activity, the 'moments' or turning points marking the cycle's quarters—one at the middle of each hemicycle—will be distinctly different in polarity and direction from one another. While each marks the midpoint of a hemicycle, that is, the moment at which the activity or direction predominating during the hemicycle reaches its maximum intensity, very broadly speaking, one marks the end of the beginning of the total cycle, and the other marks the beginning of the end.

In order to transfer these generalizations about cycles to the particular situation of astrological aspects, we must first get in touch, and stay in touch, with the facts of planetary relationship: as seen from the Earth, two planets come together in the sky, separate and conjoin again. The lunation cycle—the cycle between the Sun and Moon producing for observers on Earth the spectacle of the phases of the Moon—is the prototype or model for all cycles of aspects, which are phase-relationships between moving celestial bodies. For not only are the successive stages of the soli-lunar relationship defined by the increasing and decreasing distances between the Sun and Moon; added significance is given to each stage of the soli-lunar relationship if we interpret the shape of the Moon as a symbol of what the relationship implies at each phase.

No matter how we divide up the cycle of relationships, what names or numbers we give its various phases or aspects, the basic facts of celestial motions and planetary interrelationships remain the same. There is no complication or confusion regarding them. Controversy and confusion arise only when astrologers try to explain and agree upon just what angular values constitute *bona fide* aspects and what they specifically mean, especially when they occur between particular planets.

Practically all astrologers agree on the use of at least the so-called Ptolemaic aspects, the conjunction, sextile, trine, square and opposition (although few realize that Ptolemy was not actually referring to angular relationships between planets when he named them, but rather to relations among signs of the zodiac). Some astrologers go along with the Ptolemaic approach that the conjunction is 'neutral', depending upon whether 'malefic' of 'benefic' planets are involved, the trine and sextile invariably 'good' or 'favorable,' and the square and opposition just as emphatically and universally 'evil' or 'unfortunate'—or, in more modern parlance, at least stressful or uncomfortably tense. Other astrologers, ourselves included, do not agree that an aspect must be either good, bad or indifferent. From our point of view, an aspect, any aspect, is what it *is*—a necessary phase of a process, building upon the phase having gone before, forming a foundation for the phases to come after. No phase integral and necessary to an organic process can be good or bad in an ethical, moral or even a general sense.

While some astrologers advocate *only* the use of the five above-named 'major' aspects, others also use the quincunx or inconjunct (150° aspect now increasing in popularity after having been omitted from most textbooks in this and the last centuries, as it was considered by the earliest writers not as an aspect *per se* but as a 'non-relationship'[7]), and its companion-aspect, the semi-sextile (30°). Some astrologers also use semi-squares and sesquiquadrates, 45° and 135° aspects sometimes referred to as 'minor' aspects along with a series based on the quintile (72°) which was apparently advocated or renewed by Kepler. Some astrologers have considered the quintile to be as 'favorable' as a trine; others have considered it, along with such aspects as the septile (51³/₇°) and novile (40°), too 'esoteric' or 'specialized' to be of general value. Some astrologers deny the validity of these and other so-called minor aspects altogether. At the small end of the angular value spectrum, the term 'micro-aspects' has recently been coined to refer to arcs smaller than 7½ degrees which have been found to be significant through harmonic analysis.

If the reader is still with us after such a litany—which for brevity's sake includes only technical, not interpretive disagreements—we'll ask the obvious question: How did such confusion and general disagreement come about, and what can be done to alleviate it? The crux of the matter, we believe, is not merely deciding what angular values are significant and what they mean. It is rather

---

[1]*Ptolemy, op. cit.*, Ch. XIX, p. 40.

whether one believes that there is only one valid procedure for generating astrological aspects, or whether there are several, each procedure of generation referring to a different way of interpreting the flow of process at different levels.

A basic example of how the existing confusion arose can be shown against the lunation cycle. Like all cycles, it naturally divides itself into two hemicycles during which the Moon waxes and wanes. The hemicycles are further divided into two quarters each by the straight-edged shape of the Quarter Moons cutting across the night-sky. The fact that at the First Quarter the Moon crosses the orbit of the Earth going outward (away from the Sun), and at Last Quarter returns within it (toward the Sun), gives added symbolic significance to the quadrature of the cycle, as do the absence of the light of the Moon at New Moon and the fullness of the Moon-disc at the cycle's culmination.

On the one hand, however, the appearance and disappearance of the Crescent and 'De-crescent' Moons can be taken, along with two other 'matching' points inferred between First Quarter and Full Moon and Full Moon and Last Quarter, to mark four other turning points in the cycle. These, when superimposed upon the basic quadrature of lunation phases, map out a basic eightfold structure. On the other hand, if one realizes that the Moon is approximately 30° or the space of one zodiacal sign away from the Sun during the Crescent phases, one may infer a basic twelve-fold structure behind the lunation cycle. In fact, this—together with the realization that the seasonal year could be approximately equated with twelve lunations or months of about 30 days each, and the fact that the 30° arc between the New Moon and Crescent was the span of just about one of these lunations—is probably how twelvefoldness came to dominate astrology entirely. But does that make a twelvefold schema of the lunation cycle any more valid or intrinsically 'correct' than an eightfold division of it?

The twelvefold structure when applied to interplanetary relationships generates the astrological aspects conjunction (0°), semi-sextile (30°), sextile (60°), square (90°), trine (120°), quincunx (150°), opposition (180°). The eightfold approach generates the semi-square (45°) and sesquiquadrate (135°), but does not include the semi-sextile and sextile, the trine and quincunx. If one can divide the cycle by 8 or by 12, why not by any other number? Number 3 generates angular values of 120°, the trine also generated by the twelvefold approach. But what about a number like 5, which generates angular values not coinciding with any natural divisions of the cycle? We could, of course, generate all the angular values we'd care to, then superimpose the resulting schema on one another, keeping the aspects which are common to all or most and discounting the rest. If we did so, we would wind up back where we started, with the five Ptolemaic aspects, conjunction, sextile and trine, square and opposition—and no doubt also with the definite good/bad, favorable/unfavorable interpretation of them, because in the process of multiple divisions and superimpositions, we would have lost all sense of process and unfoldment over time. . . which is exactly what happened.

It seems to us, and is the track we will be following in this book, that each schema of generating aspects and each number-principle forming its foundation has its own validity at its own level. In relation to the process generating it, every aspect has its own meaning. But no matter how many arcs we divide a *circle* of aspects into, we must always refer them back and understand them in relation to the *cycle* or process whereby the relationship of two planets to one another develops *over time through* space. Each phase of a cycle, no matter how many phases the cycle is divided into, has its own place and function in the overall process of whatever is developing through the cycle. And every angular value, while not necessarily marking a definite turning point or aspect in a developmental process, is nevertheless part of a phase, which in turn is part of the total cycle. Moreover, in actual practice there are indeed horoscopes whose overall planetary pattern or predominating configuration stresses eightfoldness, or fivefoldness, squares, rectangles or triangles of various kinds. Each must be read and understood in terms of its own dynamic, in terms of the principles underlying its own structure. It must be assessed in terms of its own integrity, not in terms of a more or less rigid formula of interpretation imposed on it by the interpreter.

Thus, only a deep, essentially intuitive understanding of the principles of cyclic unfoldment, number and form—in that order—will do. We have to start by trying to gain a thorough understanding of the way interplanetary cycles unfold over time, how a *series* of aspects operates, one after another. Then we can try to fathom the meaning of the numerical principles underlying the further divisions of cycles into various phases and apply these principles to actual configurations of aspects in birth-charts. In all cases, we have to try to understand the dynamic direction of aspects, what they imply in birth-charts as a challenge or directive to live one's own process, to become able to take some necessary 'next step.'

2.
Familiar Aspects: Involution/Devolution

I. GROWTH THROUGH SPONTANEOUS ACTIVITY

The first half of any cyclic process is dominated by 'life' or necessity. Something new—whatever it may be—needs or is karmically impelled to be born. It has to struggle to overcome the inertia and 'unfinished business' of the past out of which it is to be born; it has to gradually steady and focus itself; establish itself in the world in a definite way; sever its connection to whatever in the formative period of its life molded and conditioned it but now hinders it from fulfilling its highest potentialities; integrate itself into its environment as harmoniously as possible; and finally, come to as full a fruition as possible in order to actually satisfy the need for which it was born, grew and developed.

This is a basic outline of the first half of any cyclic process. It is called the *involutionary* hemicycle, because a spiritual potentiality or karmic necessity *involves* or incorporates itself in matter, in the world of actual forms, during this half of the process. In terms of human beings, 'actual forms' can refer to forms of behavior, talents or capabilities, or to more concrete productions such as works of art, life-works, a business firm, an interpersonal relationship or family unit, etc. In the world of nature, 'taking actual form' is expressed in the process whereby a seed germinates and develops into a mature, flowering and, eventually, seed-producing plant. Regardless of what is developing, or the vehicle or form through which it develops, the first hemicycle of any process refers to a series of phases in which spontaneous growth in answer to a need occurs. The need may be an 'inner' one, that is, within the organism in whose life the growing is taking place, or an 'outer' one, a need in or of the environment—which can be social or psychic as well as physical and natural. Something grows and develops during the first hemicycle of a process because the need exists for what it can potentially become.

Spontaneous growth in answer to a need is subjective, instinctual and unself-conscious, carried along, as it were, on a wave of nature-born impulsions. A slender green shoot reaches up through the dark crust of earth into light. Sinking roots, soaring stem, reaching branches, light-collecting leaves... exquisite flower—each in turn is planthood's answer to the warmth of Sun, the love of caressing breezes and nourishing, moist earth. A baby grows in the same way. He explores, first, his own body, then the possibilities of his immediate, multi-colored surroundings because 'life' in him is intrigued. *Human* life grows and explores itself, not yet knowing it is itself, *through him*. He, and all humanity behind and 'in' him, struggle to master wiggly, wobbly limbs and walk upright; he babbles, then speaks, and 'humanhood' not yet 'I' expresses itself through his lips. To exteriorize what is latent within; to allow it to express itself *through* one by building the necessary forms and structures to contain it and mastering the necessary motions and tasks: this is the involutionary challenge. Through such a process, the universal within rushes out and incarnates in the particular. And in the process, the form-builder awakens. Reflected in the fruit of his labor he discovers and recognizes himself 'I'.

In this involutionary process, life moves forth spontaneously in the simplest kind of rhythm, one step after another, each step adding itself to the preceding ones in sheer impulsiveness of being: one, one plus one, one plus one plus one, etc. The arithmetic progression thus formed is an exuberant rhythm of expansion and conquest. Such a rhythm is found in the series of astrological aspects occurring between two planets' conjunction and opposition, between the time they come together in the sky and the time they face each other at opposite ends of the horizon, as far apart as they can be. It is the rhythm of the waxing Moon, each 30° Crescent-step adding itself to itself from New Moon to Full Moon. It is the rhythm of solar progress through the year, each step defining the limits of a zodiacal signs month after month following the vernal equinox—the symbolic beginning of natural activity and biological growth.

Translated into aspects, such a rhythm spanning the involutionary hemicycle contains six phases or steps—from 0° to 30°, 30° to 60°, 60° to 90°, 90° to 120°, 120° to 150°, 150° to 180°. Seven aspects—an important number in all occult traditions—are formed:

conjunction, semi-sextile (30°), sextile (60°), square (90°), trine (120°), quincunx (150°), opposition (180°). During the waxing hemicycle of the lunation cycle, the Moon grows in size, and similarly, during the 'waxing' hemicycle of aspects between two planets, their angular distances from one another—the size of the aspects— also increase. But just as important as the aspects themselves are the *phases* of interrelationship between aspect formation. Growth and development occur between aspects; aspects are turning points which given structure and direction to the process of growth.

A cycle of aspects between two planets refers to the process whereby the functional activities represented by each planet grow and develop in co-operation with one another. Some life-task or function that cannot be performed by either planet's function alone must be developed by both together. At the conjunction beginning the cycle of aspects, the functional activity represented by the slower planet gives, as it were, a new direction, orientation or creative impetus to the activities represented by the faster planet. As the faster planet moves away from the slower, it 'carries out' this new impulse, incorporating it into its activities. New forms—forms of behavior, interpersonal relating or relationships, sociocultural forms such as institutions, or more concrete forms like objects—are engendered along the way.

As the faster planet moves farther away from the slower planet, it—like the waxing Moon in relation to the Sun—reflects more and more of the slower planet's 'light.' The faster planet becomes increasingly capable of incorporating the meaning of the slower planet's activities into its own. Finally, at the opposition between the two planets, the symbolical Full Moon, the faster planet has become in a sense the 'equal' of the slower planet, fully manifesting in its own way the new direction given to its activities at the conjunction, reflecting back to Earth the fullness of its accomplishments.

For example, when related to human activity, a cycle of aspects between Venus and Mars refers to the need and opportunity to bring the personal-emotional nature to a new level of functioning or self-expression. This may mean giving a new value to the capacity for personal-emotional self-expression, or expressing oneself in new fields or at new levels of activities. At the Venus/Mars conjunction, the outward-bound activity-orientation of Mars gives a new direction and impetus to Venus' inwardly directed sense of value. In the earliest stages of the relationship between the two planets, the new orientation must focus itself at the level of subjective experience and overcome the inertia of past patterns of feeling and behaving. As the personal-emotional nature steadies itself at the new level or in the new direction, it must express itself as an objective factor. To do so it takes on or produces forms, the form of a relationship between persons; or perhaps another kind of creative, self-expressive ability, as in the arts, develops. The personal-emotional development or reorientation thus becomes embodied in its creations. At the Venus/Mars opposition—the cycle's culmination—these forms have become, as it were, a mirror: the personal-emotional nature having created them is plainly or elaborately reflected in its creations. Through the involutionary process, what began subjectively and unconsciously has become objectively manifest and self-conscious.

Every person is born at some stage of the Venus/Mars cycle, although for now we are concerned only with the 'waxing' or involutionary phases of such a process. A particular phase in the process of personal-emotional development is 'frozen' into everyone's chart at birth, and the natal phase-relationship between Venus and Mars refers to the basic stage of personal-emotional development or self-expression which must be fulfilled, i.e., made actual, over the course of the person's life.

The same is true regarding every other possible planetary pair, for there are no times when two planets are not related in some way. They are all in the solar system together; they are all part of the whole planetary pattern. Two planets are therefore always *in some phase of cyclic relationship* with one another. They become in *particularly significant relationship* when their angular distance from one another measures to certain values. They then form 'aspects,' which refer to definite steps and/or turning points in the process. In other words, Mars and Jupiter, say, are just as related when they are separated by 100° as when they are separated by 120°. But when their relationship comes to measure in the vicinity of 120°, the *quality* of it takes on a particular significance; actions related to these two planetary functions should—because it is necessary for them to—lead to more easily recognized and definable types of results.

Nothing else is meant by the fact that two planets form a trine or any other type of aspect: the association of functions represented by the aspecting planets should lead to a particular type of result because that is what is *needed* at a particular phase of a developing process.

An aspect's presence in a natal chart attests to the fact that the need for a particular kind of becoming exists, and that the capacity for it is also there; life co-operates by 'setting the stage' and providing the necessary opportunities and challenges, even though some of these may come in the guise of crisis or neurosis, hardly recognizable for what they truly are. Again, all planets, their mutual aspects or phase-relationships not in exact aspect are integrated together into the whole of every birth-chart. Each need and potentiality of being and becoming provides an impetus, foundation and resources with which to work for all the rest—such interaction being most focal between and among patterns of interrelated aspects, i.e., configurations in which several aspects are involved.

Here we are perhaps getting a little ahead of ourselves. For before discussing interrelated aspects we should first ask, "What are the phases of becoming, the developmental steps marked by aspects of the involutionary hemicycle? How does each operate when focalized into a birth-chart?"

PHASE 1 — SUBJECTIVE BEING

Just as a seed can be considered either a starting point or an end-product, so too may the conjunction be considered the first or the last of the series of aspects. And like a seed, an exact conjunction refers to a 'moment' of pure potentiality. In practice, however, *exact* conjunctions are very rare, there almost always being some number of minutes, however few, either short or over two planets' occupying the same longitudinal position. In traditional terms, a usual conjunction (that is, one between planets separated by no more than 7° or, at the most 10°) can be either *applying* or *separating*. In the former instance, the faster planet moves toward the slower, toward the conjunction that will end the current cycle. In the latter case, the faster planet moves away from the slower, thus away from the conjunction beginning a new cycle of relationships and beginning the involutionary hemicycle of aspects. Both types of conjunctions refer to the need and capacity for a very special type of activity: activity close to the source. The applying conjunction refers to activity nearly withdrawn into subjective synthesis at the end of a cycle; the separating conjunction refers to activity still very subjective (beginning of a cycle).

As an applying conjunction forms to end a cycle, the need the next opening cycle will attempt to fulfill becomes, as it were, 'set' or formulated in a particular way. When the conjunction is exact, it represents the actual release of a new energy or power, of a new possibility of developing what the two planets represent together at a new level or in some new field—in order to satisfy the needs left unfulfilled by the previous cycle, in order to build upon its accomplishments in a progressive way. As the conjunction separates, the potency released at the moment of exact conjunction is symbolically distributed. At this bare beginning of the cycle, however, everything toward which the new release is directed exists only as a potentiality which *has* to be developed. The conjunction beginning a cycle is the symbolic New Moon—the absence of the Moon from the night-sky. This means pure subjectivity, for there is as yet nothing outward to reflect anything back to the consciousness at first wholly preoccupied with its subjective experience of new power and possibilities.

Because a process is only starting to operate, the person in whose chart a (or several) conjunction(s) appears may seem to be overly concerned with the functions represented by the conjoining planets. Such subjective experience almost inevitably includes an element of confusion and, psychologically speaking, projection. The activities and consciousness of the person with an involuntary conjunction in his or her birth-chart may reveal an inability to distinguish between inner wishes, dreams or feelings and actual realities in the outer world. For if one were able to consciously sort out new possibilities, plan to go in a particular direction and act to start 'getting there,' one would not be barely beginning a new cycle. By definition one would be much farther along in a process. New possibilities just barely beginning to be subjectively felt are *meant* to be fascinating, although they can be obsessively so, as well as overwhelming. This is especially so at the beginning of a cycle when a rush of new possibilities is almost inevitably juxtaposed against the lingering patterns—however obsolete or binding—of the past.

The first category or type of relationships between planets— i.e., when two planets are from 0° to 30° apart, from conjunction to semi-sextile—therefore present the need to focus new possibilities at an existential level. This necessarily means having to meet and at least tentatively overcome the pressure of the past, or at the very least to render its 'ghosts' psychologically ineffectual. In so doing, one born with planets in conjunction gradually discovers the limits and the special purpose of the beginning of the particular cycle, at least insofar as it can be felt or apprehended in his or her life.

Two factors are especially important regarding conjunctions in natal charts: house position of the conjunction and how the conjunction is integrated into the overall planetary pattern. Through the experiences represented by the conjunction's house, the person can best, and will be challenged to, *exemplify*—i.e., focus at the existential level in his or her life—the new possibilities represented by the conjunction. These experiences become a source of the power and material with which other related planets and aspects operate. The zodiacal sign in which the conjunction occurs merely indicates the type of quality of power—potency—being released.

A full and conscious understanding of what a conjunction refers to is entirely a secondary matter for the person in whose chart one or several appear. *Activity* is more significant than consciousness during the waxing or involutionary hemicycle. For activity, at first spontaneous, instinct-ruled or even compulsive, is what will eventually 'awaken' or given birth to a new level of consciousness, in a new way, at the opposition. Consciousness thus evoked will develop and evolve through the second or 'waning' hemicycle of the process. Thus, the most significant meaning that can be given to a conjunction is an actional, or rather pre-actional one—to *allow* the potency it denotes to manifest in one's life, especially in the area of life indicated by the house in which the conjunction falls.

A conjunction in a birth-chart can be seen, figuratively speaking, as a 'well-spring' through which potency 'close to the source' —and therefore relatively unpolluted—can flow into one's life, *if* one allows it to happen. The conjunction's aspects and phase-relationships with the other planets reveal how that potency 'wants' naturally to be distributed in other areas of life; where, if there are other aspects, especially oppositions, involved, the results of allowing the conjunction's potency to operate in one's life can be more objectively manifest and consciously known and interpreted.

Disagreement about allowable orbs notwithstanding, we should perhaps enlarge our conception about conjunctions, and learn to see aspects in a birth-chart as having been dynamically formed, that is, as stations along a continuum of meaningful relationships. Two planets in the same sign (or even in adjacent signs and not yet 30° apart) still carry the quality of the beginning of a cycle. They are still distributing the 'close to the source' potency of what was released at the exact conjunction in a relatively spontaneous way. If a third planet 'waxing' away from the two conjoining ones happens to aspect or broadly oppose the degrees on and following which the separating conjunction has spanned, the third planet's function (and house) can act to focus or objectively manifest the possibilities—still in their formative phases—of what the conjunction released. In other words, a planet opposing even a widely separating conjunction (perhaps *especially* a widely separating conjunction, for its potency is more 'widely' distributed and its subjectivity less intense) helps to focus and challenge to actual manifestation the power and possibilities released and made available through the conjunction. This is perhaps most dramatic when conjunctions of historical significance (Jupiter/Saturn; Saturn with Uranus, Neptune or Pluto; Uranus with Neptune or Pluto; Neptune/Pluto, etc.) aspect and therefore need to be in some way, depending on the aspect, focused through 'personal' planets in natal charts.

PHASE 2 — FOCUSING

Phase 2 begins when the relationship between two planets spans 30°, the faster planet being now 30° ahead of the slower one. In the soli-lunar cycle, this approximately coincides with the appearance of the Crescent Moon—literally 'the growing one'— usually about two-plus days after New Moon. What gives added significance to the Crescent phase is that a dim outline of the full Moon-disc very often surrounds the brightly lit slim Crescent. This vague outline of the Full Moon is not, however, the result only of the developing relationship between the Sun and Moon per se. The light surrounding the Crescent is not the same lunar-reflected solar light as illuminates the silver sliver. It is solar light reflected first onto Earth, then onto the Moon—thus, "Earth-shine."*

The symbolism of the Crescent Moon is thus complex and many-sided. First, its appearance simply indicates that the cycle between the Sun and Moon has proceeded far enough for some of what the cycle represents to be seen, that is, objectively manifest. The Crescent or beginning of Phase 2 signals the end of the period of extreme subjectivity symbolized by the New Moon and Phase 1. At least some of the power released at the conjunction can and must be 'put to work' in Phase 2. Complementing the Crescent, symbol of beginning, the dim outline of the Full Moon surrounding it foreshadows, as it were, the culmination of the cycle. As the relationship between the two planetary functions begins to manifest outwardly, some vague hint of 'where it may be going' may be dimly perceived. This vision, however imprecise it may be at this point, is meant to be an enticing promise of fulfillment to come. Such enticement may be necessary, since Phase 1 fascination with new power and possibilities may have worn off by now; as subjectivity lessens, more mundane concerns make themselves felt.

Because this presentiment of fulfillment is symbolized by Earth-shine, however, it has a special meaning. Not only has the soli-lunar relationship developed sufficiently to be perceived (the Crescent Moon), it has developed enough to *include* a third, most important factor, the Earth. While cycles of relationship most obviously involve two moving bodies other than Earth, they are nevertheless viewed *from* Earth and given meaning in *human* terms, according to what they present to human consciousness from its point of view on Earth, and according to the human capacity—developed in the Earth's biosphere—to render celestial phenomena meaningful. The Crescent Moon surrounded by Earth-shine thus refers to the symbolic 'awakening' of the Earth to soli-lunar development thus far. The Earth, the home of Man, is the symbol of Man. Here, its reflected light symbolizes his vaguely dawning first awareness that he *needs* to grow and develop in a new direction, however imprecisely he envisions it. The Earth-shine refers to man's capacity to *partici-*

---

*cf. *The Lunation Cycle* by Dane Rudhyar (Shambhala Publications: 1971).

pate in subsequent phases of the now three-way developing relationship. However uncertain their efficacy or outcome, the imaginal and actional capacities are stirred into manifestation during this phase of a cycle. One can and must play one's part in coming developments.

Ideally then, the semi-sextile in a birth-chart represents a very natural initial focusing of a vision of something toward which to work and aspire. The power of imagination awakens, and with it a desire to manifest the substance of one's imaginings. The question is at first, "How to?" but at this phase it is premature. Images of possibilities must first become *focused*. The question might rather be, "Whence do the images arise?" In Phase 2 of the involutionary hemicycle, they 'descend' as it were to the level of personal experience from the level of superpersonal potency. What was purely potential in the beginning takes the first step toward directly involving itself in actual form. Effective action *follows* imagination, and imagination forms and focuses *will* so that subsequent action can be controlled and purposeful. Everyday activities referring to planets in Phase 2 relationship should be imbued with a sense of greater possibilities. The semi-sextile is thus no more a 'weak sextile' than the sextile is a 'weak trine.' Every definite and clear-cut relation has its meaning and is one link in the chain of relations.

As Phase 2 progresses, an urge to mobilization surfaces and intensifies, especially around the middle of the phase, when the two planets are separated by about 45°—in a magnetic field, an angle of maximum intensity of forces. Here imaginal and actional momentum is tested in two ways. Whenever one takes or even contemplates taking a step toward some future fulfillment, all the pastward resistance or inertia within one rebels and refuses to take the step. Resistance here can mean simple uncertainty or hesitation expectable at the beginning of a cycle, or it can refer to more deeply entrenched patterns of fear or preference which are carry-overs from a past that has yet to be entirely assimilated. Fear must be met; prideful preference must give way to the promptings of greater possibilities.

This becomes essential as the second challenge of Phase 2 is met. As the person with planets in Phase 2 relationship (especially in or near semi-square) matures and emerges from subjective enthrallment with a sense of new powers, he or she encounters the 'real world' for the first time. As subjective dreams and wishes are seen beside existential realities, some degree of shock or surprise may be experienced. Two 'worlds,' inner and outer, must be reconciled; peace must be made between the two. Frustration, engendered by the apparent gap between some imagined 'utopia' and the outer, inferior, perhaps inflexible reality one faces, should not be allowed to team-up with and feed inner resistance. If this occurs, the capacity for futureward activity becomes at least temporarily paralyzed, and a premature sense of frustration develops. If, however, the focusing of vision so necessary and indeed natural in Phase 2 has been allowed to occur, outer obstacles overcome or humbly side-stepped by faith in a more long-term process nurture rather than thwart a growing sense of capability.

Here again, no aspect or phase-relationship exists in a birth-chart by itself. What is important is the relationship of all planets and relationships to one another. Excellent examples of focal Phase 2 relationships are found in the life and chart of Alan Watts, the British-born Zen scholar and promoter of Oriental philosophies in the West. First, Pluto and Neptune, both in Watts' seventh house, are approaching semi-sextile, being at his birth about 28½° apart. Because these two planets move so slowly, this Pluto/Neptune relationship is common enough in the horoscopes of persons born in the years surrounding Watts' birth in 1915. But Watts' Sun in the first house at 15° Capricorn broadly opposes them both—or more properly, opposes the midpoint of the forming semi-sextile. In this way, it potentially focuses into Watts' individual being and destiny what the Pluto/Neptune semi-sextile represented. Watts' Moon is also in Phase 2 relationship with Neptune; it is in the eighth house, about 42°—a semi-square—ahead of Neptune.

The Pluto/Neptune conjunction before Watts' birth released in 1891-92 the potency for an almost 500-year-long process of universalization, which in our century has manifested through Phases 1 and 2 as an increasing globalization of human activity and consciousness. Watts, the quintessential, almost provincial Englishman by birth and education, nevertheless played a significant role in what he himself considered the most significant development of the 20th century: the meeting of Christianity and Buddhism in the

West. He wrote extensively about Zen and Eastern thought, long before it became fashionable to do so or to sit zazen or practice meditation. In fact, his life-work contributed greatly to bringing such practices to the attention of Westerners, especially in America where almost the whole of his adult life was spent.

Watts' work, however, was in no way divorced from his own 'personal,' everyday life and essential being; as the Pluto/Neptune/Sun configuration required, it was focused *through* them. Watts felt that he had to help bridge the philosophical, psychological gulf between East and West in the outer, academic and intellectual world, but he in fact had also to reconcile the two approaches and overcome the cultural inertia within himself. He tried to accomplish the former—and wound up doing the latter instead, thus paving the way for an outer, social and religious integration to follow later—by becoming an Anglican priest in 1945. He hoped to bring what he felt was the wisdom of the East into the Western Church. He nevertheless left the ministry some five years later, having realized that the social and religious institutions of the time were not broad enough to accommodate his purpose. Yet in spite of outer obstacles, a vision of possibilities had become firmly focused within him, and like a stone dropped into the middle of a pond, the ripples spread in widening circles.

The waxing semi-square relationship between Watts' Moon and Neptune was perhaps less happily manifest during his life. Married and disillusioningly divorced several times, he could never seem to reconcile the outer realities of a monogamous society with his subjective wishes and dreams. Nevertheless, he lived his relationships in his own way—viz. the title of his autobiography—endeavoring as best he could to overcome the inertia of obsolete patterns of response and relationship. *

Before moving on to consider Phase 3 of cyclic relationships between planets, we can illustrate another important point using Alan Watts' chart as an example. (It may be a premature digression for some students, but it may be helpful for others at this point.) Being able to see how a birth-chart forms dynamically, can be a great aid

---

*cf. *In My Own Way* by Alan Watts

in becoming able to interpret it significantly. For understanding from a truly process-oriented point of view the dynamics behind aspect and chart formation can lead to understanding dynamic processes of human development. Understanding what the Pluto/Neptune conjunction historically represented, 'watching' it separate and release its potentiality through the first decades of the 20th century; visualizing the Sun coming 'round to oppose the middle of its span at Watts' birth, potentially focusing some aspect of the developing Pluto/Neptune cycle in and through him and his life (even watching the Moon conjoining the Sun before his birth, the soli-lunar cycle developing, passing over and including the Pluto/Neptune semi-sextile by the time of Watts' birth); and understanding at least some aspect of Watts' life as a manifestation of the Pluto/Neptune/Sun potentiality: all these steps in thinking are process-oriented keys to interpreting Watts' life and chart. Once the principles behind such a many-sided 'seeing' are fully assimilated, they 'work' for interpreting all charts and lives.

PHASE 3 — ORGANIZING

Phase 3 begins with the astrological aspect sextile, but no distinctive shape is produced at this phase of the lunation cycle. Instead, the Moon gradually increases in size, reflecting more and more of the Sun's light to Earth. Similarly, during this phase of the cyclic process between two planets, gradual growth and expansion continue on the basis of the initial release of power (Phase 1) and its subsequent focusing and the overcoming of inner resistance (Phase 2).

While the first phase (0° to 30°) refers to the actual release of new potentialities and the subjective, captivating sense of new power and possibilities attending such a release, the second phase (30° to 60°) can represent a reaction to it. The release of power must become focused, resistance to the focusing arises and must be overcome during Phase 2. During Phase 3, both 'action' and 'reaction' must be integrated within a wider, more inclusive field of activity. This means that at the sextile, the creative impulse, having at least somewhat freed itself from the pressures of the past, and having at least tentatively acquired some kind of form (or direction), these forms can begin to take advantage of environmental opportunities for their growth and development. They can begin to become more focused and useful within the environment in which the cycle is developing—and opportunities for their development *will* present themselves, if all has gone well with the previous phases, because the initial release of power symbolized by the conjunction was *in answer to a need* which must begin to become concretely fulfilled.

Forms focused during Phase 2 can begin to take on a life of their own. By analogy, this is similar to the way a seed germinates and develops into a maturing plant. Phase 1 and 2 polarize each other as the rootlet is polarized by the germ whose upspringing it supports. Phase 3 then adds branches in both directions. Roots branch out to explore the depths, seeking a broader base of nourishment; leaves unfold to capture and transform radiant 'light' into 'life.' The new possibilities, by now at least partial or tentative actualities, anchor themselves in the realm of objectivity.

The sextile is thus a relation indicating a syncretic capacity, the capability to draw upon and synthesize materials from a number of sources. It thus refers to the capacity for the practical type of organization which makes everyday life possible and significant. Involutionarily speaking, organization means differentiation. Each developing organism must learn to do what it does best. It becomes a specialist. As specialization occurs, a particular organism becomes increasingly able to work with materials available from a wider variety of sources, and to organize them according to the direction of growth in which the cycle is proceeding.

In birth-charts, semi-sextiles usually link planets in zodiacal signs of opposite polarity and in adjacent houses. Adjacent signs and houses are in Phase 1 and 2 relationship to one another. Like any Phase 1 and 2 relationships, they stand in relation to one another as action and reaction. Sextiles, however, usually link planets in signs of the same polarity and in houses separated by an intervening house: inclusion is the key. As the subjectively-felt creative impulse beginning the cycle matures enough to include external realities, the environment accommodates and includes the steadily growing forms.

When interpreting sextiles—actually all aspects—in birth-charts, we should realize that what they represent is, in a sense, cumulative. A particular aspect focused in a birth-chart refers to a specific kind of developmental step which must be taken during the life of the person whose birth-chart it is. The implication is that the previous steps leading to that particular aspect are somehow—historically, hereditarily and/or karmically—condensed into some kind of past which is nevertheless active as a foundation for the present and unfolding life-pattern. On the other hand, the dictum 'ontology repeats phylogeny' is as valid in relation to human development *ex utero* as it is in relation to the development of a fetus in the womb. We see this working in cases where young children manifest some special kind of talent early in life. Often, it vanishes or 'goes underground'—the child loses interest in it in favor of other, perhaps more fashionable pursuits—around puberty or adolescence. Depending, of course, on the child's birth-chart and life-pattern, this may refer to an old form which has become obsolete and must be allowed to disintegrate or to become transformed into something else. Or, in order to reawaken the talent at a more adult level or to allow it to become transformed, the youth may then have to pass through a developmental process similar to the one we are discussing here—as it were, from the 'beginning,' symbolically a conjunction, regardless of any natal aspect.

Thus, while every aspect refers to a phase of a larger interplanetary process (some including yet also encompassing one human life-span), it also refers to a personal 'mini-process' which must be gone through during a person's life. Presumably, this is because every new birth is, in a sense, a conjunction—a release of new potentialities which must be actualized through a process of structured growth and development. This 'mini-process' involves all the biological and psychological growing and developing we do in order to become able and willing to take the steps to which particular aspects in our chart refer. The actual outworking and schedule of this 'mini-process,' its timing and the circumstances through which it develops, is what progressions and transits in relation to the natal chart refer to. In other words, in order to actualize fully, say, a sextile in a birth-chart, one must allow the subjective sense of possibility or capability to surface in the psyche (conjunction) as one matures. Inner resistance must often be overcome, one's talents must be allowed to develop and express themselves through form (Phases 1 and 2), and a certain kind of 'shock' at dealing with the 'real world' may have to be experienced. Then (Phase 3), when environmental (relational, social, historical, etc.) opportunities present themselves, one must be willing to take advantage of them—or at least not be too quick to say "No," or "I can't." The importance of allowing this mini-process to run its course becomes increasingly significant as squares—Phase 4—in aspect relationships are reached.

PHASE 4 — DECIDING

The square (90° aspect) marks an especially important turning point in a cycle. In the soli-lunar cycle, it is marked by the distinctive shape of the First Quarter Moon. The growing inside curve of the Crescent Moon has now become a straight line, a cutting edge slicing its way across the night-sky. What gives added significance to this phase in the lunation cycle is that when the Moon reaches about a 90° angular distance from the Sun, it crosses the orbit of the Earth, and moves away from the Sun and the place of the previous soli-lunar conjunction (New Moon), going toward the orbit of Mars and the place where the Full Moon will occur. The lunation cycle symbolism thus implies cutting away on two accounts, for the straight edge of the Quarter Moon not only cuts across the night-sky, but also across the Earth's orbit. In human terms, cutting away literally translates as 'de-cision.' It means a release from 'source,' because at First Quarter the Moon is no longer pushed, as it were, by the power released at conjunction, but is geared toward or 'drawn on' to the opposition by the 'promise' of the Full Moon.

This basic 'change of gears' occurs in any cycle at the 'waxing square'—that is, when a faster planet is, say, 82° to 98° ahead of a slower one and moving away from it—and it can be more clearly seen if we picture the developing cycle as a vibration or wave. What results is a figure called a sinusoid, which looks something like a horizontal letter S, or two half-circumferences of opposite polarities, one below and one above a line of equilibrium represented by the cycle's conjunction and opposition. The involutionary hemicycle with which we are concerned here is represented by the hemicircle below the line of equilibrium.

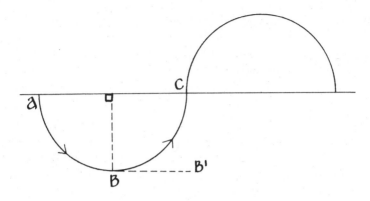

figure 2-1

Looking at this figure, it is clear that if we start from A as a point of departure, we will, on reaching B, have completed one quarter of the cycle—a 90° arc. The two points A and B are related by an angle of 90° —a waxing square. In terms of the involutionary process, it is easy to infer from such a picture that the creative impulse involving itself in form since the conjunction beginning the cycle (A) reaches the apex of its involvement at the square (B); the involutionary process 'bottoms out,' as it were. If the process is to proceed to a full, healthy culmination (C), however, not only a 'bottoming out,' but a basic change in direction is necessary. Further motion along the arc AB will not lead *toward* C but away from it. Activity AB must now be redirected to BC, by overcoming the inertia of motion (momentum) AB and the pull of centrifugal force leading 'off track' to what we have marked as B'.

We can envision this situation metaphorically by picturing a car traveling along the sinusoid figure, about to turn the corner of the waxing square. The car is impelled into the curve by its own momentum and the angle of the road. But about halfway through the turn, the driver must take over the steering mechanism. If he fails to do so, centrifugal force will pull his car off track and perhaps crash it. This can be averted only by a successful self-steering maneuver which changes the direction of the car's motion away from B' and definitely orients it toward C. The car emerging from the curve is of course 'the same' car, unchanged in its structure and appearance.

But the driver's capacity to steer the course before him—which is nevertheless not 'his own' in the sense of being his personality's or ego's creation—has been challenged by the experience and perhaps irrevocably transformed.

At one level, we can understand from the foregoing that a person with important waxing squares in his or her birth-chart has at various times in his or her life to meet 'squarely' the need for clear-cut decision—to allow the situation to be faced to develop by not shrinking from opportunities (Phase 3) or being narrowly bound to an attitude of resistance (Phase 2). When an opportunity to 'seize the moment' presents itself, even if it takes the form of a crisis or requires severance from well-familiar, comfortable patterns—*especially* if it requires such repudiation of whatever of one's past conditioning has become obsolete—the key to 'squaring' oneself with life can be summed up in two words and an exclamation point: "Do it!"

But what really is implied and at stake in such a crisis?

We can think of it as a 'crisis in action' requiring definite acts of self-assertion able to break the momentum of obsolete past conditioning. If the 'ghosts' of the past had to be met and at least tentatively overcome at earlier phases of the process (particularly during Phase 2 and at the interplanetary semi-square), they must definitely be banished at the square. If the inertia of past patterns antedating the beginning of this new cycle had to be checked early on, or worked out by meeting and working through past-conditioned psychological projection, such inertia must definitely be broken now. In other words, whatever in the past focused, molded and conditioned earlier forms through which the process operated at that time and was thereby brought to its present state, but which now hinders further development toward the fulfillment of the cycle, must be repudiated. This means a basic reorientation away from subservience to and dependence upon the past—no matter how beautiful the tradition or satisfying the sense of security—toward a reliance on a deeply felt and experienced intuition of what some future, more autonomously achieved fulfillment could be. It means the need for a definite kind of emergence into maturity where the planetary functions involved in the square are concerned. It means the need for taking a stand, becoming committed, and acting out the commitment. The waxing square can thus be called an aspect of individualization. It forces one to emerge from the womb of parentage, of culture and tradition, to stand on one's own feet and foundation, facing the world as a true individual rather than merely as a particular person —a specimen of one's lineage and times.

Behind this individualizing 'crisis in action'—behind the need for this kind of future-oriented, self-assertive, decisive action—is also what we can think of as a 'crisis in incarnation.' For incarnation, or the taking on of form, is the aim of the involutionary process. Having focused and steadied itself through earlier phases of the process, the creative impulse beginning the cycle now needs to be given definite form to actually operate as an objective factor in the world. Having at least tentatively overcome the inertia of the past (Phase 2) and adapted itself to operating through available material in current environmental conditions (Phase 3), the creative impulse seeks definite manifestation.

When such a phase is reached in a cycle between two planets, it means that through earlier phases of the cyclic process the functions represented by the planets have been sufficiently steadied in relation to one another, within some tentative form, to definitely take on a solid anchorage in the world of physical and social realities. The person with a significant waxing square in his or her birth-chart is called upon to be such an anchor, the vehicle or 'focalizer' through whom a definite kind of *form-building activity* can operate, relating the two planetary functions and preparing the way for the culmination of their relationship.

But how is this need for definite form-building activity different from what we encountered as 'focusing in form' in earlier phases of the process? Why call this need for 'incarnation' a 'crisis'? Answers to these questions can be approached through understanding the meaning of the term crisis, which comes from the Greek *crino*, "to decide." De-cision, in turn, literally means "cutting away," and any crisis or decision involves choosing among alternatives, leaving one or some of them behind and embracing others. At least two factors present themselves in any crisis or decision, but the most fundamental choice at stake in major turning points of life is not between the two or more mutually exclusive *outer* possibilities we are presented

47

with. Most deeply and fundamentally, it is between two basic *inner* qualities, one of which eventually predominates as the spirit in which all outer decisions are made. The two inner qualities are courage and fear. Behind all more superficial choices, the waxing square as a turning point in an overall process, which spans yet also encompasses our present life-cycle, presents the 'choice' between these two.

Let us stress here that the kind of decision symbolically called for by waxing squares in a birth-chart need not take the form of traumatic, or even dramatic events, encounters or psychological crises. We often make what turn out to be the most significant decisions of our lives without realizing how important they are or to what they will lead. When major life decisions do come in the form of crisis, it is often an indication that some more fundamental decision had not previously been courageously taken, or that some underlying, essential life-issue has been met with inertia or in a spirit of fear. So-called "sins of omission"—especially those of which we remain largely unconscious, so deeply ingrained is the fear and inertia called up in response to meeting the situations engendering them—are often far more dire in their consequences than "sins of commission." What we fail to do out of fear, either when it is necessary for *it* to be done or for *us* to be able deliberately to do it, often comes back to 'haunt' us in a sharper or more menacing form than what we may have actually or even wrongly done out of ignorance or misunderstanding.

Any waxing-square crisis not met, or met in a negative, fearful way, engenders not only consequences which have themselves to be met and corrected, but also more fear—which in turn forces us to meet other eventualities in a negative way, thereby creating a vicious, self-perpetuating pattern. When fear comes to dominate a person's actions, feelings and will, all growth and forward motion—imperative and ideally vigorous at this phase of the cycle—ceases. Outward or severe inner crises may be necessary to 'force the issue,' as it were. They have the possibility of creating in us perhaps sufficient tension, or even desperation, to enable us to break the bonds of our own fear or inertia and take a step we would otherwise be unable or unwilling to take. Crises help us avoid the pitfalls of so-called "sins of omission" by forcing us to do *something*—doing anything being better than doing nothing whenever fear and inertia have reached paralyzing proportions.

In saying all this, we do not mean to stress the crisis-producing aspect of the waxing square at the expense of its constructive—form-building—side, for both are important at this phase of the process. In order for any new structure to be built—safely and to last to fulfill its function—deep foundations must be dug to support it. As high as the proposed structure is to soar, that deep must the foundations go. They must rest on a bedrock of conscious and courageous commitment, not on the shifting sands of changing personal moods and whims. Such excavation is often difficult work. Tools grind against encrustations, dirt flies and the builder's knuckles—or worse—are inevitably skinned and battered. His back aches and his muscles may protest, but his is useful, practical work. The waxing square, unlike the succeeding trine which can be overly idealistic, is an aspect of practicality, of having to deal in concrete ways with the planetary functions involved.

In actual practice, one must be extremely careful to distinguish between this waxing, involutionary square—when, again, the faster planet is *ahead* of the slower and separating from it—and the waning square which will occur during the second hemicycle. In addition, here as with the semi-sextile, semi-square and sextile, the terms *applying* and *separating* should not be confused with the terms *waxing* and *waning*. Only in relation to the conjunction are the terms applying and waning or separating and waxing synonymous. Thus, there are, in a sense, four kinds of squares: applying and separating waxing squares, and applying and separating waning squares.

If we call planet *x* the faster planet, and planet *y* the slower, a waxing square forms between them when, say, planet *x* is in Cancer and planet *y* is in Aries. The same type of waxing square occurs when *y* is at the beginning of Aquarius and *x* is at the end of Aries. The waxing square is *applying* when *x* in Cancer is at 10° and *y* in Aries is at 15°—there are 85° between them, but this distance is increasing to 90°. The same is true of *x* at 27° Aries and *y* at 2° Aquarius. There are also 85° separating the pair, but there will soon be 90°. Waxing squares *separate* when, after the planets have exactly squared one another, more than 90° separates *x* and *y*, with *x* still ahead of *y*. *X* at 20° Cancer is separating from a waxing square with *y* when *y* is at

17° Aries. X at 7° Taurus separates from waxing square with y when y is at 5° Aquarius.*

The applying waxing square and the separating waxing square symbolize different phases in the decision-making process. The applying waxing square archetypally refers to a turning point in the process which has not yet been reached, to a decision which has not yet been made. The person with such an aspect in his or her chart has to 'steer through the curve,' as it were, and make the decision. A separating waxing square indicates that a decision has, on some level, already been taken and a direction committed to. It is up to the person with such an aspect in his or her horoscope to work out that commitment, to involve himself or herself in the building process proper.

PHASE 5 — EXPRESSING

The trine (120° aspect) begins the fifth step or phase of the involutionary hemicycle. In the soli-lunar cycle, no distinct shape of the Moon is produced, for after having, as it were, stepped across the Earth's orbit, it continues gradually to grow. What had been a concave curve at the Crescent and a straight line at First Quarter has now become convex. The 'direction' of the cycle is definitely outward now. This fifth step in the cycle thus refers to creative expression and outward application. It represents the means and the opportunities, arising as a result of committed and deliberate action toward an end felt and acknowledged to be necessary, to integrate what is now more autonomously developing into a workable and productive way of life. What was released as a potential answer to a need at the conjunction should by now have become established enough to begin to fulfill that need, at least for the person in whose life the development is occurring.

From a process-oriented point of view, aspects in natal charts are, in a sense, cumulative. They represent the next step to be taken

---

*As we'll see later on, this is a very different picture from what occurs at *waning* squares, when from a process-oriented point of view planets are separated by more or less than 270°, and waning squares can also be applying and separating. An applying waning square would occur with x at 10° Capricorn and y at 15° Aries. A separating waning square would occur when, after the exact square between x and y, x had reached, say, 20° Capricorn, and y had moved to 17° Aries.

on the foundation of earlier phases which have already occurred. Because they operate in terms of what we have called a 'mini-process,' recapitulating these earlier phases and focusing them into the present life-situation, a person with significant waxing trines in his or her horoscope may appear to have to meet and take major life-decisions whether or not waxing squares are also central. But as previously mentioned, one often makes what turns out to be a very significant decision without realizing the decision is anything extraordinary. At the time the decision is made there is no way of knowing what larger implications a seemingly minor matter may eventually have. Such a pattern is typical of what can be expected in association with waxing trines, because this aspect follows and therefore qualitatively includes or builds upon the waxing square. Something in us responds to a challenge or opportunity, but at this phase of the cyclic process, it may not be necessary—or even desirable from a more inclusive perspective—for that 'something' to be the conscious 'I' or ego. This is still the involutionary hemicycle, during which spontaneous activity is most important, more important than consciousness or understanding.

In the subjective experience of a person with waxing trines in his or her birth-chart, decisions may thus carry an aura of pleasant inevitability, or feel as if they have already been made. Such a person often has the feeling of merely 'going through the motions' when making decisions, of meeting a situation whose outcome, while uncertain in terms of the form it will take, is nonetheless never really in question in terms of the response the person will offer. After the hard decisions of the waxing square have been taken and outer obstacles surmounted, one can begin to envision an ideal of 'where' the process is going. One can be fascinated and carried along by this idealism.

A contemporary psycho-spiritual guide has summed up in psychological terms this involutionary process focused into every natal trine:

> *The process of growth begins with an image of its goal, though this image does not consciously direct itself. It simply appears. Even when it is not in the visual form of a specific image, it is present; and it expresses itself then as a nonconscious knowing of what is true* in principle. *It is present as an*

image of the new condition which the psyche is engaged in bringing to actuality. It is a goal that is an active factor in the person because it is a potentiality working to fulfill itself. Neither the goal nor the manner of its fulfillment are thought out in advance; nor are they rationally decided upon. The entire pattern discloses itself as it acts itself out; and often it is only in the course of this enactment that the person discovers the nature of the goal he is truly seeking...

Many instances of this come to mind in the lives of creative persons. One thinks, for example, of Herman Melville as a young man going to sea on a whaling ship with no possible way of knowing that the seeds were being planted for one of the world's great expeditions into the dimension of symbols. The writing of Moby Dick *lay completely in the future, but something drew him forward towards it. His experience at that time, as throughout the later creative years of his life, was as though one of his legs stepped forward on its own without his deciding it, and the other leg was forced to follow and step a little further. Thus, he was drawn on towards attainments without limit, never knowing the ending nor even the immediate goal. He did not decide it, and yet something within him forced it to be.* *

The astrological significance of Dr. Progoff's thoughts is increased when we realize that the Sun and Moon formed a waxing trine at Melville's birth—and that the Sun also trines Saturn.

Nevertheless, even such a trine is no more a 'given' in a birth-chart or life than a square or sextile. An immature, recalcitrant or rigid ego can pervert or call a halt to even the most potentially creative processes in life. One with involutionary trines in his or her horoscope must be willing to follow the rhythm set by his or her process as it unfolds. Like Melville, he or she must allow the necessary steps to be taken, one 'foot' to follow the other. For even Melville's novel didn't actually write itself. On an archetypal level, it may have formed and focused itself in his consciousness seemingly without effort on his part. Yet his was the hand that actually wrote out

---

*Ira Progoff, *The Symbolic and the Real* (New York, Julian Press, 1963), pp. 76-77.

the words, page after page after page. His was the patience and perseverance through which creative expression could operate.

These last mentioned qualities—patience and perseverance—are crucial to a successful and actually productive Phase 5 relationship between planets. For at the middle of the phase, the sesquiquadrate or sesqui-square (135° aspect) occurs. It performs a similar function in the second quarter of the cycle as the semi-square (45° aspect) did in the first quarter. At the middle of Phase 2, the momentum of barely nascent imaginal and actional stirrings is intensified and tested; at the middle of Phase 5, the decision and commitment elicited by the waxing square is tested. What has been committed to at the square takes on, as it were, a 'life of its own' during Phase 4. During Phase 5 it has the possibility of fully expressing itself. But it does so in an environment whose realities have to be met, acknowledged and taken into account. Just as the semi-square represented the 'shock' of a first encounter with a 'real world' challenging the extreme subjectivity of the conjunction, the sesqui-quadrate refers to a similar awakening, now to the realities—both inner and outer—of what was implied in the decision made at the square.

The trine uses and thus exhausts the dynamic energy definitely focused and directed in a particular way at the square. As the sesquiquadrate, a 'second wind' is required. The practicality of the square and the idealism associated with the trine must work together to overcome whatever obstacles appear to slow progress toward the accomplishment of a goal more clearly perceived now than ever before. This phase of the cycle requires forceful but controlled striving and outreaching; substantive growth, a general keynote of Phase 5, thereby follows.

PHASE 6 — IMPROVING

The quincunx or inconjunct (150° aspect) brings the means and opportunities represented by the trine to a more specific focus, and it begins the sixth and final phase of the first hemicycle of activity. Whatever adjustments in expression, action or application are necessary to bring the whole cycle to successful culmination at the opposition should now be made. In this sense, the quincunx is a 'last chance' aspect. For the opposition represents a definite end—and therefore potential crystallization—of whatever precedes it. Metaphorically, it is like taking a timed examination in school. When the bell rings to signal the end of the period, one is finished and hands in his paper, whether he has gone through all the material or not. The results are in—*Iacta alea est*—and on that basis one will pass on to the next form or not.

Subjectively, the quincunx often manifests as a sense of dissatisfaction—dissatisfaction with self in a psychologically mature person, blaming and frustration with others in the person not yet awakened to and accepting of the realities of what surrounds him or her. Such acceptance does not need to imply passivity or the willingness to accept what one knows and believes to be wrong. It simply means awareness, on the basis of which one can act appropriately to correct or improve what in oneself or in one's environment falls short of what seems possible and desirable.

This sense of dissatisfaction with self arising at the quincunx is, however, a new and significant development, for a real sense of 'self' is just beginning to dawn. The struggle to improve (Phase 6), to consciously overcome resistance and shortcomings (Phase 5), to 'steer one's own course' (Phase 4) during the second quarter of the process begins to give one a sense of being alone in one's strivings, of being separate. This awareness, however, is not a true and full expression of selfhood. For individual selfhood ideally and archetypally will begin to blossom only as the opposition forms and after the cycle culminates. The sense of separateness experienced at the quincunx is preliminary to it.

The person with significant quincunxes in his or her birth-chart may experience either an exaggerated sense of self-importance or an undue preoccupation with shortcomings. Underlying both may be a compensating yearning for belongingness, for unconditional acceptance which, regardless of actual circumstances, may seem insatiable. But since it goes hand in hand with true selfhood, true relatedness is only achieved at and after the cycle culminates. The kind of belongingness sought and possible before the opposition forms may represent instead a longing to 'return to the womb'—to the subjectivity of the conjunction—and dissolve the structures of selfhood that have been slowly and perhaps painfully taking form during the involutionary process. Thus, while self-improvement is the significant task of Phase 6, the emphasis needs to be on *improvement* rather than narcissistically on *self*. The person with planets in quincunx relationships is asked to meet and assimilate experiences which have the power to adjust and refine the expression of what is symbolized by the two planetary functions involved.

This improving, refining activity paves the way for the cycle's culmination, the opposition (180° aspect) which both ends the first hemicycle of activity and begins the second. The distinction between applying and separating aspects is again crucial. Two planets nearing but less than 180° apart form an applying opposition ending the first hemicycle. Two planets having already exactly opposed one another and now (or at birth) separated by more than 180° form a separating opposition which occurs at the very beginning of the second hemicycle. Here, as the first hemicycle ends, we are primarily concerned with the former, and will take up the matter of the latter in Part II of this chapter and in Chapter 4.

In the case of the applying opposition, something needs to be brought to fulfillment, to objective manifestation—or rather, something objective in relation to the two planetary functions involved needs to be *allowed* to fulfill itself through the life-pattern of the person whose chart contains an opposition, always a most significant aspect and basic axis. This is still the involutionary process whereby a creative, spirit-born impulse acts spontaneously through us, in answer to a need—*if* we let it. 'Letting it' has a different quality and different implications at each step of the way, that is, each aspect of the involutionary series requires of us a different kind of co-operation or, at the very least, non-hindrance.

This kind of non-interference with integral, spontaneous processes becomes more difficult the more one becomes aware of oneself as a separate 'I' or ego having definite desires and dislikes. Indeed, the more one is conditioned, as in our culture, to think of himself *exclusively* as a separate, 'rugged individual' (who is nevertheless not an 'individual' in the deepest sense of the term, but merely conditioned to be as 'rugged' as he fears, or is taught to imagine, everyone else is), the more difficult an accepting non-violence to natural processes becomes. Such an attitude is often dismissed out of hand or even ridiculed because it is mistakenly associated with weakness and indecision.

The kind of objectivity and personal-emotional detachment necessary to bring a cycle to successful culmination are, however, very different from weakness and indecision. They are achieved only when a person is courageous and inwardly strong enough to free himself or herself from the tyranny of unconscious projections and compulsive, conditioned behavior. The person in whose chart an applying opposition forms a significant axis is asked to meet and assimilate experiences which have the power and possibility of breaking such psychic bonds and thereby freeing and transforming the compulsive behavior tied to them. What results is not to be confused with coldness or indifference, either. For a person with an applying opposition in his or her natal chart has also the possibility of bringing to culmination and concrete, outward manifestation in his or her life something expressing a *fullness* of relationship between the opposing planetary functions.

As the exact opposition nears, the two planets, like the Sun and Moon at Full Moon, face each other from opposite sides of the Earth. The faster planet symbolically 'reflects' as much of the slower planet's 'light' as it can. Since what is represented by the faster planet has distributed, incorporated and been reoriented by the functional activities represented by the slower planet throughout the previous hemicycle of aspect-relationships, the two sets of functions together can now be called upon to do what neither separately or in relation to other planets could previously have accomplished.

Metaphors summing up the cyclic process thus far abound. What began as a stirring deep within a seed implanted in dark, humus-rich soil now culminates in a blushing bloom. What began for the newborn as the potentiality of individual selfhood culminates in midlife as a sense of identify. Having emerged as its builder and begun his labors in earnest at the symbolical waxing square, the mature individual now faces the products of his labor. He sees not only what they are, but himself, his identify, reflected in them. As the process proceeds from this moment of realization—which literally means to 'make real, ' to 'thingify'—much depends on this first meeting of 'I' and 'It' or 'The Other.' Not only what is seen, but how the seer responds to it is crucial.

Under the illumination of the symbolical Full Moon—a 'harvest Moon'—the involutionary process comes to a close.

II. GROWTH THROUGH LETTING GO

The second half of a cycle is characterized by the operation and interaction of two complementary processes. They are best characterized by the terms *devolution* and *evolution*.

Devolution is the continuation and reversal of involution, of the 'life' process begun at conjunction. At the opposition, the cycle's culmination, having exhausted the possibilities for growth inherent in the involutionary process, the vital energy fueling the cycle, like the Moon after Full Moon, begins to wane. The particular forms built as vehicles through which the cycle came to culmination begin slowly to disintegrate as they are no longer needed and the 'life force' is gradually withdrawn from them. Such is the process whereby annual vegetation withers and eventually dies after having produced flower and fruit; such is the inevitable "way of all flesh" after mid-life. And so too is one facet of any truly total and multi-level process of development. Assimilation and deconditioning must necessarily follow intense activity and experience of a new phase of growth may later proceed on as 'clean' and unambiguous a foundation as possible.

Devolution's polar complement in the second hemicycle is *evolution*. While the change from involution to devolution is natural and continuous, the change from involution to evolution requires a kind of mutation or 'quantum leap' from one level, the level of 'life,' to another—the level of 'mind' or growth in consciousness. During the second half of the cycle, the purpose of life is to develop consciousness. As the power of 'life' wanes, consciousness, awakened in the light of the symbolical Full Moon, develops. As 'life'—which operates spontaneously and unconsciously in answer to a need— devolves, 'mind,' which operates consciously toward the fulfillment of a purpose, evolves.

In this chapter we are primarily concerned with the operation of the devolutionary process, and we will discuss the evolutionary process and its special rhythm in the following chapter. Nevertheless, the operation of the two is so interwoven that, at least at first, we will have to consider them together.

The operation and interaction of these two complementary 'energy directions' is made abundantly clear in the often-used symbol of the birth-death-rebirth cycle of annual vegetation. When we outlined the involutionary process characterizing the first half of a cycle, we likened it to the process whereby an implanted seed grows into a mature plant: germ, roots, stem, branches, leaves. The culmination of the cycle—astrologically the opposition aspect—can best be symbolized by a completely formed bud, a potential flower. Contained in the nascent flower is also another kind of potentiality, the seed. While the first hemicycle develops the power of a seed to grow, the second hemicycle develops the power of a new seed to form and function.

After the cycle culminates, the seed develops within the unfolding flower. In order for it to embody the full functional capacity of a seed, two things must happen. First, fertilization must occur to form a seed; second, the seed must be released from the parent plant. Fertilization refers to the possibility of beginning the evolutionary process. It includes not only the possibility of mutation, but it also stresses interaction with the environment, for external factors (wind, insects or human beings) are in many cases necessary for cross-pollination to occur. The process leading to the release of the seed refers to the realm of devolution; as the seed forms within the flower, it in a sense kills the plant that bore it. Having produced the seed, the plant becomes an obsolescent form. The seed deprives of energy the antiquated forms which are incapable of fulfilling the new need of the time—i.e., the fertilization of the seed and its internal development. Only as the flower withers and the plant disintegrates is the seed released from bondage to the dying structure. Only when it is released can it bury itself in the soil enriched by the decaying organic matter of the plant and its preceding generations—and only then can it truly fulfill its functional potential.

The seeds released by a plant are, of course, biological seeds, insuring the perpetuation of the species the following spring. The seeds forming at the culimation of cycles of human experience are 'mind seeds'—also insuring the continuation of strictly human life, but at a level other than the purely biological. 'Mind seeds,' like plant seeds, also require fertilization and cross-pollinization. In human development this occurs through interpersonal and social relationship, and relatedness to works given special value and attention.

Like biological seed-fertilization, relationship can be both evolutionary and devolutionary in character, and at least at the beginning of the second hemicycle, these two processes are inseparable. Relationship is devolutionary insofar as through it, the limitations and shortcomings of the growing consciousness are revealed. This should lead to the evolutionary aspect of relationship in which the growing consciousness becomes aware of its heretofore unconscious and limiting values and assumptions. This evolutionary awareness in turn fuels the positive aspect of the devolutionary process in which what were unconscious values and assumptions reveal their obsolescence and are 'let go.' Relationships thus force the questioning and breakdown of taken-for-granted, habitual patterns of behaving, thinking and feeling which no longer 'work,' or elicit positive responses from working-materials, partners or associates.

Thus, evolution and devolution most constructively interact in the second half of a cyclic process when devolution takes its toll on whatever developed as temporary vehicles during the first hemicycle. These unconscious assumptions and forms of feeling and behaving were necessary to the involutionary process, but after the cycle's culmination, they become obsolete and stand in the way of conscious evolution. As these 'empty shells' are 'let go' and allowed to disintegrate, the developing consciousness is freed to give a new, more timely, appropriate and responsible rather than reactionary meaning to its purposeful participation in life and social processes and events. As objective consciousness, and the power of 'mind' to formulate meaning, develop in scope and acuity, they further challenge whatever stands in the way of the next evolutionary step.

Each half of the overall cyclic process thus essentially refers to a different realm or level of experience and development—the first

hemicycle to the outworking of 'life' through spontaneous, unconscious activity in answer to a need; the second hemicycle to conscious, mental and group-participatory evolution, part of which ne-
cessitates and is facilitated by the devolution or devaluing of what
predominated during the first hemicycle. Each of these processes—
involution, devolution, evolution—operates according to its own
rhythm and 'schedule.' Each is represented astrologically by its own
series of aspects formed according to principles exemplifying and be-
fitting it. We have already outlined the rhythm of involution domi-
nating the first hemicycle of a process, and in Chapter 3 we will
explore in full detail the 'syncopated beat' according to which conscious evolution proceeds. What we have now to do is to understand,
at least briefly, the rhythms of devolution—the inexorable continuation and reversal of the 'life' process as it operates throughout the remainder of the arithmetic series of aspects.

After the opposition, since the faster planet has moved as far away
from the slower planet as it can, it begins to return toward it—actually toward the two planets' next conjunction—and the distance between them decreases. According to the way aspects are considered
in usual astrological practice, aspects formed after the opposition decrease in size, in angular value, and the order of aspects formed during the waning or devolutionary hemicycle is essentially a reversal of
the order of aspects formed during the waxing or involutionary
hemicycle. The waning quincunx *follows* the opposition, then the
trine, square, sextile, semi-sextile and, finally, the conjunction beginning a new cycle. The semi-sextile, for example, occurs as Phase 1
of a six-phase process in the involutionary hemicycle; the semi-sextile of the second hemicycle ends both the devolutionary series and
the entire cyclic process. Similarly, the quincunx ends the involutionary series in the waxing hemicycle, but in the waning hemicycle
it is the first aspect formed after the opposition.

This reversal indicates great differences in meaning between
the (so-called) "same" aspects in the two hemicycles. Unfortunately,
practically all astrologers do consider these two types of aspects—
waxing and waning, involutionary and devolutionary—identical in
meaning. This is due to thinking of aspects merely as categories of
possible interplanetary or even zodiacal relationships, and not as

connected phases of ongoing, cyclic processes. From a process-oriented point of view, a particular aspect has significance only in terms of the place it occupies, the function it performs, in the structure of a *whole* cycle of relationships. It is quite as senseless to believe that a waxing and a waning square have the same significance as it would be to say that the summer and winter solstices have the same meaning in the seasonal cycle of the year beginning at the spring equinox. Youth has not the same character as old age, even if one sometimes speaks of a second childhood or 'adolescence in reverse.' Even if we consider the shapes of the Moon at the first and last quarters, we see that they are oriented in opposite directions. So are the Moon-crescent after the New Moon and the Moon-crescent (or decrescent) before New Moon.

If two opposite stages in planetary relationships are called by the same name and measured exclusively in terms of the same angular value, it discourages the practice of properly differentiating between their meanings. This confusing situation need not, however, be perpetuated. Rather than thinking solely in terms of a series of angular values *decreasing* after the opposition—i.e., 150°, 120°, 90°, 60°, 30°—we can also continue the series of angular values and phase relationships begun at the conjunction. What we work with then is a series of *increasing* angular values: Phase 7, opposition to quincunx (180° to 210°); Phase 8, quincunx to trine (210° to 240°); Phase 9, trine to square (240° to 270°); Phase 10, square to sextile (270° to 300°); Phase 11, sextile to semi-sextile (300° to 330°); Phase 12, semi-sextile to the conjunction beginning the next cycle (300° to 359° 59').

Both ways of considering and measuring waning aspects can be revealing. Measuring in terms of decreasing angular values tends to stress the devolutionary facet of the second hemicycle, since the emphasis is indeed on decrease and the reversal of the involutionary sequence of aspects. The decreasing angular values are actually measured in relation to the coming conjunction beginning the next cycle. The sequence from that perspective shows devolution merely as a clean-up process between two involutionary hemicycles. It stresses the devolutionary process's function of clearing up the life-arena of useless or potentially harmful debris, so that the next life-cycle can start on a clean foundation, the remains of the previous involutionary phases having been fully broken down into 'humus' which will nourish the next sequence of involutionary activity. This way of looking at the devolutionary process fails to show that the ultimately radical clearing-up process operates hand-in-hand with a process of consciousness development, without which the next involutionary process would merely repeat the past one—mistakes, failures and all. The phase-denominated, increasing angular value way of considering the second hemicycle aspects tends toward integrating at least some hint of this evolutionary process into the devolutionary sequence. It—and even more the series of aspects we will study in Chapter 3—points to the second hemicycle as a continuation of the first in the sense that 'reaping' follows a period of 'sowing.'

From another point of view, nothing is actually changed by measuring the aspects in one way or another, *as long as* one clearly recognizes that second hemicycle or waning aspects are different from first hemicycle or waxing aspects, and as long as one understands the interrelationship of major processes operating through the cycle as a whole. Generally speaking, waxing (involutionary) aspects refer to the instinctual building up of the relationship between the two planetary functions involved. During the second hemicycle, the fruit of the relationship is reclaimed. *Devolutionarily*, the emphasis is on the breakdown of the interplanetary relationship, which releases, so to speak, the 'seed essence' of the 'harvest.' What use is made of that harvest as it is released, how and for what purpose it is assimilated and incorporated into the life-pattern of the individual or the community, are concerns of the *evolutionary* process.

As an example, we can continue the illustration of the Venus/Mars cycle we began and left unfinished earlier in this chapter. To recap what we said regarding the first hemicycle of relationships between the two planets: the conjunction beginning the Venus/Mars cycle referred to the need and opportunity to bring the personal-emotional nature to a new level of functioning or self-expression. At the conjunction, the outward-bound, activity-orientation of Mars gave a new direction and impetus to Venus's inwardly directed sense of value and capacity to give form. The new orientation had, first, in the earliest stage of the relationship, to focus itself at the subjective level; then, at the waxing square, to be allowed to 'burst forth' or definitely 'incarnate' in the forms Venus built. During Phases 4, 5 and 6, a commitment to creative, autonomous endeavor had to be established, sustained and refined in order to complete the involutionary process. By the opposition, the cycle's culmination, the personal-emotional nature has become embodied in its creations, whether these manifest as actual forms such as works of art, forms of behavior, or psycho-emotional exteriorizations such as interpersonal relationships, etc. Reflected therein are the unconscious and compulsive values and desires of their creator.

The opposition between Venus and Mars refers to the need and opportunity to bring expression at the personal-emotional level to objective consciousness. This can occur only when the personal-emotional nature becomes aware of its creations as separate from itself. True relationship *with* them, rather than mere subjective reaction *to* them, becomes possible. In this relationship, objective consciousness can be born, and the forms created during the first hemicycle of activity can be consciously made to fulfill an evolutionary purpose. Before this can happen, the nascent consciousness must become aware of and overcome habitual patterns binding self-expression to instinctual, biological imperatives operating at the involutionary level.

In the first stages of the Venus/Mars cycle after the opposition then, the nascent consciousness must disidentify with the strictly biological operation of the two planetary functions. This can be accomplished primarily through interpersonal and social relationships, in which the personal-emotional nature becomes conscious of itself, of what it has become, by relating with what it has created during the first hemicycle. This relating provides awareness-stimulating feedback which forces the nascent consciousness to become aware of the values (Venus) on which activity (Mars) had previously been based. As Venus moves back toward Mars, she symbolically 'gathers in' the harvest of their relationship—a harvest of meaning giving new purpose and value (Venus) to activity (Mars) at the personal-emotional level. As this occurs, the basis on which self-expression has operated heretofore has to be re-evaluated.

At the waning square, the consciousness is thus forced to turn inward again, to question the previously taken-for-granted assumptions and values on which activity at the personal-emotional level operated. Some old forms of expression based on old values reveal themselves to be obsolete, to be out of tune with new values and purposes gradually being recognized and assimilated. The old forms of personal-emotional expression must be 'let go,' and, finally, released. As the cycle ends, consciousness at the personal-emotional level again withdraws into subjectivity. It yearns for a new creative impetus, for an opportunity to begin again, at a new level, to develop new forms of personal-emotional self-expression. The Venus/Mars conjunction beginning the next cycle refers to the release of just such a potentiality. It comes in answer to that need, and also in order to stir into actual operation the new, yet unrealized and latent capacities 'seeded' during the now-ended second hemicycle.

Again, we repeat, everyone is born at some phase of the Venus/Mars relationship, although we are now concerned only with the waning phases of the cycle—and these primarily from a devolutionary point of view. For the purpose of intellectual analysis and understanding, and in astrological textbooks such as this one, the devolutionary and evolutionary processes interacting throughout the second hemicycle can be somewhat separated. But in actual living, especially in the lives of persons in whose birth-charts waning aspects qualitatively or quantitatively predominate or form significant patterns, this is not necessarily the case. The operation of the two processes may be sequential or simultaneous, in the same or in different areas of life, clearly distinguishable from one another or not. Only the 'active intuition' of the astrologer or 'life interpreter' can pierce the 'meaning-enigma' of the client's birth-chart and life-pattern.

PHASE 7—REALIZING

Much has already been said about the metaphorical and theoretical meaning of this pivotal phase in the cyclic process. The most basic significance of an opposition in a person's birth-chart is that it defines a particular set of functional activities (planets), life-areas (houses) and modes of operation (zodiacal signs) in which the person will be challenged to repolarize his or her being. Such repolarization entails breaking away from the level of being at which 'life' holds sway. It means transferring the center of one's being from the level where what is represented by the opposing astrological factors operates unconsciously, compulsively and essentially rooted in biological imperatives, to the level of being at which 'mind'—objectivity and conscious understanding—dominates and purposefully directs activity.

Such a picture may seem very abstract and unrealistic to astrologers used to defining oppositions simply as more or less irreconcilable conflicts between what is represented by the opposing astrological factors. Oppositions may indeed manifest in people's life-patterns as such conflicts, but a truly process-oriented point of view indicates that this usual definition is not so much wrong as it is incomplete. It does not take into consideration the *meaning* of the conflict, what it is *for* in the client's life. In order to understand the situation as a whole, the astrologer/life-interpreter must go beyond this obvious and merely descriptive definition of what most significantly is a dynamic process in a person's life. He or she must ask: "What is my client to do about or with the situation confronting him or her? Is such a conflict really 'irreconcileable?' If it is not, how can it be resolved? Does its solution involve the client 'choosing' one pole of the situation—i.e., what is represented by one set of the opposing factors—over what is represented by the other?" The most basic question of all is: "What can meeting such a situation *mean in the overall development* of the client as a human being, indeed as an individual person?"

In order to answer these questions, we must realize that latent in the natures of people with Phase-7 oppositions in their birthcharts is a high degree of development of the planetary functions involved in the opposition(s). The person has been born at the apex of a cycle developing what these planets represent. While the 'seeds' for their development are within his or her nature at birth, the genetic, familial and/or social circumstances into which he or she is born provide the 'flower' or matrix within which they can develop in an actual, existential way. Such development occurs throughout the 'mini-process' of the person's maturation. As the person develops and each set of planetary functions manifests its own kind of 'fullness,' a contrast sharpens between what the two sets represent, and the polar nature of the planets is emphasized. Hence, perhaps the most challenging and potentially deeply repolarizing oppositions occur between planets whose functions are by nature polar—e.g., Sun/Moon, Sun/Saturn, Moon/Saturn, Venus/Mars, Mercury/Jupiter, Jupiter/Saturn, Saturn/Uranus, Jupiter/Neptune, Pluto/Mars.

When each set of functional activities first expresses itself in the person's life, it may seem to do so more or less independently of the expression of the other set of functions. This apparent unrelatedness or even antagonism is because the opposition emphasizes polarity in the early stages of its 'mini-process' development. Both sets of polar activities initially operate in the life-pattern unconsciously and compulsively, perhaps through the genetic constitutions or personalities of the parents, or through other circumstances over which the person has little or no control or even awareness. As conflicts and contrasts arise, they may even result in psychological complexes. In order for the purposeful, functional nature of such conflicts to operate, they must be allowed to 'come to a head.'

The person must, first, allow to come to objective manifestation what each 'side' of the opposition represents, even if it means conflict or, initially, neurosis. Then, his or her task is to allow the conflict to generate within him or her sufficient dissatisfaction—'energy' or 'fire by friction,' as it were—to enable an awareness to develop of what is at the root of the problem. In other words, the person must realize that no solution to the problem is forthcoming unless he or she is willing to find out and experience what really is behind and implied in the situation. If the person accepts to be the *field* in which the problem resolves *itself*—rather than insisting on an external or technical solution to what is really internal and not subject to the manipulations of technique—he or she has the possibility of becoming objective to both sides of the polarity. Perhaps with a little guidance, he or she can come to see and accept the wider developmental context in which the situation occurs.

Objectivity and acceptance eventually become detachment, which 'breaks the spell,' so to speak, of unconscious compulsion binding the operation of the opposing planetary functions to 'circumstance' seemingly 'outside' the person. As the person accepts to look at the situation as a dynamic, potentially growth-producing aspect of his or her life and being, both 'sides' of the conflict are integrated into a larger picture. The problem is 'solved' insofar as the person rises in consciousness to a level at which the conflict-aspect of the situation ceases to be the central factor. What takes its place is the challenge to express, harmoniously but dynamically—and above all, consciously—an integrated fullness of what had previously, in another form, conflicted.

Successful polarization thus ultimately actualizes a person's latent capacity to bring to objective manifestation a creative fullness of what is implied in the relationship between the two sets of opposing planetary functions. This brings the previous, prenatal involutionary development between the two opposing functions to culmination and 'flowering' in and through that person's life. It makes of him or her a potential agent through whom can be satisfied the need in answer to which the cycle began and proceeded. For this last-mentioned reason, it is often most valuable for the astrologer to refer back in the ephemeris to the previous, prenatal conjunction of two natally opposing planets. The zodiacal sign in which the conjunction occurred, any close, major aspects it may have made to other planets at the time, and especially the meaning of the conjunction's Sabian degree: all these are symbolic clues amplifying and making more explicit what underlies the opposition-situation, and therefore what kind of repolarization, in what arena of life, is required of the person meeting such a situation.

For the person in whose birth-chart two planets are in Phase-7 opposition, failure to meet the life-experiences they refer to in such a way as to facilitate repolarization ultimately means being swept away by the devolutionary process in which crystallization and degeneration dominate. The possibility is there for the person to become more or less permanently 'suspended' between the horns of a dilemma. In extreme cases, the result can be a sort of psychic or psychological paralysis. The devolutionary rhythm then takes its toll on whatever it is to which the person is consciously and compulsively bound. Since repolarization and birth in objective consciousness have not occurred, the person can find no meaning—no broader developmental context—within which he or she can integrate the painful 'letting go.' It rather appears to him or her as a 'no win' situation, one in which he is 'damned if he does, damned if he doesn't'—i.e., painfully bound to a conflict with no apparent solution, but afraid to let go of the conflicting elements because they have become structural factors around which coheres an otherwise unintegrated personality or life-pattern. Degeneration follows such crystallization, and as any particular situation degenerates, the tendency is for it to become essentially reconstituted in the life in another form. But past failures—the 'sins of omission'—tend to accumulate and complexify the situation. Successful repolarization becomes increasingly difficult and unlikely—but certainly not impossible.

PHASE 8—SHARING

Phase 8 begins with the waning quincunx, and it is therefore related in meaning to Phase 6, which began in the first hemicycle with the waxing quincunx. While Phase 6 represented the necessity of refining and adjusting expression, Phase 8 refers to the need to fine-tune vision, to adjust oneself to the realities of what one is now able clearly and objectively to see.

Phase 8 also occupies a similar position in the second half of the cyclic process to the one occupied by Phase 2 in the first hemicycle. For just as Phase 2 initially focused the subjective, actional possibilities released at the conjunction, Phase 8 focuses the objective possibilities of consciousness-development released at the cycle's culmination, and the ability to give meaning to experience steadies and grows. If the repolarization required during Phase 7 was not successful, Phase 8 can refer to a reaction to and/or compensation for the failure. It does so in terms of crystallization and progressive degeneration—illness or fruitless neurosis.

In the lives of person with significant Phase 8 interplanetary relationships in their birth-charts, this distinction between success and failure may not be very clear-cut. For conscious understanding can develop on the basis of what we like to call positive experience as well as on the basis of what human beings fear and consider negative. Phase 8 relationships between planets challenge the growing consciousness to go beyond such moral and ethical dualities as positive/negative, good/bad, right/wrong, etc. They refer to the need to meet experiences in such a way as to widen the scope of one's understanding to include all *necessities* in their proper relationships to one another. This may mean having to accept what *is* in lieu of wishing for what 'should be' in a moral or ethical sense—and at the same time trying to bring to consciousness and work toward what is possible, what 'can be' in a progressive, evolutionary sense. It may also mean operating, at least initially, on blind faith, or in terms of a parrot-like repetition of affirmations in which one does not wholeheartedly believe. This may be necessary as a foundation, but truly inclusive understanding eventually needs to be based on a focusing and sharpening of the kind of mind that actually sees the necessity and interprets the interrelatedness of various factors and experiences. What needs most to be 'let go' during this phase of the process is exclusion—the notion that experiences are exclusively good or bad, that one will accept growth only in particular forms. Openness and inclusiveness become increasingly necessary as the waning sesquiquadrate approaches at the midpoint of Phase 8.

The waning sesquiquadrate is related in meaning to the semi-square encountered at the midpoint of Phase 2, for the sesqui-quadrate is also a semi-square—45°—from the opposition. Here the growing consciousness naturally begins to disseminate or apply to external reality its steadying vision and understanding. As it does so, it emerges from the realm of self-referential illumination, where it is primarily concerned with itself, its own pain, pleasure or process. As its attention turns outward, it may be shocked by the realities of the 'real world' into which it is awakening. Such a shock may force it to expand its growing understanding to include external realities. Its capacity to give meaning is enhanced and broadened by such an exchange. The question prematurely asked during Phase 2 becomes appropriate and significant here: "How to?"—how to reconcile the difference between what one sees and what one internally envisions? The answer: by exchanging ideas and ideals with others, and by working with others toward the fulfillment of shared goals and needs. Such working relationships provide new materials—new understandings and unfamiliar visions—which, as Phase 8 draws to a close, must be integrated into a workable philosophy of life.

The waning sesquiquadrate is also related in meaning to its counterpart in the first hemicycle, the waxing sesquiquadrate of

Phase 5. Like the waxing sesquiquadrate, the waning sesqui-quadrate can also involve struggle, but in the second hemicycle the struggle is to understand, to let go of exclusive points of view, to include the understandings and the needs of others in one's point of view, and to begin to assimilate the meaning of what one now sees.

PHASE 9—UNDERSTANDING

As the faster planet increasingly moves back toward the slower one, it symbolically 'brings' with it the harvest of the interplanetary relationship thus far. The waning trine and Phase 9 refer to such an 'ingathering,' a harvest of meaning with which one can purposefully work. The flower may have faded as the seed develops, but the fruit, protecting the seed until it is mature enough to be released, progressively ripens. While the waxing trine creatively focused the nature of the slower planet through the expression and activities of the faster one, the polarity is reversed at the waning trine. The functional activities of the faster planet enrich and bring new meaning—and eventually the necessity for questioning and re-evaluation—to the functional nature of the slower planet.

The waning trine is also related in meaning in the second hemicycle to the sextile beginning Phase 3 in the first half of the process, for it occurs 60° after the opposition, when the planets are separated by an angular distance of 240°. Opportunities to focus growing understanding, to work constructively with others toward the actualization of a shared vision, present themselves. By taking advantage of these opportunities, the person with waning trines in his or her birth-chart discovers what his or her special integrative and expressive capabilities are. He or she thus fulfills the waning-trine challenge to focus in his or her life the harmonious, *conscious* expression of what has been developing thus far in the cycle—i.e., the 'harvest' of the interplanetary relationship. Creativity typical of the waning trine is not only based on outward expression as it was in the first hemicycle at the waxing trine. Creativity here is in addition based on 'intake' and responsiveness—on the ability to respond at the level of holistic understanding, of intuition giving meaning to the entire situation in which any event, encounter or experience occurs.

All this is primarily a concern of the evolutionary process in which the waning trine plays a significant part, and we will discuss the aspect of the situation more fully in Chapter 3. What is significant here is that especially as the waning trine separates from exact, its devolutionary facet—the catabolic side of relationship and of what has occurred since the opposition—becomes increasingly apparent. Since the opposition, consciousness has, ideally, been growing through relationship, which first acted in its evolutionary, fertilizing mode. As consciousness increasingly focuses, and 'mind' becomes formed enough to be able to give constructive meaning to 'life' or experience—no matter what it may be—this growth turns destructive, as it were, of the cohesiveness of what was built up during the first hemicycle. In other words, through Phases 7, 8 and 9 in general, relationship and the need to understand and integrate in meaning all experiences have pointed up the necessity to question the basis on which one previously acted. This is why waning trines in birth-charts often refer to involvement in relationships which turn out to be upsetting to the status quo. The most obvious encumberances of consciousness brought over from the first hemicycle—assumptions, dogmatic ethical assertions, taken-for-granted values and beliefs, etc.—must be recognized as such and 'let go.'

Just as in the first hemicycle the waxing square forced one to dig down to bedrock in order to build on a solid foundation, the waning square forming at the end of Phase 9 forces the growing consciousness to plumb the depths of what it rests upon. From the opposition, and particularly from the waning trine, to the waning square, the growth of understanding undermines the foundations on which activity previously operated. As the waning square approaches, old forms of relating, feeling or behaving—or more concrete forms such as tools, social institutions, etc.—reveal their inappropriateness in the light of new understanding. They no longer fit in with new ways of thinking, nor do they elicit positive results from the material with which one is working or from partners or associates to whom one is related. As the waning square forms, a tension toward the definite breakdown of all that has become obsolete develops. What was an actional crisis in the first hemicycle becomes in the second a crisis at the level of understanding and values—a challenge to radical re-valuation out of which new insights, new values and a new philosophical basis can eventually emerge. Persons born with planets in Phase 9 relationship nearing Phase 10 relationship are challenged to meet and assimilate experiences helping to focus in their lives just such an ideological crisis.

PHASE 10—REVALUING

Like the waxing square (90°), the waning square (270°) is a particularly important turning point in a cycle. In the lunation cycle, the beginning of this phase is marked by the distinctive shape of the Last Quarter Moon, the first definite shape formed after Full Moon. What had been the round fullness of the Moon-disc has gradually diminished to a hemicircle, reminiscent again, as at First Quarter, of a straight-edged scythe slicing across the night-sky. The straight-edge of the Last Quarter Moon is oriented in the opposite direction than the First Quarter Moon's. Here again, also as at First Quarter, the Moon crosses the Earth's orbit. But now it comes back within it, moving toward the orbit of Venus, toward the Sun and the place where the next soli-lunar conjunction (New Moon) will occur.

The lunation symbolism again implies cutting away—'decision.' The crisis or decision is not at the actional level, at the level of 'life,' as it was at First Quarter. It is now at the level of consciousness, of understanding—of 'mind'—a philosophical, ideological parting of the ways. When the Moon crosses the orbit of the Earth going 'inward'—toward the next New Moon—the cycle is symbolically no longer operating on the actional momentum established at First Quarter and reaching culmination at Full Moon. it is rather 'drawn on,' as it were, by the promise of the next conjunction, the Moon's reunion with the Sun. As the Moon crosses the orbit of the Earth, it symbolically begins the return to 'source.' Renewal will soon be necessary, and possible.

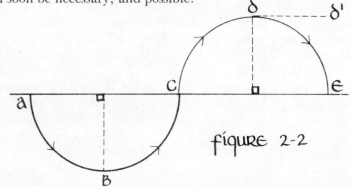

fiquRE 2-2

The sinusoid figure again provides a graphic illustration of these significant points. After the involutionary process 'turned the corner' of the waxing square (B) and stabilized in the direction of the cycle's culmination (C), motion in this general direction continued, even after the line dividing the two hemicircles from one another was passed. Before the opposition (C), the direction of activity was 'outward,' toward developing objectivity and becoming conscious—in terms of the individualizing process, toward actualizing the potentiality of individual selfhood. After the opposition (C), consciousness develops, at least at first, along the same lines it 'awakened': relationship. The initial upward thrust of the second hemicircle seems to imply a kind of 'ascent' or expression of consciousness. A relatively minor 'course correction' occurs at the waning sesquiquadrate, midway between the opposition and the waning square (D). The waning square presents another significant turning point. Now, our metaphorical driver steers into the curve fully conscious. Midway through it, he is forced, as it were, to yield to centripedal force, to allow his car to be pulled inward, back toward source, the next conjunction (A^1), rather than 'off track' to D^1. The decision here does not involve 'taking over' as it did at First Quarter; now it involves—in its devolutionary aspect—'letting go.'

Thus, the last quarter square is, like the first quarter, a moment of crisis and reorientation. The decision now involves 'cutting away' at the level of consciousness: severance from whatever in an individual is still rooted in a taken-for-granted collective past. For the beliefs, dogmas and assumptions beginning to be questioned at the close of Phase 9 are those inherited from parents and collective, tradition-perpetuating institutions such as churches and schools. From the devolutionary point of view, the person with significant waning squares in his or her birth-chart is challenged to recognize and root out internally whatever is still bound to this collective past. If such severance does not occur, bondage to the collective past forces the person to meet experience on the basis of handed-down solutions and techniques which cannot provide valid and workable ways of meeting present problems because they developed in a different, no longer existing context, in response to a different set of circumstances, needs and available materials.

Like a seed forming and drawing nourishment from a dying plant, a person's mind is fed and formed by collective images impressed upon it since birth. In the development of a seed, a moment comes when its connection to its parent plant must be severed, or else both the seed and the remains of the plant will return to the soil together. If the seed is not separated far enough from the parent plant, the strong chemicals released by the decomposing structure may pierce the seed's protective covering and render it ineffectual, unable to weather the winter and germinate in the spring. So too must a person who aspires to true individuality and inclusive understanding sever his psychic connection with collective-cultural values and beliefs.

Thus, the person with significant waning squares in his or her birth-chart is called upon to be the vehicle or 'focalizer' through whom some kind of reorientation or 'revolution in consciousness' can operate—no matter how limited or wide in scope its effects may turn out to be. The person will, first, be challenged to probe deeply into taken-for-granted beliefs and values—his or her 'own' and those of the culture having impressed itself on consciousness since birth. Some set of life-events or circumstances will prompt such probing. They are significant in themselves insofar as they reveal the general area in which the person must confront what is at the root of consciousness. The outcome of the situation, whatever the actual circumstances may be, depends on this inner probing being carried out and not evaded. It must be done not only courageously, but, above all, honestly.

This last-mentioned quality of consciousness is perhaps the key to meeting successfully the challenge of the waning square. For something—some set of values, beliefs, ideas—to which one is attached has outlived its usefulness and has become obsolete; mental structures, like the flowers of spring and the husks of autumn, come and go according to the eternal rhythms of birthing and dying. The inexorable rhythm of life, of change, decrees that whatever is obsolete will, in time, disintegrate. But whether it does so while one's being and consciousness are still attached to it, depending on it to fulfill some function it can no longer perform—or whether the old structures fail and disintegrate after one has 'moved on' to operate on the basis of more vibrant and life-giving foundations—ultimately depends upon the degree to which one is truly honest with oneself when confronted with the need to re-assess and re-evaluate one's basic beliefs.

If one does *not* meet such a confrontation honestly, one remains attached to obsolete ideas, and no-longer-valid assumptions and images structure one's thinking and behavior. Solutions to life's problems founded upon such values fail to 'work.' Time after time, they fail to produce the kind of results one hoped would follow. Anger, resentment, resignation, bitterness: such is the harvest of the failure to let go when letting go was necessary and appropriate. Self-righteousness and a tragic sense of isolation can develop in a rigid, crystallized ego, which mistakenly thinks itself victorious over change. Degenerative diseases, whether of mind, body or both, nevertheless set in. In the long run, change always wins.

If, on the other hand, one *does* meet such a confrontation with one's values and beliefs honestly—which may or may not occur the first time it comes up—some cherished images inevitably emerge tarnished, revealed as 'rusting' and obsolescent if not completely obsolete. From the devolutionary point of view, the second part of the waning-square challenge is indeed to let them go, and in some cases, to help to hasten their demise both in oneself and in others. The person having successfully faced the first challenge of the waning square is thus asked, for ultimately constructive purposes, to be part of a destructive, or destructuring process, which helps to break down whatever in himself, his community or society is no longer positively contributing to evolutionary progress, but instead stands in the way.

We have stressed here the devolutionary or 'catabolic' facet of the waning square, but in actual practice one should neither dwell on nor minimize its difficult side. What a waning square refers to in a person's life must be seen in the context of a whole process, in terms of its function of impelling someone to question the meaning of everything accepted since birth. This is, unquestionably, a difficult task, especially if one resists doing it when it is necessary. To question everything, however, does not mean that one is required to discard everything, to "throw the baby out with the dirty bath." On the contrary, the waning square is a kind of winnowing mechanism of the cyclic process, asking us to separate the kernel of experience from the husk. One does not throw out the kernels, just the husks—but of course one must be able to tell the difference, and not be attached to the husks simply because they have seemingly 'always been there' and one has become used to seeing them.

This kind of mental focusing and discriminatory ability—using the term discriminatory in its original and positive sense, not as it has recently been popularized sociopolitically—results from meeting the ideological crisis of the last quarter 'squarely.' It provides the foundation on which the waning square can also operate in a positive, evolutionary way. As a person meets the crisis of the waning square, focuses in on some basic issues and breaks away from unquestioned subservience to collective dogmas, that person becomes ready and able to contribute positively to the harvest of human experience. The mind is open and free, yet also sufficiently focused to release new images—'kernels' or 'seeds'—'mind-seeds'—pregnant with truly evolutionary possibilities. Having met and assimilated experiences both catabolic and focusing at the level of mind, the person embraces the possibility of becoming more than merely a member of a 'demolition-derby' team. He or she becomes, potentially, an architect of a new future.

The necessity to begin reorganizing consciousness around such new, but as yet vague and indefinite images increases as the waning sextile, the beginning of Phase 11, approaches.

PHASE 11—REORGANIZING

After the Last Quarter phase of the soli-lunar cycle, the Moon continues to wane, to move within the Earth's orbit back toward the Sun—back toward 'source.' The directional momentum established at Last Quarter stabilizes. Symbolically, consciousness has been forced inward, back on itself for radical reassessment and revaluation. Yearned for now are new images around which consciousness can reorganize, a new or renewed connection to some vital wellspring of energy and archetypes.

The aspect beginning Phase 11 is the waning sextile, occurring when two planets are separated by an angular distance of 300 degress. It is related in meaning to both the waxing sextile beginning

Phase 2 of the overall cycle, and to the waxing trine beginning Phase 5; for the waning sextile is both 120° from the opposition or the fifth aspect formed during the second hemicycle, and 60° or two 'steps' before the next conjunction. Significant also is the fact that in this second hemicycle the sextile follows the square, while it preceeded it in the first half of the cycle.

While the waxing sextile referred to the need and latent ability to spontaneously organize inchoate materials into new forms which revealed their purpose as they developed, the waning sextile refers to the need and latent ability to reorganize understanding having been disrupted by a radical crisis of revaluation at the waning square. The most significant question surrounding this reorganization is, "Around what set of new or renewed images will reorganization take shape? To what source or 'resource' will the increasingly subjective consciousness turn, to fill what it experiences as a vacuum, an inner emptiness created when obsolete values and ideas were recognized as such and rooted out? From whence will revitalizing images arise? Whither will they lead?"

Such are the kinds of questions the waning sextile poses and challenges us to answer. Depending upon our point of view, on the perspective from which we view this aspect, the answers we offer differ. On one hand, we can look at the waning sextile primarily from the point of view of its beginning Phase 11 of the overall process, as the phase following the waning square's 'crisis in consciousness.' Having reassessed and found wanting many sociocultural values and fashions in 'thinking-feeling' of relatively recent vintage, consciousness may seek renewal in the very ancient past—symbolically, the conjunction long ago beginning the now-ending cycle. In an attempt to drink again of clear and unpolluted waters close to source, consciousness goes, as it were, upstream, against the flow, to seek whatever may remain of the spirit behind the original creative impulse.

If, on the other hand, we consider the waning sextile primarily as a sort of second-hemicycle trine—120° or five 'steps' from the cycle's culmination—consciousness may seek its new foundation in the present, depending upon its own and its associates' resources and understanding, as these have developed since the cycle's culmination, on the foundation of what was realized then. The 'source' to which consciousness turns is symbolically the opposition, and its focus is on the present rather than the past, on meeting current problems—perhaps, symbolically, trying to clean up the 'river' having become dirtied and polluted by the residual effects of past mistakes, whether these have been 'sins' of comission or of omission.

From yet a third point of view, we can consider the waning sextile primarily as two 'steps' before the *next* conjunction. The attempt at reorganization then turns consciousness toward the future, opens and prepares it for it. Rather than seeking an unpolluted source upstream, or trying to clean up any particular 'harbor,' this solution follows the flow to the sea, to the Source of all sources, Ocean of all potentialities. The deepest possibility here is some kind of prophetic anticipation—a sort of psychic pre-echo such as occurs acoustically on LP records sometimes—in which new images are intuited or resonated to 'in advance,' images so new that a cycle developing what is potential in them will not begin until after the coming conjunction definitely releases them.

All of the above refer to possibilities for the person in whose birth-chart waning sextiles predominate or form significant patterns. To recapitulate an ancient past, undoubtedly very beautiful and vibrant at its far-distant source; to solidify and express a present built on and at the expense of that past; to anticipate a future in which both are resolved yet superceded: these are the possibilities of what waning sextiles can mean in relation to the planetary functions involved. The key to all is *re*organization, with an emphasis on the *re*. For there is no prophetic anticipation of new images unless old ones have definitely been let go. There is no truly now-oriented expression unless 'now' is no longer merely an extension or possible repetition of the past. There is not even any true recapitulation of the ancient past unless what is revived is really of source—eternal and ageless, not dated and of limited applicability.

Some form of creative expression often results from or stimulates reorganization of consciousness in the life of a person with planets in Phase 11 relationship in his or her birth-chart. Creativity is latent in his or her nature, for the waning sextile is, as we've pointed out, the 'trine' of the second hemicycle—120° or the fifth 'step' after the opposition. But what is expressed and the spirit behind its expression now are not the same as the ebullient creativity typical of the waxing trine. The term creative isn't quite right either, because rather than bringing something new into existence, creativity at the waning sextile deals more with reorganizing or rearranging old materials in an especially evocative way. What are evoked are indeed new possibilities—possibilities so new as to be 'seed possibilities'—conveyed through forms so radically different from anything produced under prevailing principles of esthetic or intellectual organization that they can only be called 'seed forms.'

Seed forms are the bare, spare, essentialized and condensed expressions of the end of a cycle. They at once recapitulate the ancient yet eternal past in which the cycle was rooted, pose the unsolved problems of the present, and anticipate as yet unknown and unknowable future solutions. They are conveyors—*evocateurs*—of understanding and vision rather than concrete forms serving utilitarian purposes. They may be philosophical or psychological systems, or symbolic and evocative works of art. Whatever they are, they are geared to a future of which their creator can see only the structural outline or prenatal glow. They carry consciousness to its limits, to the threshold of what can be known and consciously apprehended about the future. Their function is to implant in the minds of their creators and public alike the seeds for future development.

As Phase 11 proceeds, the waning semi-square forms. It is 45°—again an angle of maximum intensity of forces in a magnetic field—from both the waning square and the coming conjunction. It is related in meaning to both the waxing semi-square and sesquiquadrate, for it also occurs 135° after the opposition. What is symbolized midway through Phase 11 is almost the mirror-reverse of what was significant during Phases 2 and 5. In the first half of the cycle, nascent future possibilities had to focus themselves, meet and at least tentatively overcome the inertia of the past (Phase 2). Actional capacities were stirred into motion, and expression became outward, vigorous and potentially explosive by the middle of Phase 5 (waxing sesquiquadrate). Now, as the cycle ends, consciousness turns increasingly toward whatever it intuits as a new or renewed source of creative potentiality. While the creator (or appreciator) of

seed forms may feel himself or herself to be the product of the past—
which indeed he or she is—his or her deepest identification should be
increasingly with the future, unborn though it may be. Creativity
may thus be intensely subjective and potentially implosive, for the
person focusing the waning semisquare phase of the cycle in his or
her life and birthchart identifies with a future which few others can
imagine or relate to. The person will be inwardly impelled to scatter
seeds of potential rebirth—'seed ideas,' 'seed forms'—while being
challenged to embody seedhood or seedlikeness.

Thus, the functional activities represented by the semi-
squaring planets, the fields of experience represented by the natal
houses they occupy, will be those through which the challenge to
'seedhood' will come. The environment in which the person operates
may be hostile or relatively receptive to the futureward vision he or
she endeavors to embody and exteriorize—most likely the former. In
either case, the person with planets in waning semi-square relationship will be challenged to become outwardly self-sufficient and inwardly dedicated—like a seed, totally self-contained and con-
secrated to participating in a process which is understood and accepted as far greater than the span of the person's own life and consciousness. Like Moses and the Promised Land, the seed-man or
-woman of even the most prophetic vision cannot actually 'enter' the
future. The pressure of karma, of the unfinished business of the past
of which the person is indeed the product, is too great. At this phase
of the process, all one can—and must—do is to see and point the
way.

This most humbling of all 'lessons' increasingly hits home as
Phase 12, the final phase in the process, begins.

PHASE 12—RELEASING

The waning semi-sextile begins the final 'step' of the psychlic*
process. In the lunation cycle, the Moon is again a slim Crescent, or
more properly, de-Crescent, for it is oriented in the opposite direction from the Crescent beginning the cycle. The inverted lunar Crescent rises for a few days ahead of the Sun announcing the new day.

---

*This was an interesting typographical error that I thought I would leave here.—LR

Like the Phoenix descending into consuming flames from which it will rise again, the Moon is soon caught in the firey embrace of the Sun, and disappears from view until after New Moon. What occurs between the two Crescents, when the Moon is absent from the night-sky and darkness prevails, is thus unseen—a mystery—a most profound transition between a cycle now ending and another yet to begin.

In more human terms, the Moon's absence from the night-sky symbolizes the subjectivity to which consciousness returns at the end of a cycle. It has, ideally, utterly repudiated reliance upon what is external and traditional, dedicating itself instead to cultivating a vision of an unborn but increasingly compelling future sustaining it from within. Outwardly, deeper issues may seem, mysteriously, to take care of themselves, to be subsumed in a largely unconscious process of inner assimilation and transition. Problems of daily living must still be met, and since traditional solutions are no longer relied upon, answers and the inspiration for new approaches must be sought within.

On one hand, such an inner search can mean an anarchic 'every man for himself': "Don't bother me, I'm doing my own thing." While each individual must seek an inner source of inspiration, at the collective level alternatives replacing traditional approaches to daily living will arise, and they will come through especially open and enterprising individuals. Some individuals rising to the challenge of seedhood during the last phases of a cycle manage to both free themselves from collective cultural domination and 'return' to serve the collective by becoming dedicated channels through whom new images can be implanted in human consciousness. They do not become caught up in the kind of atomistic individuality possible when traditional constraints have been abandoned. Neither do they spurn the possibility of being actively related to a greater whole or greater process in favor of "doing their own thing."

In birth-charts, waning semi-sextiles are not usually considered significant aspects, possibly because they refer to matters not usually requiring a great deal of conscious attention or even understanding from the person in whose chart they occur. This is often true unless —and this is a significant unless—the Phase 12 interplanetary relationship is particularly focal in the birth-chart's overall planetary pattern (gestalt), in more exteriorizing aspect to a third planet, or very close to (in orb of) conjunction. An example of the first instance would be, say, a see-saw* chart in which two planets in waning semi-sextile occupy one half of the pattern. An example of the second instance would be what occur if faster planet A were 30° behind slower planet B, and either one or the midpoint of both were aspected, say squared, opposed or trined, etc., by planet C. Such situations would tend to bring out into the open a process of assimilation and qualities of being which would otherwise remain more internal or subjective.

In these types of situations we see lived out (at least potentially) the inner workings of what otherwise occurs subjectively when a cycle ends. The person whose chart contains significant Phase 12 interplanetary relationships—especially as they approach conjunction —develops and matures to focus in his or her being the essence of both the accomplishments or 'successes' and the unfinished business or relative failures of the entire now-ending cycle. Both sides of such a polarity are latent in his or her being. Here the task is living out the two. This means manifesting in more or less objective or subjective ways both the assimilated harvest of a by-now degenerated past and an openness to an as-yet unknown and uncertain future which is, ideally, increasingly acknowledged to be necessary.

Thus, at the close of the cycle, as at the beginning, consciousness and activity are poised, as it were, midway between past and future. An internal polarization at final conjunction complements the one we saw operating at the interplanetary opposition. The more deeply one probes past experience for new solutions and inspiration, the more wanting and empty of vital, compelling meaning past experience reveals itself to be. The more consciousness tries to project itself into the future, to intuit in some relatively definite way what a new creative impetus might bring and mean, the more it falls back upon itself. Since it has been formed and molded by the past, a steady vision of a truly new future will always elude it: old bottles should not be used to hold new wine. A truly new future is always more than merely an extrapolation of the past.

---

*cf. *Person-Centered Astrology* by Dane Rudhyar, p. 175ff.

This Catch-22 characterizing the end of the cycle can manifest in a variety of ways in the lives of persons whose birth-charts contain significant waning conjunctions. Such people often learn to deeply mistrust the traditional past represented by the conjoining planetary functions and operating in the natal house occupied by their conjunction. Whether through rebellion or inner compulsion, they may be driven to seek new directions for these functions' expression. As long as a person is the product of the past and/or rebels against it, he or she is bound to that past. The connection to the past cannot be truly left behind until one comes in touch with a vision of a future so compelling that it irresistibly dynamizes being, consciousness, activity and incinerates pastward ties. Like Moses and the Promised Land, a person cannot 'enter' or even envision a truly new future—in that future's own terms—until and unless the past *in him or her* is released.

The kind of release providing the 'way out' of the end-cycle Catch-22 is more than a simple, conscious letting go. It is deeper, indeed more mysterious. It is one thing for a dying plant to release seeds; it is another for the seed to 'release' the plant that bore it, to allow it to die. Yet it is precisely this more internalized release which enables the seed-in-the end to become—*after* a period of dormancy—the seed-in-the-beginning. The two are not the same: this spring's germs are not 'the same' plants as died last fall, nor will this summer's roses be 'the same' flowers that blossomed last year.

What then transforms the 'seed-in-the-end' into the 'seed-in-the-beginning?' What is the 'out' of the Catch-22 past/future polarization ending the cycle? What calls down into the realm of human consciousness and experience a creative release of truly new potentiality? We may say with St. John, "In the beginning was the Word," but the creative Word is always what it is—a particular, focused spiritual impulse—in answer to *a need*, a need clearly focused and formulated at the end of a cycle which acts as a vessel, as both an emptiness needing filling and as a container capable of receiving and holding a creative downpour. As the vessel is formed, to such a shape will the malleable, molten contents conform later on.

Thus, it is useless for the person caught in the end-cycle polarization to turn exclusively to either the past for solutions or the future for inspiration. The person with a (or several) waning conjunction in the birth-chart is instead challenged to identify being, consciousness and activity with *the need* for a new creative impluse in which both the past and future are united. Such a person lives the duality inherent in the end of the cycle, and his or her life and being give form and formulation to what is needed next. This need—as it is lived is what will summon forth the release of truly new potentialities beginning the next cycle. To the quality of the way the need is formulated, the quality of spiritual impulse answers. It gives to the unfinished business and decaying remains of the past an opportunity to become reincorporated into living structures in a transformed way.

Just as one can call half-empty or half-full a 12-ounce glass containing 6 ounces—or concentrate on figure or ground, or the image of a chalice or the two profiles forming it—so too can a need be lived in one of two basic attitudes. One can focus upon the facet of personal lack, on emptiness, confusion and frustration. Or, one can emphasize the quality of meta-personal service behind making oneself a vessel fit to call forth and receive a new potential fullness. To live an open-ended need instead of a closed solution either culled or extrapolated from past experience represents the greatest release and deepest 'letting go' of all. It is to sacrifice what the personal ego wants and envisions for what the higher, transpersonal intuition senses but cannot grasp. It is to die into the lesser so that the greater can later be born and, like a seed, to allow a kind of 'empty,' dormant interlude between two cycles to do its mysterious work.

As the cycle comes to a close, Oroboros curves back upon himself, swallowing his own tail. The seed-in-the-beginning has now become the seed-in-the-end, waiting to be transformed into a seed-in-the-beginning. It occurs not 'again,' for all is new—and yet the same: eternal, Aeonic. So subjective and protectively self-enveloped has consciousness become that it cannot communicate the difference, nor needs it to. It is and does the difference and the sameness of the task: Seedhood waits . . . and waits. It is not 'patient,' for it knows not that time, an objective measure, passes. It is one with the inner rhythm of the cycle. In spring, warm Sun, caressing breeze and rain, blessed rain, will be answered by a green, upspringing germ. Again, yet ever anew.

3.
Less Familiar Aspects: Evolution

GROWTH THROUGH MEANING AND CONSCIOUS PROCESS

One of the main drawbacks in astrology is that there are too many things taken for granted, even by the most expert astrologers, without a sufficiently thorough enquiry into the principles or postulates underlying the various practices in everyday use. Why should only a few angular values—0°, 30°, 60°, 90°, 120°, (sometimes) 150°, and 180°—in most cases be honored as the only ones entitled to be called and considered aspects? If others, like the quintile (72°) or sesquiquadrate (135°), are considered, is there any reason for doing so—and for either taking or not taking into account other angular values such as 36° or 40°? Is there no way of understanding the complete cyclic process within which *all* angular values find their place and meaning so that such questions can be answered consistently?

In order to do so, we must understand that the series of angular values based on multiples of 30° best describes the successive phases in the process of growth and decay characterizing the 'life'-cycle. We have seen that 'life' operates in its positive, anabolic, building mode during the first half of a process. This first hemicycle is best characterized as what we have called the involutionary process, and it refers to the realm of instinctual activity and nature-born impulsions. Life moves forward in the simplest kind of arithmetical progression, one step adding itself to the preceding one in sheer impulsiveness of being: one, one plus one, one plus one plus one, etc. It is a rhythm of expansion and conquest. It is the rhythm of solar progress through the year, which defines the limits of the zodiacal signs month after month.

With the opposition aspect, a new realm is potentially reached. On one hand, the rhythm of 'life' continues, but in its catabolic, devolutionary mode. On the other hand, a process of consciousness evolution may begin, based upon but not exclusively limited by what has grown and developed during the first hemicycle involutionary process. We have previously referred to this twofold nature of the second hemicycle by likening it to what occurs in the vegetable kingdom when a plant has already flowered and gone to seed. The analogy is more apt and instructive at the level of involution and devolution than it is in terms of the evolutionary process, for while the evolution of consciousness in human beings can be generally likened to the development of a seed in the second half of the yearly cycle of vegetation, it should be obvious that the disparity between the level at which plants operate and the realm in which human minds function is so great as to render the analogy useful only for very broad, structural or inspirational purposes.

The distinguishing characteristic of the human potential is that human beings have the capacity to go beyond merely biological functioning. This ability develops as human beings (1) become objectively aware of life-currents, (2) give conscious meaning to them, and therefore (3) assume responsibility for their actions and reactions. Yet so great is the difference between involution and evolution, between the realm of 'life' and realm of 'mind', that even these last-mentioned capacities, fully actualized, are only the first three phases of the evolutionary process which begins at the culmination of a cycle—its opposition or symbolical Full Moon. At all such symbolical culminations, birth in consciousness is theoretically reached, i.e., it becomes *possible*. It becomes actual *if* the kind of radical repolarization or reorientation we have spoken about previously is successful. When this does occur, the tide turns, the subjective impulsiveness of expanding life stops. The 'I' meets the 'Other.' The subject meets the object, and for the first time becomes fully aware of the relationship—of the fact of being inextricably related to the outer world and 'reality.'

It is on the basis of this awareness of relationship that 'mind' develops. Conscious objectivity is the foundation of intelligence, and it is rooted in duality and contrast. As the self consciously faces the world and other selves, the instinctual feeling of wholeness of being characterizing involution is superceded by an increasing feeling of 'dividedness' produced by an increasing involvement in a myriad of relationships involving ever more numerous facets of being.

Astrologically, this means that all progress, until the end of the cycle, will be symbolized by a process of division, not addition, of angular values, and the series of aspects thus derived is rooted in the opposition rather than in the conjunction. From the opposition, the half-way point of the cycle, the circle is divided into thirds, fourths, fifths, sixths, sevenths, eighths, and so on. The sequence of aspects is thus: opposition, trine, square, quintile, sextile, septile, octile (or semi-square), novile (or nonagen), decile (or semi-quintile), etc.

Among the aspects of this series are the less-familiar, less often used and understood aspects. There are also some aspects which we have already encountered in our study of aspects formed by the ad-ditive process. Now, however, aspects have been obtained by a fun-damentally different process, and they are no longer related solely to the conjunction beginning the cycle. They can be understood signifi-cantly only if they are related to their source, the opposition—that is, to the basic factor of *awareness* produced by the dualism inherent in all conscious perception of external reality.

In order to understand the less-familiar aspects and the second-hemicycle meaning of more generally used aspects also found in the first hemicycle, we have first to understand the opposition from which the new process proceeds—that is, to understand the nature of awareness, how it develops, and more specifically, how each of the aspects of the second hemicycle, in its own specialized way, re-fers to a particular stage in the evolution of awareness and conscious-ness. In order to do so, we can approach these aspects in two basic ways within the framework of a third, encompassing and unifying idea. (1) As we divide the circle (cycle) into successively smaller, symbolically more specialized arcs (phases), we can rely on our sense of the archetypal and *qualitative meaning of number*—numerology —to guide us in determining the meaning of each arc (phase) so de-rived. (2) We can look to the traditional, symbolic meanings of the *geometric forms* we would inscribe in a circle if we connected by lines the demarcations of the arcs obtained by the division process. But (3), underlying both these approaches, the numerological and the geometrical, we must retain the basic sense of *process* which we attribute to any whole cycle. Only within a whole cyclic process—which the two-dimensional circle merely *represents*—can any phase (or arc), however derived, be given meaning.

THE OPPOSITION AND THE QUINCUNX

Dividing a circle into two parts creates a diameter and two points on the circumference separated by a 180° angle. Characteristic of this angular value (yet little attention is paid to it) is the fact that whether one starts from one of the two points or the other, there is the same distance between them—which is not the case with any other aspect. The opposition thus describes a type of relationship which is entirely unique, in a class by itself. This distinctive relationship is what underlies consciousness and the development of the thinking mind.

Consciousness, as we in the West understand the term today, implies and depends upon duality and separation—the division between an inner and an outer realm. Our thinking proceeds on the basis of such dualities—'I' and the 'Other', 'in here' and 'out there'—or other categories such as hot and cold, joy and pain, good and bad. Even more fundamentally, if there were no symbolic diamter separating 'I' from 'Other,' there could be no 'I' as the thinker, and there could be no 'Other' or categories to think about, because everything would be One, and One would not be conscious of itself or anything else.

Thus, the diameter represented by the opposition separates 'I' from the 'Other.' Only as 'I' sees the 'Other' can it distinguish and define itself. At the stage of mental development represented by the opposition aspect, only the bare fact of awareness—of 'I' as separate from some 'Other'—exists at first. The subject faces the object; separating them is thin layer of skin or the organs of sensation and perception. A person awakens and sees wall, bed, chairs. He—we—takes this for granted and does not usually question what it means or how it happens. In a sense, all philosophy is a many-sided attempt to discover, or rather interpret, what is implied in this 'seeing,' through which are defined both the object seen and the 'I' that sees. Neither exists without the other, fundamentally speaking, on the plane where this 'seeing' occurs.

But 'seeing' is not understanding. It is a *prerequisite* for understanding, and if evolutionary progress is to occur, seeing must *lead to* understanding. Thus, the diameter represented by the opposition divides, but separation can be absolute and irreconcilable, or it can be an impetus compelling us to find a way of meaningfully relating two things or the subject and object that appear to be separate. Any opposition can therefore be approached in two ways or stages: from the point of view of unbridgeable differences leading to confrontation, or in terms of a separation that exists for the purpose of providing a foundation for a new level of relatedness to develop—whether this relatedness is between persons, between a person and society, between two facets of a personality or two areas of a person's life. Thus, the quality of consciousness latent in the opposition aspect grows in acuity and precision at the first stage of its development by laying stress on contrasts and differences. At the next stage, it grows by trying to relate and integrate the two halves of the field of experience symbolically divided by the opposition aspect.

When the subject faces the object, one cannot be altered without the other also being changed. Any change of 'shape' on one side of a boundary line necessarily modifies the shape of the space on the other side of the line. No one can transform himself or herself without changing the universe. Does this sound abstract and metaphysical? It should not, for it deals with the most practical of all facts: there can be no change in the outer world and in society unless the individual's subjective being is altered, for better or for worse. This is the challenge of the opposition: to allow the 'seeing' of the 'Other' to alter one's subjective being, and therefore to alter the world in which one lives.

Such an alteration is 'progressive' (i.e., in the direction of universal or personal evolution) or 'regressive'—that is, degenerative. One can move toward a new experience or meeting in a positive, creative and open way, as in, "Let me see what this is, include it in my experience, give it a meaning." Or, one can recoil in fear: "I don't want to see or deal with that." In the first case, the opposition symbolically becomes a trine; the Two becomes Three. The duality is bridged, and we will see later on that the trine has geometrically the tendency to connect in a definite way the two sides of the circle differentiated by the opposition.

In the second case, the opposition symbolically regresses to a quincunx. Here, the quincunx carries the negative connotations of a fearfully or antagonistically met sixth-house experience: personal maladjustment, sickness, enforced labor, repairing the results of past mistakes, inefficiency or omissions. A similar process often operates at mid-life, during the early or middle forties—the symbolical opposition of the human life-span. If a person cannot meet whatever then confronts him or her, internally or externally, in a positive, progressive way, and feel secure about moving into the second half of life, some form of behavioral or emotional regression may occur. It can take the form of a quasi-adolescent love affair, perhaps with a much younger person, or an emotional and out-of-proportion sense of dissatisfaction with one's job, career or lot in life. In any case, behavior more appropriate to an earlier stage of development reveals a more or less unchangeable inability to move on to life's next phases. If the regressive behavior becomes a permanent feature of the personality, disillusionment, frustration and maladaption are almost sure to follow. Sometimes, however, such a regression is not only temporary but therapeutic: something missed can be picked up, and the cycle can afterward proceed to the kind of healthy conclusion it could not previously reach, owing to the developmental omission. Thus, while from this point of view the quincunx carries an unpleasant meaning, it need not be considered absolutely 'bad.' For whatever reason, some adjustments have to be made, some untaken step passed through at last.

When looking at any particular quincunx, however, an astrologer has no way of knowing whether it is functioning as a 'waxing' aspect following a trine in the first hemicycle, or as a symbolic falling back after an opposition. Here we are not primarily discussing facts to be applied directly to chart delineation, but trying to understand an overall picture, a process-oriented *context* within which holistic life-interpretation and astrological guidance can intuitively occur. By understanding the archetypal possibilities and pitfalls of all the various stages of a process, we can understand not only particular aspects when confronted by them—either in natal charts, progressions or transits—but more importantly, we can recognize their analogues *in life*, whether or not they come alongside the 'proper' or 'expectable' astrological configurations.

We should keep in mind that when speaking of the quincunx, we have now three basic ways or contexts within which we can understand such an aspect: in the involutionary series as a 150° angular value beginning the sixth 30° step, in the devolutionary series as a 210° angular value beginning the eighth 30° step, and in the evolutionary series as an opposition having fallen back 30°.

THE TRINE

When the Two becomes Three, what does the trine add to the opposition? The first intuition or vision of a goal. The subject facing the object realizes that he or she can use the object for some purpose. In the opposition there is only awareness; conceivably, anything or nothing could happen. Either the subject or the object could transform itself and thus change the other forcibly. Under the pressure of life or evolutionary growth, however, the state of perfectly even (albeit often tense) equilibrium represented by the opposition cannot last. The inner or the outer must win. We have seen that this essentially means that either the subject (you or I) will shrink from the outer object or person, in which case the object 'wins' and there is regression for the ego. Or, the subject will move toward the object in order to use it, to include it in his life-experience and make it serve a purpose—in which case both the ego and the object are victorious over fear and inertia, and the opposition becomes a trine.

In order to fulfill such a victory, the subject has actually transcended the battle; it has seen some purpose for a relationship with whatever is confronting it. The bare 'fact' of awareness (opposition) becomes transfigured into 'purpose' as the opposition leads to a trine. The total experience (the whole circle) is no longer merely divided into two opposite factors (hemi-circles); a third factor now links the two. This is the factor of purpose and, at a higher level, of meaning, for meaning always deals with referring something to a higher, more inclusive whole. The trine thus forces one to ask in regard to what one becomes aware of at the opposition: "Where does it fit in my life? How do I fit in with it? Where do we both fit into a larger view? How can we most meaningfully use our relationship?" The trine always presents a challenge to have a vision of what is *possible*.

Geometrically, division by 3 produces the triangle. Triangles were probably at first sacred symbols, perhaps connected with the shape of volcanic mountains and thus with the mysterious spouting forth of fire—which is also symbolic, especially in relation to the myth of Prometheus, of the power of Mind. Two other kinds of triangles were sharply differentiated in archaic geometry as well: the descending equilateral triangle pointing down from its base (or standing on its apex) and the rectangular triangle, of which Pythagoras made a strongly mystical use, beside it being the subject of his famous theorem concerning the square of the hypoteneuse (5) being equal to the sum of the squares of the other two sides (3 and 4).

The first kind of triangle can be, as we have mentioned above, associated with volcanic mountains, fire and Mind. It was exemplified in the American and Egyptian pyramids (*pyr* is the root of the term for fire, *pyros*, in Greek). The rectangular triangle is to be considered, on the other hand, the result of halving a square or rectangle—and as such is a symbol of polarization and of creative interplay, the hypoteneuse representing the divine power through which the integration of two polarities can be effected. In the Pythagorean formulation, the side number 3 represented Man, and that numbering 4 the material world or Fate. The hypoteneuse, 5, symbolized the creative power of Providence through which Man can overcome Fate and adjust the material world to his need.

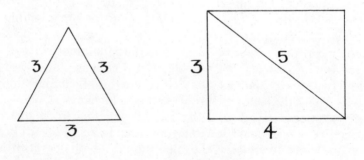

fíqure 3-1

This numerical symbolism, undoubtedly far older than Pythagoras, is most important. In astrology the trine aspect was introduced into the fate-oriented (because unalterable) fourfold time-pattern of cycles, such as the year or the lunation cycle. The trine represented Man as the constructive power able through the use of his intellect to bring purpose and meaning to the instinctual and seemingly purposeless 'wheel of life and death'—symbol of all natural processes and of fate in Buddhist philosophy and elsewhere. The number 3 is thus the symbol of active intelligence; multiplied by itself, 9, it represents, as we will see, the establishment of human consciousness in the realm of pure intelligence and the growth of the psycho-mental 'body' which, collectively speaking, is civilization, and in the spiritually victorious individual the 'Diamond-' or 'Christ-Body.' The down pointing equilateral triangle is what is specifically, geometrically produced at this point in our astrological series of aspects. Its base, from which it is 'suspended,' joins the two sides of the circle differentiated by the opposition, and in so doing allows a new *vision of the whole* to incarnate.

As the self is able constructively to respond to this incarnation of purpose and meaning, one not only displays the faculty of vision and understanding (often-used keywords for the trine), but also *experiences ideas*. On this basis, the self actually begins to transform the outer world and all the relationships in which it has accepted to participate. Significant relationship can also be with one's own talents and capabilities, which one recognizes at the opposition. However, as the self seeks to meet the outer world (or its companion) in terms of ideas and mental vision, the inertia of the whole universe resists the transforming thoughts.

In other words, whenever we take a positive step toward embracing a new experience, vision or relationship (fulfilled evolutionary trine), we are changed. As we are changed and intend to use our new relationship or view of reality, so too is the world around us in some way changed. The natural process then is that everything in our environment, and everything in us, that is still inertial and fearful, that doesn't want to be changed, stands up and hollers: "Stop!"

In order to overcome this inertia, a further step must be taken: the square. The circle must be further divided into four quarters, resulting in the *cross of action*. Vision must become action; purpose must carry the sword of decision; mind must summon will in order to fight for the triumph of creative thought over inner and outer inertia. The Three becomes Four; the trine leads to the square—otherwise it degenerates into the sesquidrate, a 'reactionary' aspect which we will discuss in both its positive and negative dimensions later on.

For now let us say that in relation to the challenge of moving from the trine to the square, the sesquiquadrate operates in much the same way as the quincunx did in relation to the transition from opposition to trine. At this stage, as at the opposition, one can also experience defeat—the defeat of the idealist or dreamer who fails to break through the 'shoulds' or taboos of past traditions and through discouragement, fears or a sense of futility. Ideally, the fully awakened consciousness (opposition) is so fascinated by its new vision or the 'incarnation' of meaning (trine) that sheer conviction or devotion carries it through the fear or inertia. If such a vision fails sufficiently to take hold of the consciousness, what results is a period in which one has to struggle—or re-struggle—through the inertia, inner or outer, blocking the transition between trine and square.

THE SQUARE

The next step leads to the square aspect. Geometrically, dividing by 4 produces the cross within the circle, a very potent symbol which has been used in all eras and by all religions or techniques for psycho-spiritual integration. It is a figure in which two oppositions mutually bisect each other at 90° angles, and similarly, the square can also be considered an opposition divided by 2.

More will be said later on concerning the astrological grand cross formed when two interplanetary oppositions mutually bisect each other producing four squares. For now let us say that the cross within the circle stands essentially for the focusing of universal energies through a particular bi-polar form. The circle represents the lens, and the cross drawn through it the means to focalize with extreme accuracy the image projected. We find such a figure on camera or telescope lenses, and it also constitutes the essential structure of a birth-chart.

In the birth-chart, the meridian is analagous to the spine of a human figure standing with open arms; the line of the arms symbolizes the horizon. Although much has recently been made of the rise of kundalini power from the base of the spine to a spiritual center at or above the crown of the head, the line of the spinal column can also be considered a channel through which spiritual energies *descend* into the human form. As they do, they are symbolically distributed through the figure's outstretched arms; through them the descending spiritual energies (meridian) are made to permeate in an individual way a particular field of being defined by the horizon.

The cross within the circle is thus a symbol of concrete incarnation, of the actual form given to what previously existed at the level of vision or archetypal Idea (trine). Likewise, the geometric square constructed by linking with straight lines the four arms of the cross has since time immemorial been a symbol of solidity, of actual, material form. In its negative aspect as a square inertially resting on its base, it may refer to the imprisonment of spirit in matter. A more positive meaning has traditionally been given to the swastika, a whirling cross (as indicated by small lines trailing from each arm) pictured poised in mid-motion, balanced on the tip of one arm. The incarnation of spiritual energies symbolized by the square aspect is thus not only concrete, but always moving from one stage of equilibrium to the next; it is a symbol of incarnation in action.

Such a meaning becomes more apparent when we consider the square as an opposition divided by 2. We have seen that the opposition is produced by dividing the whole circle by 2, and further division by 2 produces the square. Generally speaking, division by 2 establishes a contrast or rapport between subject and object, spirit and matter, self and not-self. Wherever this operation generates a new aspect, we will find that what was mostly subjective activity becomes a type of activity in which some objective factor is a strongly influential factor. At the level of the square, this objective factor is the heavy, inertial, and sometimes unworkable nature of matter, against which the subject must summon his will to impress upon it the vision conceived under the trine.

In the first or involutionary half of a cycle, the square *precedes* the trine. It represents the need to clear the ground of all obsolete structures before the building operation of an integrated, harmonious way of life can begin in earnest. At the level of involution, such integration can only be intellectual and compulsively or instinctually actional; and it can only be achieved after the severance or decision challenged by the square has been successfully accomplished. In the evolutionary series, the square *follows* and builds upon the trine—i.e., conscious, mental awakening. It represents the stage at which concretization of the ideal or idea envisioned at the trine is necessary and possible.

While it is possible and quite simple to differentiate between a waxing and waning square in a birth-chart, it is not possible to know from the chart if a particular waning square is evolutionary or devolutionary. For a 'last quarter' square to be interpreted as evolutionary, the *person* in whose chart is appears must be able in life to positively relate its meaning to the opposition (or Full Moon) that preceded it—that is, to the beginning of real awareness and individualized consciousness. Like all aspects in the evolutionary series, the square refers to a definite, differentiated stage or level of consciousness and potential achievement. By contrast, an aspect in the involutionary series is not to be considered a definite stage of consciousness or potential achievement *per se*. Rather than a set reality which is latent and which must be actualized, it represents the beginning of a new phase in the gradual focusing of power released in an initial act (the conjunction or New Moon). What counts most in the first hemicycle is what occurs *between* aspects, i.e., the continuous development of an impulse—thus the process of development itself, potentially leading to the successively differentiated stages of consciousness and achievement represented by the evolutionary series.

When, in the evolutionary second hemicycle, one considers aspects the results of dividing the circle—which is now seen as a whole—what is important is *the station reached* as the result of the dividing operation. It represents a set and definite category or level of human activity or realizations. What is significant during this hemicycle is the *use* to which are put the ability to understand ever more inclusively (trine) and the ability to act in an increasingly focalized and effective manner (square). What matters is the overall meaning one gives to a certain capacity (represented by the aspect) in one's life, what one makes of and produces with that capacity.

The trine thus symbolizes the capacity for an ideological or visionary type of activity; the square follows up with an architectural type of activity in which a concrete model is built—for example, the by-laws of an organization, the musical score of a symphony, the plaster model of a building, etc. Then comes the task of actually demonstrating the power to formulate the plan for others. The level of creative formulation is reached: the quintile.

Before proceeding to consider the quintile, we should first try to integrate for practice what has been said so far regarding the opposition, trine and square. To do so before leaving the square category is most appropriate, insofar as the vision or purpose for action conceived or received under the trine should be anchored—at least in intent—to the physical world at the square.

When looking at the overall pattern of a natal chart, we should consider any oppositions in it as dividing the field of experience represented by the houses into two. An opposition also has a particular orientation within the angles of the chart, which are two 'oppositions' inherent in the framework of the chart itself—the Ascendant/Descendant axis (horizon) and the Midheaven/axis (Meridian). Aspects crossing an opposition and thus bridging the two hemicycles divided by it can reveal the best way a person could include and begin to integrate in life the basic relationship or confrontation (internal or external) represented by the opposition. When trines cross the opposition and link the two hemicircles thus divided, they indicate the capacity for including in understanding the two polarities of the opposition; squares indicate the necessity for an actional solution to the problem.

Although traditional delineations prize the presence and abundance of trines in a horoscope, from the overall, process-oriented and therefore cumulative point of view we are presenting here, it is not important whether or how many trines appear in a chart. Any evolutionary aspect other than an opposition or a trine itself implies the level of the trine having been reached some time in the past—although it is probably best not to consider this 'past' as merely per-

sonal history or even from a personal reincarnational point of view.*
The primary significance of trines in a birth-chart lies far more in
how they link hemispheres divided by oppositions or the natal horizon or meridian. When they are connected to squares, they may
reveal the nature of the vision—thus what is possible—underlying a
challenge to action in a person's life; or, for a person having difficulty meeting some life-challenge, they may reveal what could be a
source of strength and inspiration. Trines can also reveal how basic
life-confrontations or relationships represented by an opposition can
be most meaningfully and productively understood.

From this point of view, we can see that what is usually called a
'kite' (Diagram 3-2) can be a particularly constructive configuration, and this will become clearer when we study the sextile from a
geometric point of view later on. For now, we can see that the basic
polarity AB is resolved in each hemisphere through C and D, while
the relationship CD bridges and concretely links the two hemispheres divided by AB. If either C or D were to be in waning square
to a fifth planet (E), or if a T-square were to be formed by a planet
(F) squaring both A and B, a configuration particularly dynamic
and potentially creative of concrete results is produced.

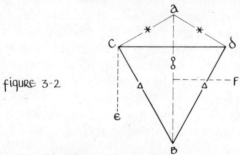

fiquRE 3-2

---

*Many people have had the experience that what they were living through was actually,
though in some indefinable manner, the consequence of antecedent causes—i.e., of events long
ago. One may of course *interpret* such a strange feeling by accepting the hypothesis of reincarnation. But the conception of reincarnation can be understood in several ways, and not only
from the more or less popularized point of view current today. In any case, we can say that our
present is at least partially conditioned by the past—by the past of our parents (what they have
experienced and the way they have responded or reacted to it as well as their 'unlived lives'), by
the ancestral traditions and prejudices which have been stamped upon our receptive minds in
early childhood, and by the evolutionary past of mankind.

All configurations in birth-charts are not so neat and symmetrical, and yet all aspects in a chart—especially major and basic ones like oppositions, trines and squares—are related to one another, if not directly and geometrically, in terms of the actual interrelationship of functions and activities in a person's *actual life-process*. The reason an astrologer studies aspects from an overall, process-oriented perspective is to train the mind to respond to and think in terms of principles of universal and human development. As a result, the practitioner sees meaning not only in the geometric and symbolic aspects of a natal chart, but also in what becomes to him or her the transparent and also symbolic, dynamic aspects of the client's life and being.

THE QUINTILE

The quintile (72° aspect) is the first aspect in the evolutionary series not also found in the involutionary/devolutionary sequence. It is produced by dividing the whole circle into five segments. This operation results in a pentagram, pentagon or five-pointed star. These stand as symbols of creative (or "five-limbed") Man. The five-pointed star is an expression of Man's 'starry' (the literal meaning of the term astral) being. In traditional symbolism, the star is considered in two aspects: one, the upward-pointing star, and the other down-pointing. The latter identifies the 'fifth limb' with the sex organ, through which the power of biological generation is expressed; the former identifies it with the spiritual power of the creative mind centered in the head—in a sense, the power of utterance, the power of the Word.

The upward-pointing star thus emphasizes the connection between human mentality and the function of imagination. In the down-pointing star, imagination arouses and sustains the generative functions in the realm of material production and pleasure. It symbolizes creation and building for their own sake, or under the spur of material goals—which ultimately leads to self-destruction. It leads to self-destruction because the generative power of life or material productivity belongs to the involutionary—not evolutionary—process. What is important by the time the level of the quintiles is reached is not the 'mindless' proliferation of life-forms, but fulfillment of the truly human potential achieved by exercising the faculty of conscious mental creation. Thus, the upward-pointing star shows the whole human organism transformed into a dynamo generating power to sustain the creative will, indeed the 'light' of the 'starry' being. This star radiates light; similarly, the truly creative person emanates a world-transforming energy. He or she has not only had vision (trine) and given it definite form (square), but is also able to fecundate with it the substance of society, the collective mentality of fellow human beings.

When we approach quintiles in birth-charts and especially, as we will see in a moment, quintile-based patterns, we are *not* looking for literally upward or downward pointing star-patterns. We should instead realize that a quintile can operate—if it operates at all—in one of two basic directions or polarities. The polarization is similar to what we found at the opposition: the evolutionary process either progresses or regresses. Here progress is symbolically identified with the head, with the spiritual-mental or conscious aspect of man, with the activation of Vibration Five or Mind—which is a spirit-emanated power to be used in the context of a large evolutionary process. Mind at the level of the quintile or Vibration Five does not mean mere memory, or the simple (or even complex) association of sense perceptions into intellectual patterns—no matter how superficially satisfying or even exciting such activity may be. When fully developed, it leads to truly creative (not merely productive) activity— that is, activity in terms of creative spirit, activity therefore transparent to individual purpose.

Regression, on the other hand, identifies creativity with an earlier process: the generation of 'life.' Such an emphasis is inappropriate at this phase of the process, because the power of 'life' coupled with some degree of individualization seeks only its own self-perpetuation and aggrandisement. Moreover, since the quintile is the first aspect of the evolutionary series not also found in the devolutionary sequence, it contains the potentiality of victory over nature or materiality, whose tendency at this stage of the devolutionary process is toward disintegration and uniformity (entropy). While the victory that must be won is a mental victory, the urge toward it may run amok if the consciousness has not completely realigned its 'allegiance' from the 'life'- and matter-bound involutionary/devolutionary process. Since the challenge of the square was to overcome inertia—the inner mental inertia of old, inherited assumptions of what can and cannot, should and should not be done—a dynamic momentum of conquest and overcoming had to be established. It in turn may develop its own inertia (resistance to change), and a pattern of activity for the sake of activity may develop. The consciousness may restlessly yearn for activity only for the sake of the excitement of the actor, and at the level of the quintile, this is most likely to be in terms of intellectual, rather than truly mental, excitement and activity.

Such a pattern reveals a temporary or permanent inability to function positively at the level of the quintile. Moreover, it can thwart the process of transition from the quintile to the sextile. As we will see later on, the level of activity represented by the sextile brings the individualized consciousness to a point at which it should feel the need to participate in self-encompassing processes of universal evolution by expressing its own essential genius in harmonious relation to these larger processes.

Thus, Vibration Five, Mind, can operate in one of two ways: in terms of purely material, intellectual or selfish desires (regression), or by expressing one's creative genius (progression or forward evolutionary motion). The expression of genius becomes possible only after what is represented by the square has been 'squarely' met, and a definite reorientation of consciousness and activity away from conquest and overcoming necessary at the level of the square has been accomplished. Something truly creative can be brought into being only after the inertia of the past that prevented it has been overcome (square) and the new possibility thus liberated is recognized as something that can indeed happen or be done. This recognition, moreover, must occur in a new context—the context of a truly evolutionary process in which human beings create in conscious, individualized and mental ways.

Practically speaking, this means that when two or more planets (or the horizon and meridian) in a birth-chart form quintiles—and they should be no more than 2° or 3° over or short of exact, and preferably less—the types of activity the planets signify in the total life and personality can potentially open doors to the influx of creative spirit. But the potentiality may not be actualized if some stronger or more basic factor in the life or chart effectively blocks this influx or the expression of it, or if the person has not yet fully met the challenge to forceful, individualizing action presented by the square— that is, if he or she has not yet emerged from the sea of collective activity and consciousness.

These last-mentioned considerations are the primary reasons why astrologers tend not to use the quintile aspect. The vast majority of their clients (and many astrologers themselves) have not, as yet, truly individualized out of the collective social and psychic matrix. Most human beings on the planet today can go no further than the level represented by the square. As we will see more clearly when we consider the sextile, they cannot respond positively to evolutionary processes of spiritual integration beyond the level represented by the Four.

Even if a person can function effectively at the level of the quintile or Five, it does not mean that the person will necessarily prove to be a 'genius' in the almost colloquial sense of the term. Conversely, all so-called geniuses do not have birth-charts with outstanding quintiles. This is simply because many (or most) of those whom we sometimes rather indiscriminately call geniuses are not real creative spirits, but merely 're-arrangers' of previous patterns of being, dispensing to society what satisfies its traditional desires and appetites. In other cases, a great Personage who truly transforms society can be said to operate in a manner transcending the realm of genius as we understand the term here, as for example, the mouthpiece of some cosmic or divine power (an Avatar).

Nevertheless, every person whose acts reveal the power and purpose of the 'star' which symbolizes his or her essential individuality can be considered a genius. The person may not produce great works of art or give birth to scientific theories. But in some way, he or she reveals spirit at work—and spirit can act as destroyer of obsolete structures as well as projector of new archetypes of living and new structures of social or esthetical organization. Such destruction and/or projection can also operate on a continuum of scales, from the very personal to the most public and world-wide. The quintile presents the challenge to actualize the innate potentiality of one's own creative genius—however brilliant or inconspicuous the flame of it may be.

Since the quintile is one of the less familiar and less often used aspects, a few examples might help to clarify its meaning. While we cannot go into great interpretive depth here, we can at least point to a few examples which the serious student is urged to follow up and examine more closely. We can begin by mentioning the chart of Franklin Delano Roosevelt, which contains several quintile-based aspects as well as a number of other significant unfamiliar aspects. The basic quintile element here is the 71½° aspect between the 10th house Moon and the rising Uranus; Mercury is also nearly 69° away from Saturn, and the Sun/Moon and Uranus/Sun angles measure about 145° (bi-quintile) each. These bi-quintiles mean that a five-pointed star is partially outlined by the Sun, Moon and Uranus. Two unmarked points are left, one of which (0° Sagittarius) is near the Moon's North Node (5°41' Sagittarius). The other is about 23° Aries —the exact degree of the New Moon of April 12, 1945, the day of Roosevelt's death.

Thus, at the death of this leader whose significance was world-wide, the New Moon completed the five-pointed star linking an elevated Moon, a rising Uranus, a third house North Node, a fifth house Sun (conjunct Venus and the Part of Fortune): this is indeed a most remarkable star! The Sun/Moon/Uranus configuration is a symbol of transformation potentially achieved through self-exertion and self-conquest and by passing *through* a deep, personal crisis. We can thus see what the five-pointed star suggests in the life of a man who gained the power to lead humanity in a time of global crisis by virtue of the victory he had won over his own personal tragedy—and the additional quintile between Mercury and Saturn links the sixth house of personal crisis with the eighth house of personal transformation. This victory was the substance of F.D.R.'s 'genius'; through it he was able to let his 'star' shine forth and incorporate itself into a world-destiny.

Of course, no discussion of indications of 'genius,' especially the kind that expresses itself mentally, would be complete without Albert Einstein coming to mind. Here, as in F.D.R.'s chart, three points of a five-pointed star are outlined, and what is more, they link the two hemispheres of Einstein's chart divided by a Jupiter/Uranus opposition between the 3rd and 9th houses. The basic quintile is between Mars and Mercury/Saturn. Both Mars and Mercury/Saturn are bi-quintile Uranus, one 'end' of the basic opposition. Jupiter thus falls nearly, but not quite exactly, at the midpoint of the Mars, Mercury/Saturn quintile, and Jupiter is also quintile Neptune. The Mercury/Saturn conjunction is at the midpoint of the Jupiter/Neptune quintile, thus semi-quintile to both. (We will see later on how the division of the quintile into the semi-quintile—implying the division of the circle by 10—releases in specific ways the creative power of mind represented by the quintile.) It should come as no surprise to find such a veritable array of quintile-based aspects in the chart of a scientist whose work stands as the threshold of the Atomic Age and whose very being has come to symbolize 'genius.'

We might mention one point as we become more involved with examples of less-familiar aspects in the lives of well-known persons. Very often students' responses to such examples as Roosevelt and Einstein is, "OK, that's fine, but what does something about their charts have to do with my chart or my next door neighbor's?" It is important to realize that when someone is born—with whatever aspects—there is no differentiation among babies as to any particular one 'having' a special destiny to fulfill. Old wives tales and birth-omens notwithstanding, a baby is not born with a sign saying "This is the one who is going to be significant." In the next hospital delivery room or down the block from where just about anyone was born, there was also another baby being born with a very similar chart. Aspects between planets are rather long-lasting and appear in many horoscopes of babies born over a period of several days or even weeks. Granted, the house positions of the aspecting planets change, but even these change relatively slowly, considering the numbers of babies born every hour in large cities. When we realize what all these considerations imply, we should conclude that an astrologer must give to all clients the highest and most comprehensive vision of birth-potentialities possible. The more an astrologer or client sees and understands is possible, the more the person will be able to actually realize and accomplish. The more one settles for a limited point of view—"This in my or his life or chart could only mean this or that, and only on a personal level," or "It couldn't refer to anything truly significant in a large, humanitarian way"—the less one will be able actually to accomplish and fulfill. We use astrology most constructively and creatively when we gain from it a sense of what is indeed possible for us at the highest levels of our potentialities. Seeing that, the challenge is then to keep our eyes open to life itself, to be able to respond appropriately when some event or chain of circumstances seems to say, "Hey, remember that quintile—or septile? If you are able or want to do anything about it, here's an opportunity."

THE SEXTILE

The next step in the series of evolutionary aspects is represented by the waning sextile or 60° aspect. This is a familiar aspect also belonging to the involutionary/devolutionary series. In the evolutionary series, the sextile is the level reached after the quintile. It results when the circile is divided by six, and it can also be understood as a trine divided by two. Geometrically, division by six produces a six-pointed star made up two interlaced equilateral triangles.

In the six-pointed star or Solomon's Seal, one triangle points downward, the other up. Two trines, two kinds of understanding and vision—are potentially integrated here. On the one hand, the sextile therefore refers to the ability to offer integrative solutions to bi-polar problems sometimes necessitating the harmonization of different approaches to solving them. On the other hand, the down-pointing triangle refers to the descent or incarnation of spirit; the upward-pointing triangle refers to the ascent of matter, to its readiness to receive the spiritual descent. Interlaced together, they symbolize the very involutionary and evolutionary processes we are studying, and in this sense the sextile markes the completion of the process. What tried to 'incarnate' at the trine, and could then only manifest as vision and understanding; what had to overcome the inertia of habit and matter at the square, and the restlessness of the intellect at the quintile, can now, at the sextile be met and embraced by an ascending material form: a human organism (involutionary process), awakened consciousness (opposition) imbued with a sense of purpose (trine), a focused will (square) and mind (quintile) can now receive and work with the downflow. The level of consciousness and activity reached at the sextile is thus one at which spirit and matter can be integrated through *adequate management and organizational genius.*

As at previous stages in the evolutionary process, success in actualizing the potentialities represented by the sextile is not guaranteed. The manager or organizer can become so caught up in his own machinations and talents that he fails to recognize the workings of spirit behind and through his acts. This can lead to a fateful egocentrism or to a lazy, easy-going type of consciousness which seeks the line of least exertion and thus fails to integrate creative power with the material need that is calling forth the descent of spirit-released power. When this negative possibility operates, the polarities of spirit and matter become reversed: spirit that should have become incorporated and active as a solution to the need of an evolving material organism (a human being, a society), loses interest, as it were, in matter, and flies back to its 'heavenly' or purely subjective realm —while matter, which should keep evolving upward toward the spirit, falls back to the state of disintegration and chaos without enlightened management. Spirit then goes 'up'; matter falls 'down'— and following this reversal of creative polarity, the two cannot again attempt integration in the present cycle. The 'marriage of heaven and earth' is broken; divorce ensues, often under the compulsion of hatred—which is just as binding as love and which therefore will of necessity call forth a new cycle in order to 'try again.' One can only hope that the karmic burden of the failure is not so heavy that it cannot be overcome in the opening phases of the following cycle, or that at least part of it may yet be dissipated in the closing phases of the now-ending cycle.

The sextile can also be considered as a trine divided in two. At the level of the square, we saw that bisection does not apply only to the division of the circle into two halves (opposition). We found its basic meaning reappearing in a somewhat modified form, and it will come up again when we consider the octile (semi-square) and decile (semi-quintile). Here we find that bisection again establishes a contrast, relationship and/or rapport between self and not-self, subject and object. Now, after the quintile, this rapport is established between the creative subject (the 'genius' expressing an individual destiny or universal truth) and society at large, or a receptive segment of it.

At the level of the quintile, there is no real working relationship between creator and public, leader and led, the fashioning of a spirit-energized mind and the racial organism of body and psyche subjected to the creative release, usually under some kind of strain. The motto of a creator operating strictly at the level of the quintile may be, "Art for art's sake." The individual who is entirely absorbed in being creative does not take into consideration what the creative expressions will bring to humanity—of if the person does, it is only insofar as the reactions of society will affect his or her ability to create further.

It was a great achievement for the individual Einstein to 'create' the formula upon which the controlled release of atomic energy depends, but humanity is now faced and must live with the reality of nuclear power in a variety of forms. If our world-civilization succumbs to an atomic disaster of one kind or another, or to the hysteria of fear and uncertainty the danger of one has produced, the genius of Einstein and his colleagues may indeed appear to future generations as catastrophically destructive—because of having come as a premature 'gift' to an immature society. Such a realization made Einstein and many other prominent atomic physicists of the post-War years to take the lead in trying to educate people and governments into an awareness of the political and social changes which the scientists' genius made necessary, if humankind is to survive. What is necessary is a complete shift of the level of consciousness of modern men and women, especially of those who provide leadership and set examples of supposedly constructive behavior for their societies. This shift in level of consciousness can be symbolized astrologically as a change from an emphasized quintile-type of consciousness to one in which the characteristics of quintiles *and* sextiles are integrated.

What this means is that at the level of the sextile, not only sheer creativeness (quintile) is important, but also the *effect* of the creative expression upon the outer world and society. If the creative approach to life represented by the quintile is to be made truly spiritual and fully constructive at the sextile, it must take into consideration the need of the world. The essential nature of spirit is to act only in response to need. The spiritual action is always a necessary action free from all unnecessary elements—just as the truly great work of art or elegant solution to a problem is one which contains only necessary elements from which nothing can be subtracted without impairing the harmony and beauty of the whole. Truly spiritual activity at the level of the sextile must therefore be attuned to the purpose of the whole—to what some may call Tao or 'the flow,' others, 'God's will'—or at least to the purpose of a particular life-cycle.

Waning sextiles thus produce an unprecedented evolutionary challenge today. They are most apt to operate at first in their devolutionary mode, as the need for reorganization following a crisis in consciousness. This is because the vast majority of human beings actually have little to do with the level of consciousness represented by the quintile. They can go no further than the level of the square—or, to put it differently, they cannot respond to evolutionary processes of spiritual integration beyond the stage (or Vibration) Four. Only a mentally positive minority can respond to those creative processes symbolized by the five-fold differentiation of the circle, the five-pointed star or pentagram and the Vibration Five. It is this 'elite' which today must experience a 'change of gears' from a dominant, mentally restless Vibration Five to a vibration in which the principle of characteristic response to life's challenges represented by the Five and the Six will become integrated.

As consciousness truly progresses in the evolutionary series, it moves on by way of ever-greater inclusiveness—that is, when reaching the level Six it does not (or should not) abandon the powers of creativity gained at level Five. The problem is to integrate the new powers (Six) with the old ones (Five). Similarly, when humanity as a whole shifts from the level Four to the level Five, it does so only gradually, by stressing successive 'overtones' rather than by jumping from one 'fundamental' to the next. Today we are witnessing a twofold process: on one hand, the majority of humanity is slowly shifting the focus of its mass-consciousness from the level Four to the level Five (witness the extreme emphasis on 'individual rights'); on the other, the already mentally developed minority is hesitantly beginning to incorporate into its approach to experience features characteristic of the level Six.

These features are the ones which Jesus came to announce and to exemplify. His coming sounded the keynote of a new 26,000-year cycle of precession which began at the inception of both Christianity and the Roman Empire. These features are also expressed astrologically in the sextile—but the sextile considered as a step in the series of evolutionary aspects whose keynote can be best defined as *creation in understanding.*

In terms of involutionary (i.e., instinctual and unconscious) activity, the sextile represents balanced and practically effective action resulting from the ability to link two polar rhythms of masculine and feminine impulses. This is because the involutionary sextile includes two consecutive zodiacal signs of contrasting polarity, for example Aries and Taurus, from Aries 1° to Gemini 1°. It therefore represents a complete, bi-polar type of activity, which is nevertheless subjective, because it does not include a view of the whole circle. In terms of evolutionary (that is, conscious and integrative) responses to life, the sextile is also a symbol of practical effectiveness, but this effectiveness operates at the level of creative mental processes and is the result of the conscious integration of the will to create with the human need that made the creation necessary. It is fully effective because activity at the level of the evolutionary sextile includes a clear and compassionate understanding of that which *called forth* the creative act—thus of the human need, whether it be personal or collective.

Rarely, but occasionally, one sees a chart with a full pattern of six sextiles, two interlaced grand trines. Two are in our files. One is the chart of a young man (23 at the time of consultation) who had not at that time found his 'place' in life. He has apparently taken the line of least resistance and exertion, always managing to 'scrape by' on all levels, but little more. The other is the chart of a woman, now past mid-life. She has led a most varied and interesting life of accomplishment in terms of both social and spiritual values. It is interesting to note that at the root of the life-challenges faced by both people, has been the question of relatedness: two interlinked grand trines, six sextiles around the circle, *automatically* imply three oppositions. In the case of the young man, his relationship to his own diabetic body and to God has been focal. In the case of the woman, interpersonal relationship and relationship to a Teacher and a Work have been and continue to be significant.

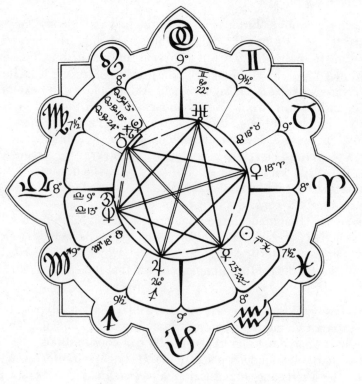

figure 3-3

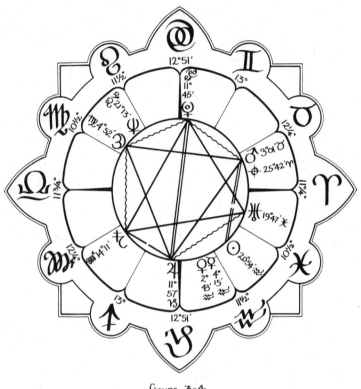

figure 3-4

THE SEPTILE

When we come to the aspect which follows the sextile in the evolutionary series, we find it based on a division of the circle of wholeness into seven equal parts. Such a division produces an angular value which cannot be measured exactly in degrees, minutes or seconds of arc: 51° 25' 42" *plus*. Converted into decimals it is 51.4285714285714... It is thus an 'irrational' value. If we inquire into the occult meaning of numbers we find out that the number Seven producing this value is a very special kind of number indeed.

Perhaps the simplest way to interpret the character of number Seven is to say that it represents what remains after the Six has operated fully. The meaning of such a remainder is clearly shown in the geometrical element *pi*, which measures the relationship between the circumference and diameter of a circle. This relationship is an 'irrational' one in that it does not measure to any whole number, being 3.14159 etc., and it is also a most 'occult' value.

If instead of the diameter we consider the radius of a circle in relation to its circumference, we readily see that more than six radii are necessary to make a circumference. This 'more' constitutes the 'remains' or 'leftover' after the sixth period of any cycle is completed. The Seven refers to the part of *pi* that goes on forever, to what is left over beyond three diameters or six radii—the indefinable *plus* required for a whole circle, which also gives it the opportunity to become a spiral.

In order to take care of that 'left over' a seventh period is necessary, and this seventh period is actually the seed-beginning of a new cycle. In the new cycle, the 'left over' of the old cycle will be given a new chance to become integrated and to progress in the vast scheme of universal evolution. Besides the kind of leftovers that remain unintegrated from the preceding six phases—whatever has not as yet managed to become integrated—there are also leftovers that can't possibly be integrated because they are toxins or negative by-products of the cycle. Rather than being integrated, these have to be neutralized and eliminated so that they will not poison the succeeding cycle now beginning to seed.

Every cycle has its 'left over'—and materials which could not be assimilated to spirit, which the consciousness of the person operating under the Six could not understand or provide for creatively. At the close of the sixth period the actual cycle is ended, as far as outward and normally visible manifestations go; but to the need of the disintegrating remains (or 'manure') of the closed cycle, some new type of spirit-born realization answers—and this realization eventually leads to the birth of a new cycle.

What should be realized in full consciousness during this seventh period (reminiscent of the Biblical 'Seventh Day') is not essentially that everything was well with the work done, but that there is never an end to creative activity and that there are always ashes to take care of after the fire of life has subsided. What the Seven tells to human beings is that no account can be closed forever; that six radii do not make exactly the length of the circumference; that nature (human and otherwise) is not simply rational, and that it cannot fit into strictly rationalistic or mental patterns. There are fractional numbers ad infinitum to take care of—the never-ending decimals of the septile and the value *pi*.

To realize these things and to incorporate this realization into the structure of one's inner being is to operate at the level of the septile. It is to force oneself to be immortal—that is, to stride over the close of the cycle in order to become a seed ready to sacrifice itself in order to be the foundation of a new vegetation, when spring comes again. The number Seven is thus the key to personal immortality—to identifying oneself with the entire cycle, with the eternal. In a negative sense, it can refer to identification with atomicization, with the process of disintegration inevitable at the close of the cycle.

In order to be at all significant, a septile aspect must be very close to exact. If we count it as a 51½° angle, two planets form a septile only if they are from 50 to 53 degrees apart. A lesser distance should be considered a semi-square; a greater distance is a sextile.

In addition to its outstanding quintiles, Franklin D. Roosevelt's chart contains most significant septiles. Mars is just short of being 51 degrees ahead of Saturn; and the Moon which is in sextile to Saturn, forms a septile to Neptune (about 52°) and to Jupiter (if the time of birth was at the later hour recorded, it seems, in his father's diary). As Jupiter and Neptune are very close and their conjunction of obvious importance in F.D.R.'s life, we can say that the Moon is in septile to this conjunction, whether the earlier or later birth-time is accepted.

According to Marc Jones, the key meaning of the septile is 'fatality,' and in the exact septile of Mars (retrograde) and Saturn we can see how fatality worked in its strange and mysterious ways to bring tragedy and fame to F.D.R. Mars and the Moon are in the tenth house, and the septiles they control clearly deal with Roosevelt's public life, his death in office, etc. But there is far more to these septiles than fatality—or this term has to be made to cover a greater depth of meaning than is usually the case. In the septile we find a potential gate to immortality, as well as the possible assumption of a collective and historical destiny—a potentiality only, we must stress.

Lenin's chart contains a septile of Jupiter (26° 9' Taurus) to Uranus (Cancer 18° 16'). He also died from overexertion in office. In the case of the composer and super-star archetype Franz Lizst, the septile of Sun and Moon did not produce tragedy, except if we consider the abuse of vital forces and the over-spending of self as one. In Henry Ford's chart Mars in Leo (conjunct Regulus) is septile Jupiter in Libra (20½ °). Under the circumstances, this could be considered a compelling destiny of wealth and social power. A similar remark could be made concerning Andrew Carnegie's septile between Mars (a symbol of iron and steel) and Neptune; the septile linking his Moon and Venus presumably refers to his fame as a prototype of the large-scale American philanthropist and culture-patron.

In the case of Evangeline Adams, Venus rising is in septile to Pluto in the second house, and we might even consider the almost 54° aspect of her Sun to Neptune a septile, especially in view of the obvious correlation between Neptune and what turned out to be her astrological 'mission.' Similarly, the 53½ ° aspect between Uranus and Mercury in George Bernard Shaw's chart seems a valid septile indication of what became his world-wide influence as a writer and humorist. Another significant illustration is found in Edgar Allan Poe's septile between Neptune and his Sun/Mercury conjunction, for the Neptunian factor—often linked to fantasy, mysticism. . . and alcohol!—influenced his vitality and his literary work, bringing both tragedy and fame. The septile between Neptune and Jupiter in Walt Whitman's chart had what seems to be a happier outcome—an evident symbol of the expansive social vision that made the bard of American democracy forever great.

A more contemporary example is the chart of California's charismatic Governor Jerry Brown—who has been known to claim to have "an essence" rather than an "image." His horoscope displays the outline of four points of a seven-pointed star. The Sun is septile Jupiter, which in turn is tri-septile Neptune. Neptune in turn is septile Pluto. The chart of the spiritual teacher Krishnamurti is also an interesting example. Here the Moon and Saturn are septile as are the Sun and Mars. These septiles are made more interesting as they define the two ends of an overall see-saw configuration;* all the planets of the chart are contained within one septile or another. President Jimmy Carter's chart has also a prominent septile between Mercury and the first house Moon. Transiting Uranus was on the degree of this Moon during the (1979) Camp David meetings with Anwar Sadat and Menachem Begin. The Moon rules the President's Midheaven, while Mercury, in the eleventh house (transformation of social structures), rules also the ninth (religious or philosophical ideology).

The chart of the contemporary 'consciousness movement' figure Ram Das also provides an example of an interesting, if obvious in meaning, septile. Rising Jupiter is 51½° behind Neptune at the nadir—a quite clear-cut statement regarding social participation (Jupiter also rules the Midheaven) and drugs, meditation and altered states of consciousness. Since Jupiter also co-rules the sixth house (crises of personal transformation), and Neptune is in the third (mental functioning), the issues of mystical experience and spiritual discipleship are highlighted (no pun intended!).

These examples, however limited their scope, lead us to believe that it can be shown on good evidence that wherever a septile is found in a chart, *and* the individual is able to realize at least to some

---

*cf. *Person-Centered Astrology*, "First Steps in the Study of Birth-Charts" (New York: ASI: 1980) by Dane Rudhyar for an in-depth discussion of overall chart shapes (*Gestalt*).

extent its positive implications, the septile indicates the direction in which the individual is led to his or her destiny by some outstanding achievement or compulsion—the former being dependent upon a typical kind of inner attitude. One can probably also say that the septile implies some kind of psychological complex or spiritual compulsion—and in that sense it may be called an expression of 'fate.' What seems to be fate or fatality to the living and striving or suffering personality may be differently interpreted in relation to spirit, which transcends (while including) the particular personality. Spirit compels the inclusion of whatever remains valuable in what has previously been devalued or denied. In a more mundane sense, the garbage has always to be taken out, and leftovers cooked into new meals. The longer they stay around, the more difficult it is to dispose of them pleasantly or creatively. In a larger view, there are deaths (large and small) that are sacrificial gifts, and not somber tragedies, simply because they are geared to the vast cycle of human evolution, and as such are tokens of immortality.

THE OCTILE OR SEMI-SQUARE
AND THE SESQUIQUADRATE

If, instead of two interlaced triangles inscribed in a circle, we consider two squares with all corners equidistant from one another, we have an eight-pointed star and the foundation of the semi-square, which more rarely, but equally accurately is also called an octile.

The semi-square is to the square what the sextile is to the trine, and there is no reason, whether theoretical or practical, to give less importance to the semi-square than to the sextile. The main reason why many students and practitioners of astrology pay less attention to the semi-square than to the sextile is that since the positions of the planets are expressed in terms of zodiacal degrees and signs, one can easily detect sextiles, whereas semi-squares are less obvious. This is, quite evidently, not at all a good reason, and it is hoped that the outstanding importance of semi-squares will be universally recognized and correctly interpreted. A semi-square is no more a 'lesser square' than a sextile is merely a 'lesser trine.'

Another reason for the lack of attention given to the semi-square is that while the sextile is found in both the involutionary and evolutionary series of aspects, the semi-square (or octile) occurs only in the latter. In the classical past, astrology has dealt almost exclusively with the involutionary series and thus ignored or undervalued the semi-square. But as a truly modern astrology should be occupied primarily with psychology and problems of consciousness, it is essential that it should give full significance to the evolutionary series—of which the semi-square is an integral part.

The significance of the semi-square may be derived from that of the square, in much the same way we derived that of the sextile from the trine. The vision and understanding of individuals (trine) become the gift of practical organization and management (sextile) when this vision (spiritual triangle) is related to the need of any material organism, body or collectivity (material triangle) in the midst of which this vision appears as an inspiration. The square, on the other hand, refers to the level of consciousness at which vision and understanding (trine) become transformed into the realization of the need to act, and by acting to make the ideal a concrete reality. It means, in a positive sense, a victory over inertia, fear and discouragement, because vision, in order to become reality, must overcome the ghosts of the past and the feeling of insurmountable difficulty which often accompanies the realization of a new idea.

However, this overcoming of inertia is only a potentiality at the level of the square. The need for it is felt, and *if* the individual takes and holds a positive attitude, the victory will eventually be won through the use of powers symbolized by the quintile and sextile. The precise blueprint, established at the level of the square, will be on the way to becoming an actual structure of earth-materials. We have seen that in any building operation there are always left-over materials, things that did not fit. They must be disposed of; they may be burnt or cleared away as sheer waste; or they may be kept for future use. It is to this type of operation that we have seen the septile refer.

The next step is the semi-square. The square, which referred to a realization of the need to act and to make the vision concrete, is now interlaced with a second square—much as the two triangles of spirit and matter are interlaced in the six-pointed star. The second square now represents the concrete, officially established organization or structure; but organization and structure are built in the midst of an already functioning society—that is, among people. What do the people think of it? How do they respond to what it offers them? Do they feel it meets their needs, or do they laugh at it and scorn its purpose? Do they try to destroy it, or ignore it and let it decay unused?

The semi-square refers to all such problems of exteriorization. The person of vision (trine) should not only formulate a set of ideals clearly and approach problems with creative initiative (quintile), a genius for organization (sextile) and the ability to use what is fit and to deal with what is unfit (septile); he or she should as well take into consideration the way in which others are likely (because of their past conditioning) to react. While such a person undoubtedly feels that the work will answer a real need of the people, the people must also feel that their need is being served. The semi-square thus refers to the level of consciousness and activity at which the response of the people must be integrated into the vision having become a concrete social reality—or, in another field, the reaction of the body and its organs must be integrated with a new technique of behavior based upon a new ideal of spiritual or more healthful living.

As in the case of the sextile, the semi-square must be considered from two points of view. It may mean integration, or a breakdown of policy. The new organization and its products are accepted by the people—the new apartment house finds tenants eager to move in— or, the people ignore the products and perhaps even destroy their would-be benefactor. The key to success is effective dissemination, just as, in the case of the sextile, success depended upon an effective schedule and policy of management. The most effective kind of dissemination is the kind where no propaganda is actually needed because the people's need is obviously satisfied by what is offered as an answer to it. When in time of social chaos a strong leader and his group tell the public the very words it wants to hear, or when a man like Henry Ford presents a new product which is an efficient answer to the evident need of the times, relatively little promotion is required. Yet some kind of adjustment between need and concrete answer to this need is always necessary.

The successful builder or leader is the one who plans in terms of such an adjustment, yet who does not sacrifice the integrity of the vision. The balance between opportunism and spiritual integrity is always a difficult one to reach, let alone maintain. In formulating and concretizing the ideal, it is easy for a creative person to rely too much or too little on what the people's *desire* (rather than need) may be. Many trines may make real communication with people (or whatever the vision is meant to serve) difficult, for the focus is on the vision itself, while semi-squares may mean practical success but also subservience to materialistic needs or changing fashions and a loss of long-range spiritual vision.

Through the semi-square spirit scatters itself into matter; or at least the energy of spirit is allowed to permeate an expectant, but usually not comprehending chaos. In order to convince the people (or any collection of material entities) of the value of a new organization, product or structure, the leader, inventor or author has to become 'sales manager' as well—and this is often a real crucifixion or self-sacrifice, far more crucial sometimes than the one implied in the process of making an ideal concrete in a definite structure or organization (square). The square means the *concretization* of ideas; the semi-square their *dissemination*.

These are two phases of one process. A third phase could be conceived in which the semi-square itself is divided into halves of 22½ ° each. Such an aspect could be called a semi-octile, thus paralleling the semi-sextile. It would refer to the stage of vulgarization of the ideal or spiritual vision. When the latter is spread out among the many in order to meet their everyday needs, it often loses most of its purity and integrity—yet it has nevertheless become an active force in the world.

The absence of semi-squares in a birth-chart does not necessarily mean that an individual will not be able to disseminate his or her vision or ideals. The presence of strong semi-squares shows that a special stress should be laid upon this process of dissemination, that it has the potentiality of being especially effective or related in a purposeful way to personal or psychological crises through which the individual can discover an essential truth or destiny.

In Henry Ford's chart the Sun is in semi-square to both Venus and Uranus, at the nearly exact center of the square which these two planets make. Uranus is at Gemini 24° and Venus is at Virgo 23°, while the Sun is at Leo 8°. Mercury at 4° Leo could be said to participate in these semi-squares, yet it is usually advisable not to give to the semi-square more than a three-degree orb (thus allowing from 42° to 48°). After concretizing (square) a new approach to manufacturing (form-building, aptly symbolized by Venus and Uranus), Ford sowed the idea of industrial mass-production into every corner of the modern world. In his chart, Pluto and Uranus also form a 41½° aspect which can be considered as a distant semi-square, inasmuch as Pluto squares the Moon and adds to a chain of such aspects, linking Moon, Pluto, Uranus, Sun and Venus—which thus contribute five points to an eight-pointed star.

In Andrew Carnegie's chart we also find a square divided into two halves: the square of Saturn and Neptune is bisected by Venus. In such cases, the bisecting planet should be considered the focal factor in the disseminating process; on it rests the main burden for the spread of the vision or idea. Venus in the chart of the American steel magnate and philanthropist rules the seventh and twelfth houses, and Carnegie was noted for the manner in which he established partnerships (seventh house) and built hospitals and social institutions (twelfth house). He spread his vision via a Venusian kind of activity, while Ford, with his Sun bisecting the square of Venus and Uranus, worked on the basis of his own individual center—a paternalistic autocrat.

George Bernard Shaw is again another example of such a triple configuration. The Moon and Uranus bisect a square of Jupiter and Saturn. This square of the two planets of social consciousness indicates the potential release of new ideals of social organization. Uranus's semi-squares to these two planets focus the revolutionary and challenging character of the new ideals, and the Moon contributes to this dynamic pattern a keen mental power of intellectual adjustment to social situations. Neptune is also in exact semi-square to Pluto and at the same time in sextile to the Moon and trine to Mercury. It is also sesquiquadrate (135° aspect) to the conjunction of Sun and Venus.

THE SESQUIQUADRATE OR TRI-OCTILE

A sesquiquadrate may be understood in a variety of ways. In the above-mentioned case of George Bernard Shaw it may be considered the sum of three semi-squares, thus as linking two of the points of an implied eight-pointed star. This way of interpreting a sesquiquadrate (also called sesquisquare) stresses the positive implications of the aspect. We see it then as a semi-square added to a square—as an outreaching process of disseminating ideas. It can also be understood as an opposition from which a semi-square has been taken away—and thus defined, the sesquiquadrate is one of two aspects having a very special meaning, especially in psychological terms.

The first of these aspects, as well have already seen, is the quincunx. In the involutionary series, the quincunx begins the fifth stage of outward expression. It represents thus the 'works of life,' the 'work of the world,' the extension of spontaneous activity by means of effective, yet largely unconsciously acquired and applied technique. It shows instinctual life-activities at a stage of refinement through critical and objective subservience to standards of perfection. The involutionary quincunx is thus a symbol of self-improvement.

Yet this is only its positive aspect in terms of dynamic activity. It has as well a negative aspect which results from the failure to carry this dynamic activity to the level where cooperation with other centers of dynamic activity—other individuals, men and women, and also other living organisms of the less-evolved life-kingdoms—becomes essential, after the opposition. The quincunx is then a 'falling back' from the level of the opposition—thus, as we have seen, a regressive step. It then represents sickness and whatever personal neuroses and maladjustments come because the ego has been unable or unwilling to adjust itself successfully to the demands of relationship and cooperative activity.

Similarly, the 135° aspect is, in its negative connotations, a falling back from the step required between the waning trine and the square. It then refers to the inability to put over one's idea and vision. This essentially means a failure to include the needs of others (or the need of one's body and organs) in the plans one makes—a failure in compassion and in understanding the conditions which a new plan or organization will have to meet when becoming exteriorized and ready to operate in the environment whose needs it should serve. The project and blueprints may be wonderful in and of themselves. But if they do not take into account the character of the materials which they should organize and integrate for use, or the needs of the people expected to use what results from them, the outcome is an at least temporary failure—and means for the planner a more or less acute sense of disappointment, resentment, bitterness, or even a 'persecution complex.' His public outreaching may then become overstressed, and he may fruitlessly scatter his energies.

This does not mean that a person with natal sesquiquadrates will necessarily lack outer success. The sesquiquadrate may manifest in its positive aspect as a public outreaching—a square plus a semi-square. On the other hand, a person of vision may be so identified with what he feels as a mission to get his vision across to the public that he will do practically anything to achieve recognition. He may meet the superficial demands of the public and achieve outer success. But if success is built, not on the vision, but on some kind of compromise in which that vision is lost or disfigured, it may mean a sense of futility or a real inner failure in spite of success. In such a case, the old saying "Nothing fails like success" may well apply. Therefore, in order to be truly successful, the person whose chart includes significant sesquiquadrates should be careful always to be aligned with the essence of the inner vision, and to include the needs (not merely the wants and desires) of others and of the public.

One often encounters a significant aspect pattern involving an opposition divided by a sesquiquadrate and a semi-square. The line of least resistance in such cases is to take an ineffectual, confused or self-destructive approach to the problem of consciousness represented by the opposition. The meaning of the conflict and opportunity defined by the two poles of the opposition may not be clearly or sufficiently understood, and the nature of the possible failure is indicated by the planet forming the semi-square and sesquiquadrate with the opposition. The positive approach to such a configuration involves using the function represented by the planet aspecting the opposing planets to release the meaning of the opposition—regardless of how much personal struggle, persistence or courage would be necessary. This configuration can be considered analogous to—but also in a sense the reverse of—what happens when a planet is in exact sextile/trine relationship to two planets in opposition; for the focal planet in that case can be said to integrate what is represented by the two poles of the opposition through a practical vision or ability to manage people or resources.

An example in which the two ends of an opposition are linked by both a semi-square and sesquiquadrate and a sextile/trine is found in the chart of the Danish physicist Neils Bohr. A Venus/Neptune opposition defines the chart's overall hemispheric pattern. While Jupiter (the planet of social consciousness and participation) is trine Neptune and sextile Venus, Saturn (representing authority and formal organization) is also sesquiquadrate Neptune and semi-square Venus. At the focal point of the semi-square/sesquiquadrate configuration, Saturn is on a degree (9° Cancer) referring in the Sabian series to "the first naive quest for knowledge and for an ever-elusive understanding of life." Bohr was, of course, at the forefront of vanguard research in theoretical physics during the most exciting period of that discipline's development early this century. Jupiter, at the focal point of the sextile/trine configuration, is on a degree (23° Virgo) stressing the need to "tame" powerful energies—a need Bohr recognized only too well, for he was among the first to realize the socio-political implications of the Allied effort to actually build an atomic bomb during World War II. The bomb was, of course, a great 'success,' and it was built largely through the application of ingenuity and imaginative innovation symbolized by Bohr's Venus/Neptune opposition. The failure of Bohr's (and others') efforts to have the use and regulation of atomic power internationally shared —which would have entailed the building of new social structures and authorities, astrologically represented by Jupiter and Saturn— ultimately led to the global arms race still continuing today.

Another example of the opposition/semi-square/sesquiquadrate configuration can be found in the chart of Werner Erhard, the "wizard of est." Here the fifth-house Sun opposes Saturn, which is retrograde, elevated and rules the Midheaven; and Pluto in the second house of resources is sesquiquadrate Saturn and semi-square the Sun. Pluto is also sesquiquadrate the Moon on the Descendant, which is in turn square both Saturn and the Sun, thus at the 'short

end' of a T-square. What results is an interesting connection between the two sides of the line of opposition: one side is released
through two very basic squares (Sun/Moon and Moon/Saturn), the
other through a semi-square (Sun/Pluto) and sesquiquadrate (Saturn/Pluto).

Equally interesting, however, is a pattern formed as a result of
the fact that Pluto is actually at the inverse midpoint of the square
between Saturn and the Moon. In relation to a square, this pattern is
similar to what happens when a planet is at the inverse midpoint of a
sextile, what is called a 'Yod' or 'Finger of God' configuration, resulting from two quincunxes linking two sextiling planets to a third.
In this case, two sesquiquadrates rather than quincunxes 'point' to a
third planet, and the 'base' of the configuration is a square instead of
a sextile. If there is any meaning in calling the quincunx/sextile configuration a 'Finger of God,' one might consider calling the analogous sesquiquadrate/square configuration a 'Finger of the World'—
for it challenges one to concrete action (square) that must be well-
advertised and disseminated, but which at the same time should
stand on its own as an almost self-evident answer to a pressing social
or evolutionary need. In the case of Werner Erhard, whether or not
his efforts fulfill such a challenge can only be left to the debate of his
supporters and detractors—both categories having many vocal adherents.

Another contemporary 'consciousness movement' figure whose
chart displays prominent sesquisquares is Ram Das. An almost exact
conjunction of the Sun and Uranus in the eleventh house is sesquiquadrate Neptune, which in turn is sesquiquadrate Saturn. Since
Saturn is also square the Sun/Uranus conjunction, what we have
called a 'Finger of the World' results. This whole pattern is further
integrated into the chart's overall configuration, for the Saturn/Neptune sesquiquadrate also links two oppositions, Saturn/Pluto (the
latter being also conjunct Jupiter) and Venus/Neptune. Another sesquiquadrate between the elevated Venus (ruler of the twelfth house)
and the first-house Pluto completes the rectangle structured by the
two oppositions. This is a most significant pattern which we will
study more fully in the next chapter. At this point, however, the pattern's repeated references to public life, social participation and or-

ganization, drugs and mystical experiences should help to illumine the challenges underlying Ram Das's early, seminal involvement with psychedelic drugs, altered states of consciousness, and his more recent emphasis on meditation and spiritual development.

In closing this condensed section on two interesting but usually ignored aspects, the complex chart of President Roosevelt again provides an excellent example. His fifth-house Sun is sesquiquadrate the dominant tenth-house and retrograde Mars; the eighth-house Saturn is in sesquiquadrate to rising Uranus. The two sesquiquadrates are linked by the septile between Mars and Saturn, the bi-quintile between Uranus and the Sun, and a bi-novile between Mars and Uranus. These aspects refer no doubt to the tragedy which nearly made physically impossible, and yet psychologically facilitated, his professional career. They also show how an aspect with the potentiality of defeat (the sesquiquadrate) can be made the very springboard to personal triumph and spiritual victory.

THE NOVILE

By dividing the circumference of a circle into nine equal segments, we produce the rarely used aspect called novile or nonagen (40°). The geometrical figure that results combines three equilateral triangles. The number 9 is not a primary number like 3, 5, or 7, but neither is it divisible by 2. It can, however, be divided by 3, and the novile can also be considered the result of trisecting a trine. This combination of 'threeness' gives to the novile its basic significance.

When we think about division by 3, we realize that we might also consider the sextile the result of dividing an opposition or half the circle into three 60° segments. But in order to be truly significant, the division of aspects must always be related to the entire circle—that is, to the wholeness of being, experience or a situation. If only half of the circle is considered and divided by 3, the result is the negative meaning of the sextile: a kind of trine (vision, understanding, ideal) which affects only half of life and consciousness, and leaves the other half out of the picture. It then deals with the meaningless proliferations of material nature un-illumined by spirit, or with the subjective activity of a dream-like consciousness too weak or lazy to meet and fecundate the material realities of our world. The sextile is therefore not to be considered positively as a half circumference divided into 3 segments, but instead as the result of inscribing two interlaced triangles into the whole circle.

Since the novile results from inscribing three interlaced triangles in the circle, it can be considered a characteristic product of division by three—or, to be more exact, we should really say, of *multiplying* by three, for it implies the multiplication of the triangle (and thus the segments) within the circle. One or two triangles becomes three triangles; three or six segments become nine.

In the six-pointed star, we found two triangles, and we referred one to the descent of spirit and the other to the ascent of matter. Such a duality means opposition and contrast, and three oppositions are implied in any perfect six-pointed star. But as we saw, dualities and contrasts may lead either to the rhythmic integration of opposites, or to irreconcilable cleavage. The idea of trinity, on the other hand, begins with the principle of harmonic integration within an encompassing transcendent concept, pattern or image. The world of *life*, as we know it in the biosphere, is essentially a world of dualities and conflicts which may or may not be resolved into love and into the organisms or organizations born of love. The world of *mind* is a world of trinities and threefold relationships—even the quintile based on the Five is the third aspect after the opposition in the evolutionary series. Life is based on power, mind on meaning; and the capacity to see meaning in whatever there is in the world of life is what is called intelligence—in the real and philosophical sense of the word, not in an artificial sense as in IQ or intelligence tests, etc. Meaning is envision or conceived by the mind when the dualities and conflicts of the world of life are related to and included within a third factor—God, the Universe, Self, man as a spiritual being—in reference to which these conflicts and contests for power become productive and acquire a purpose.

The nine-pointed star, as the result of the symmetrical interlacing of three equilateral triangles, raises the meaning of the Three to a higher level: 9 is the second power of 3, i.e., 3 multiplied by itself.*

---

*We can also interpret the number 4 as 2 multiplied by itself. The awareness produced by the opposition is raised to a higher level of dynamic intensity by becoming a definite blueprint for action (square). All we build is originally born out of what we have carefully observed. Perception (2) leads to conception (3), then to constructive action (4).

At the level of the Three, a human being discovers and envisions the meaning and purpose of what he or she *experiences*, and orients himself or herself toward the fulfillment of this meaning and purpose. At the level of the Nine, the individualized person discovers and envisions the meaning and purpose of what he or she *is*. The trine leads to planning for action; the novile (when at all operative in an individual's life) leads to personal rebirth—or 'Initiation'—to a basic identification of the self with the purpose this self is seen to have within the harmony of the universal Whole.

The novile thus represents the level at which complete fulfillment of individual being is possible—either as an end in itself (negative approach) or as the condition for positive emergence into an altogether new and higher realm of being (beginning with number Ten). Thus number Nine is the number of a fulfilled period of gestation (e.g., nine months of pregnancy) followed by birth. This period also contains 40 weeks, and the number 40 has been the symbol for a period of preparation for rebirth: the forty-year wandering of the Jews in the desert, and in the recent Baha'i movement, Abdul Baha's forty years of imprisonment in the town of Akka—a name meaning 'womb.' In terms of Hindu chronology, the Kali Yuga (Dark Age) lasts 400,000 years, or forty 10,000-year cycles.* Kali is the Great Mother in her dark, unconscious aspect. Kali Yuga is thus the period during which a new humanity is being carried within the collective 'womb' of the old humanity. According to Brahminical records, we have just completed the first 5,000 years of such a process having begun in February, 3,102 B.C.

We can bring the preceding ideas to the level of the interpretation of a birth-chart by seeing that the presence of noviles—or of one strongly emphasized novile—in a chart shows that the individual may come to realize, or will strive to realize, that the entire personality is a womb or matrix from which a 'higher' being—a spiritually conscious Self—should emerge. Christian mystics speak of the birth of the Christ-child within the heart as the central experience of the spiritual life. In a less exalted sense, every aspect based on 40° increments brings the possibility (not the certainty) of some 'birth out of

---

*10,000 years is astrologically the Great Cycle of Uranus. Cf. *Astrological Timing: The Transition to the New Age* (Harper & Row, New York, 1969) by Dane Rudhyar.

captivity,' some emergence into a Promised Land, whatever it be within the personality that is held captive, wandering in the 'desert' of unconsciousness and spiritual aridity. The two planets in novile aspect indicate the psychological functions which establish through their relationship the matrix-field from which the act of spiritual liberation or rebirth may occur.

For example, in the birth-chart of the Persian prophet Baha'u'llah, who claimed to be a manifestation of God, the Sun and Moon are 42° apart. This is, in a sense, a very wide novile, as in most cases no more than a degree and a half should be allowed for this aspect; but the Moon may be exactly 40° away from the Ascendant, and such an aspect would be characteristic. If a man is actually to be considered a physical incorporation of divinity, then it would be logical to expect the Sun and Moon—the two basic vital powers—to be in novile at the time of his birth. The fact that the Sun is rising (and that the Part of Fortune is thus conjunct the Moon) adds immensely to the significance of the configuration.

The complex chart of President Roosevelt again provides an example. Here, the Moon is 39° away from Pluto, and Mars is 81°—thus bi-novile—from Uranus. The 'captivity' F.D.R. underwent was of course a physical one, a literal confinement to a wheelchair after he was stricken with polio. The level at which he mobilized his energies (Mars), as well as the one at which his capacity for adaptation (Moon) and public life (tenth house) functioned, had definitely to be transformed. He was indeed presented with the opportunity—disguised as the direst of crises—to be 'reborn' out of adversity.

President Carter, whose experience of Christian rebirth in 1966 is a matter of public record, has a novile between Venus and Pluto in his chart. Both are significant, elevated planets—Pluto in the ninth house of religious and philosophical ideology, Venus in the tenth (public life and, in the deepest sense of the term, one's vocation or 'calling') and ruler of the Libra Ascendant. The experience followed Carter's first, unsuccessful attempt to become Governor of Georgia, and the symbolism is quite apropos in terms of Plutonian catharsis and regeneration.

A prominent novile also appears in the horoscope of Mohandas Gandhi. Straddling the Scorpio Ascendant, the twelfth-house Sun and first-house Mars are separated by 39½ °—an interesting configuration for the promoter of *ahimsa* (non-violent resistance). Mars is on a degree (24° Scorpio) stressing "the need to incorporate inspiring experiences and teachings into everyday living," which is exactly what the great Indian leader urged his countrymen to do. A moving testimony to the personal aspect of this challenge to rebirth is chronicled by the Mahatma himself in his autobiography, where he tells of his struggle to overcome the urges of his strong sexual nature. Equally poignant is the virtually exact novile between Albert Schweitzer's eleventh-house Venus and his first-house Sun. Striking too is the novile between the Sun and Uranus in the chart of the theosophical amanuensis Alice Bailey.

THE DECILE OR SEMI-QUINTILE

Only two or three aspects of smaller angular value than the novile are worth mentioning. The first, the semi-quintile or decile (36°) is the result of inscribing two interlaced five-pointed stars—a ten-pointed star—within the circle. One star points upward, the other downward. These two stars have traditionally been understood as the symbols of 'white' and 'black' magic—of Man as a creator focusing through his mind and his right hand the creative power of spirit—and man, the adversary of spirit, working against the tide of evolution or the 'will of God,' and after more or less prolonged period of power, being himself destroyed by the relentless pressure of the universal tide.

This traditional interpretation of the two stars does not, however, exhaust the meaning of their relationship. Insofar as the semi-quintile is concerned, we shall say that the upward pointing star represents true creativity, while the downpointing star represents the 'art for art's sake' approach—creation, or rather mere production, for merely the sake of the producer's ego or of the formalistic approach of a disintegrating or crystallized culture. Formalism in all creative expressions means focusing on the outer pattern, the circumference—style without substance. Indeed, it is the negation of creativity, of the flow of spirit from a center—a flow conditioned by the need to bring more harmony and fuller living into the world. The true creative act is an act of compassion for whatever is chaotic and unintegrated.

The 'art for art's sake' type of attitude removes the creative act from its central source, the spirit within, and considers not the 'act' but the technical excellence or defects of a finished product or state of being, which must conform to some traditional or fashionable pattern of perfection. Technique as an end in iself is the death-song of creative activity, whether in the realm of the arts or in any field in life—for example in the building of a refined and intellectual ego which is also seen as an end in itself, or in politics when the importance of so-called public opinion polls and the advice of advertising and public relations specialists eclipse the real social and cultural issues at stake. Nevertheless, technique has great value and cannot be ignored. It is to the techniques of the old, disintegrating culture that people prophetically anticipating the release of a new creative impulse must go in order initially to acquire skill in focusing it.

The semi-quintile also refers to the relationship between a new creative impulse and old techniques or traditional 'know how'—just as the semi-square refers to the relationship between the new structure or organization and the public which will have to receive and use it. This relationship between a new creative impulse and an old technique is what is meant by 'talent' in the deepest sense of the word. To have talent is to be able to incorporate a creative impulse into a technique.

The problem here is how to prevent the old technique from perverting and deviating the new creative impulse, while not swinging to the other extreme and scorning technique altogether, under the pretense that any technique would pollute the anticipated and longed-for creative flow in its inspirational purity. Talent, however, has come most often in our society to mean mere technical skill—for our civilization worships technicians and specialists, whether what they make leads to a richer, spirit-oriented life or binds human beings to senseless, automated and indeed in the long-run counterproductive patterns.

In President Carter's chart, the Sun and Moon are semi-quintile, while Mars and Jupiter are quintile. Carter has, of course, a background in engineering, and is noted for his grasp of technical matters, particularly concerning the complexities of nuclear power and weapons systems. In contrast to the sweeping social vision of, say, a Roosevelt, Carter's approach to issues is more pragmatic and detail-oriented; he depends upon technique and technical solutions rather than on a more philsophical approach. Combining the two approaches in a more obvious way is R. Buckminster Fuller, the scientist-inventor who has become a leading figure in the 'New Age' movement. His Sun and Pluto are probably close to semi-quintile (we have only a solar chart with which to work), while the Sun is also at one point of a grand trine involving the Moon and Uranus.

In relation to the semi-quintile, we mention again a horoscope we previously pointed out in relation to the quintile. Albert Einstein's quintile between Jupiter and Neptune is bisected by a conjunction of Mercury and Saturn (and the Part of Fortune), and no doubt symbolizes, on the one hand, Einstein's capacity for the kind of painstaking, cautious work required during his fruitless search for a unified field theory. On the other hand, it may also refer to his essential conservativism, expressed both in his staunch resistance to accepting the cosmological implications of quantum mechanics, and in his speaking out against the use of atomic power after World War II.

THE SEMI-SEXTILE

Next after the semi-quintile comes the semi-sextile or 30° aspect—the span of one zodiacal sign and thus the basic step in the involutionary/devolutionary series of aspects. The semi-sextile in the evolutionary series is, on the other hand, practically the last of these aspects. It is produced by inscribing a dodecagon (or twelve-sided figure) in the circle of wholeness. This operation, according to the Pythagoreans, was the key to the perfection of cosmic order.

The twelve-pointed star within the circle can be interpreted as the product of interlacing two hexagons (six-sided figures), three squares or four triangles. It has thus a threefold foundation in terms of vision and meaning (trine), concrete structure (square), and organizational activity (sextile). It is all these things *brought to the level of everyday activity* in all organisms. It is vision, meaning and purpose (3), expressed functionally and concretely through structures of all types (4). It is structure (4) discovering its functional meaning (3) in terms of experience. It is organization and management (6) all the way down the line to the foreman of the factory—the delegate of the top managers in the very midst of the workers, the 'materials' to be organized (2). In short, the semi-sextile can be said to refer to actual functional activity and to the everyday experience of the person who has to prove in terms of practical results all he or she envisioned, knew, built and organized.

THE SMALLER ANGULAR VALUES

If we now try to understand the meaning of lesser angular values in the evolutionary series—aspects smaller than the semi-sextile—we should come to the conclusion that they refer to disintegrative or catabolic processes. We have already mentioned the semi-octile (or semi-semi-square, 22½°) as referring to the *vulgarization* of an idea having been made a concrete structure for everyday common use—that is, to the process following which a spirit-conditioned value, by indiscriminate common use, becomes materialized and abused. One could find similar meanings for other small angular values—for example, the semi-semi-sextile (15°), as referring to the automatism of habit and a consequent loss of meaning and value. On the other hand, although the series for all practical purposes ends with the semi-sextile, semi-octile or semi-semi-sextile, it can, theoretically be continued *ad infinitum*, the angular values always decreasing and approaching 0° but never actually reaching it. In terms of the old cycle, the next conjunction implies the final act of death, a release of the life-principle from a worn-out organism which is no longer useful. In this case, the end of the life-cycle corresponding to the very small aspects of the evolutionary series (18°, 15°, 10°, etc.) is not actually a preparation for rebirth, but the final phases of a disintegrative process.

On the other hand, increasingly smaller angular values can represent preparation for a new birth in individualized consciousness, especially if the ending cycle has been at least relatively successful. The smaller the aspect, the greater the number of sides have the inscribed polygons to which they correspond. The larger this number, *the more closely the inscribed polygon comes to being a circle.* The difference in area between an equilateral triangle or square and the circle within which they are inscribed is quite considerable. This difference decreases as the inscribed figure gains sides. It is very small if we think of a polygon with 360 sides, each representing a 1° angle.

No polygon, however numerous its sides, will ever equal the circle in area. But the circle is the mystic ideal, the ultimate goal rather than the present reality. A mysterious 'something' is needed for this goal to be realized in actuality, for the many-sided polygon (the end of the cycle) to become the whole circle (time fulfilled, eternity, personal immortality). This something is the gift of the Initiator, the God-spark, at the true Initiation. It is the gift of immortality, of identification with the eternal, thanks to which the end of a cycle becomes the conscious rebeginning of the next.

In the new cycle, the process of involution and progressive differentiation begins again. It does so on the basis of the success or relative failure of the preceeding evolutionary process. If this process has been at least somewhat successful, we see its continuation astrologically when we superimpose the geometrically-based, opposition- or awareness-rooted aspects of the evolutionary series on the addition-based, conjunction-rooted aspects of the involutionary series. Figure 3-5 illustrates this superimposition.

In human terms, we can say that once a person's consciousness can resonate to and operate at the level represented by, say Number or vibration Five, the person can actualize a quintile-type of creativity in a new involutionary process stressing spontaneous activity. Such a 'waxing' quintile follows the sextile in Phase 3 of the first hemicycle, and the type of creativity it symbolizes arises from and depends upon practical organizational abilities and the capacity to draw on and synthesize material from a number of sources. The waxing bi-quintile—another point on the five-pointed star—falls in Phase 5 of the first hemicycle. It follows the waxing trine and sesquiquadrate, referring to a type of potential creative expression built upon idealistic vision and the capacity to persevere and be willing to stay with a problem or situation until a way of working it through can be found. The semi-quintile or decile occurs near the beginning of Phase 2, after the semi-sextile. It refers to an instinctive, perhaps

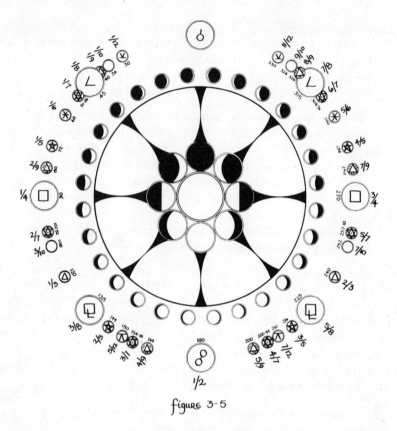

figure 3-5

automatic application of an old technique, carried forward or inherited from the previous, now-ending cycle, which may nevertheless prove valuable in focusing the new direction stabilizing during Phase 2.

Similar reasoning can shed light on the meaning of other evolutionary aspects in the 'waxing' hemicycle. The first aspect of the septile series (51³⁄₇°) falls after the semi-square and before the sextile, indicating the necessity to eliminate or neutralize whatever was left out of the resolution between the 'ghosts' of the past and potentialities of the future met at the semi-square before a new organizational capacity is allowed to operate. The second septile-based aspect (biseptile, 102⁶⁄₇°) follows the waxing square, also symbolizing a similar necessity in relation to the 'de-cision' made at the square. A tri-septile (154⅖°) falls between the quincunx and an aspect of the novile series (quad-novile, 160°) near the beginning of Phase 6. It deals with the need to eliminate the leftovers from the process of adjustment and refinement begun at the waxing quincunx, and its 'fate-ordained' action can be a prelude to inner rebirth (novile) preceeding the cycle's outward culmination (opposition).

The novile series, too, interacts with involutionary aspects in a similar way. A novile follows the semi-sextile and semi-quintile or decile, and precedes the semi-square of Phase 2. The bi-novile comes between the quintile of Phase 3 and the square beginning Phase 4. The waxing tri-novile coincides with the waxing trine beginning Phase 5. And, as we have already seen, the quad-novile follows the tri-septile in Phase 6 and immediately precedes the new opposition beginning Phase 7 and, potentially, a new evolutionary process.

As there are always cycles within cycles within cycles—cycles so encompassing that what we human beings consider large processes are but sub-cycles within them—there are always new beginnings, potentially at least, at ever higher, more inclusive levels of activity and consciousness. A closed circle is not a fact of ever-surging life. It presupposes objectivity, the power to contemplate, as it were from above, a completed cycle—the power of Man to remember and give meaning to his experiences. The first condition of readiness to move to ever more inclusive levels is to envision the process as a possibility, for no one can ever consciously reach what has not been previously visualized as a possibility.

4.
Special Conjunctions and Oppositions: Retrogradation

A TIME FOR REORIENTATION

When involution gives way to evolution, or vice versa, what is required is a definite change in the level of activity and consciousness. When a planet operates most focally in terms of its own kind of functional activities—that is, in its cyclic relationship with the Sun—a period of transition is required for the deep-seated change to occur. Astrologically, such a situation is represented by the planet's retrogradation—a phenomenon which is usually not well-understood because it is not usually seen in its proper, i.e., cyclic and process-oriented context. For retrogradation is nothing more nor less than *a phase of an overall sequence of relationships* between a planet and the Sun.

From a process-oriented point of view, the retrograde periods of planets can be best understood when they are considered graphic representations of certain 'aspects' the planets make to the Sun as seen and experienced from Earth. Retrogradation always occurs when the relationship between a planet and the Sun is about to change from one hemicycle to the next. Such a change occurs, as we have seen, at both the conjunction beginning a cycle of aspects and the opposition culminating the process. It refers to the need for a radical reorientation in consciousness and/or activity involving the aspecting planetary functions. In both instances, it can also include the possibility of a certain kind of 'mutation' or repolarization.

The term retrograde literally means to 'move backward.' A planet is said to retrograde when its motion appears to be contrary to the usual direction of planets in their orbits, i.e., forward in the zodiac, from lesser to greater longitude. Retrograde planets move backward in the zodiac, from greater to lesser longitude. Only the planets, never the Sun or Moon, go retrograde; but all the planets, at some point in their orbits, appear to stop, go backward for a time, stop again and resume direct motion. To ancient and pre-Copernical astronomer-astrologers, this was a most perplexing occurrence that could only be plotted and perhaps predicted on the basis of past observation, but it could not really be explained. So it remains for many students and astrologers today, who truly understand neither the cause nor the meaning of the planets' retrograde motions. The little R's and D's in the ephemeris are accepted as if there were nothing puzzling about them.

Some astrologers maintain that a planet is 'weak' when it is retrograde. Others, because a planet is as close to the Earth as it can be when it appears to move backward, assert that a retrograde planet is particularly 'strong.' Although they appear to contradict each other, neither of these views is entirely false, but neither represents the whole picture either. In order to understand the full meaning of retrogradation, it must, we repeat, be seen in context. The periods during which planets retrograde must be seen in relation to their whole cycles. The key, we cannot stress enough, is to understand that retrogradation occurs at a particular phase of each planet's cyclic relationship to the Sun when seen from Earth. How many students of astrology realize that *any planet in or near opposition to the Sun is always retrograde?!*

Actually, when seen heliocentrically (from the point of view of the Sun), there is no retrogradation; the planets always move in the same direction in their orbits. Retrogradation is an optical illusion generated by our geocentrism, by the fact that we view all celestial phenomena from the Earth's surface. Four basic factors combine to produce apparent planetary retrogradation:

(1) The above-mentioned fact that we are on the Earth, observing all celestial motions from points on its surface,

(2) the place of the Earth's orbit in the solar system and the

    Earth's orbital speed in relation to the speeds of the other planets,

(3) the fact that from our vantage point on Earth the Sun appears to move while the Earth remains stationary, and

(4) the fact that none of the other planets moves at the same speed of either the Sun (in its apparent motion) or the Earth.

All of these factors combine to produce the optical illusion we call retrogradation.

The situation is similar to what happens when a fast-moving train approaches and passes around a curve a slower-moving train travelling on tracks parallel to it. When the faster train comes up on the slower train, the slower train appears to the passengers in the faster train to stop and then move backward as the faster train passes it. When the distance between the two trains increases sufficiently, and the slower train enters the curve around which it has been passed, the slower train appears (to the passengers in the faster train) momentarily to stop again and then resume its forward motion.

Such are the mechanics of retrogradation. In order to apply them to the actual cases of the planets, Sun and Earth, we have to differentiate between two categories of planets: those closer to the Sun than the Earth and thus inside the Earth's orbit (Venus and Mercury) and those outside the Earth's orbit, Mars, Jupiter, Saturn, Uranus, Neptune and Pluto. This is because the Earth, like the faster train in the above example, passes Mercury and Venus around, so to speak, an outside track (in relation to the Sun), while it passes Mars, Jupiter, Saturn, etc. around an inside track.

The cyclic relationships between Venus and Mercury and the Sun are very special indeed. At first, when we observe the changing relationships between these planets and the Sun, we may think we have found two notable exceptions to the cyclic pattern of aspects we studied in the previous chapters. Venus and Mercury do not appear to go all the way or 'full circle' around the Sun, but rather to oscillate back and forth in relation to it, more or less carried along by the Sun in its yearly zodiacal circuit. Mercury never appears more than 28° of arc away from the Sun, while Venus's maximum elongation is about 46°.

Of course, heliocentrically, Venus and Mercury do go all the way around the Sun and travel in the same direction in their orbit. Diagram 4-1 illustrates this cyclic pattern, and by studying it closely we can hope to understand the cycle it represents, the mechanics and meanings of the retrograde motions of these planets. We'll begin by first considering the instance of Mercury's cycle with the Sun.

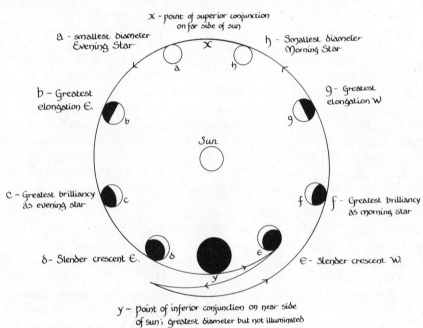

x - point of superior conjunction on far side of sun

a - smallest diameter Evening Star

h - Smallest diameter Morning Star

b - Greatest elongation E.

g - Greatest elongation W

Sun

c - Greatest brilliancy as evening star

f - Greatest brilliancy as morning star

d - Slender crescent E.

e - Slender crescent W.

y - point of inferior conjunction on near side of sun; greatest diameter but not illuminated

figure 4·1

Since Mercury's orbit is closer to the Sun than Earth's, Mercury is never seen opposing the Sun; Mercury and the Sun can never be on opposite sides of the Earth. Instead of a conjunction beginning the cycle and an opposition dividing it into two hemicycles, what constitute the two major turning points of the Mercury/Sun cycle are two conjunctions—but conjunctions very different from one another. One of them is called the 'superior conjunction.' It occurs when Mercury is on the opposite side of the Sun from the Earth. It is called the 'superior' conjunction because when it occurs Mercury is 'superior to' or 'above' the Sun. Like the Moon in relation to the Earth at Full Moon, Mercury at its superior conjunction with the Sun is as far from the Earth as it can be. It thus refers, astronomically as well as symbolically, to what we can call 'full Mercury.' Moreover, Mercury is direct (moving in its usual forward-in-the-zodiac direction) when it forms its superior conjunction with the Sun.

The other major turning point in the Sun/Mercury cycle is called the 'inferior conjunction.' It occurs when Mercury, like the Moon at New Moon, is between the Earth and the Sun, and as near the Earth as possible. It is thus considered the conjunction beginning the cycle, symbolically a 'new Mercury.' In terms of the cyclic pattern we have studied, Mercury waxes from inferior conjunction to superior conjunction—from 'new' to 'full' Mercury; after the superior conjunction, until the next inferior conjunction, Mercury wanes. It does so both astronomically and visually from our point of view on Earth, and the symbolism of the two hemicycles applies as well. As Mercury approaches its inferior conjunction with the Sun, it appears to slow in speed, to stop, and to become retrograde.

Mercury's retrogradation occurs as the inferior conjunction forms because of a number of factors. The Earth and Mercury are on the same side of the Sun, and both—let us not forget—are moving. As Mercury moves in its orbit, the Earth speeds toward and around it, coming to pass it on a parallel track in much the same way that the faster train of our earlier illustration passes a slower train. As the Earth and Mercury near one another, Mercury—like the slower train in our example—appears to slow down, stop and become retrograde. When the Earth aligns with Mercury and the Sun in such a way that they (the Sun and Mercury) occupy the same zodiacal degree (inferior conjunction, which from the point of view of the Sun would be an Earth/Mercury conjunction), Mercury is and has been (for some 10 days to 2 weeks) appearing to move backward. Around the time of the inferior conjunction, however, Mercury cannot actually be seen in the sky, for it is too close to the Sun in the daytime, blocked from view by the Sun's light, and it does not appear in the night sky, being below the horizon with the Sun.

After inferior conjunction, the Earth and Mercury move away from exact alignment. Mercury continues in retrograde motion, and because the Sun also continues its apparent motion (actually the counterpart of our own—the Earth's—actual motion), the number of zodiacal degrees between the Sun and Mercury increases. From the time of the inferior conjunction, Mercury is on the other side of the Sun from where it was when it first became retrograde. Some 5 days after the inferior conjunction, Mercury has become far enough from the Sun to be seen over the eastern horizon before sunrise: a morning star.

Several days after this first appearance (approximately 8 days to 2 weeks after the inferior conjunction), the Earth and Mercury have separated far enough for Mercury to appear to stop and resume direct motion. A little more than a week after Mercury turns direct, it reaches its greatest distance from the Sun. For approximately 20 to 30 days after its first appearance, Mercury appears as a morning star, but after having reached its greatest distance from the Sun, the two—because of the variance between the speed of Mercury and the apparent speed of the Sun—come progressively closer together. Heliocentrically, this occurs because Mercury is preparing to pass on the far side of the Sun from the Earth. Thus, about a month and a half after inferior conjunction, the superior conjunction occurs.

At the superior conjunction, Mercury passes on the far side of the Sun in direct motion. It becomes invisible as the superior conjunction forms, and afterward emerges on the other side of the Sun from where it was before superior conjunction. Thereafter, when it appears in the sky again, it rises after the Sun and remains blocked from view by the Sun's brilliance by day. A few days after the superior conjunction, having moved far enough away from the Sun, Mercury appears over the western horizon after sunset: an evening star. About a month and a half after the superior conjunction, Mercury again reaches its greatest distance from the Sun. It appears after sunset as far eastward of the western horizon and the setting Sun as it can. Several days later, a little less than three months after the superior conjunction, the Earth begins to overtake Mercury and prepares to pass it. Mercury appears to stop, in preparation for retrogradation. The inferior conjunction occurs about two weeks later, and a new cycle begins.

In a complete cycle of Mercury and the Sun (as seen from the Earth, let us not forget), there are thus the following stages:

- Inferior conjunction—'new Mercury'—Mercury retrograde
- Mercury retrograde—'waxing' and rising ahead of the Sun (morning star) for approximately 10 to 15 days
- Mercury direct—still waxing and rising ahead of the Sun (morning star) for approximately 46 days
- Superior conjunction—'full Mercury'—Mercury still direct
- Mercury direct—now 'waning'—rising after the Sun (evening star) for approximately 46 days
- Mercury retrograde—still waning and rising after the Sun (evening star) for approximately 10 to 15 days
- Inferior conjunction—Mercury remains retrograde while a new cycle begins.

These phases of the Mercury/Sun cycle can be symbolically represented as in Diagram 4-2. The important points to remember are: (1) From inferior to superior conjunction Mercury waxes; from superior conjunction to inferior conjunction it wanes. (2) The retrograde period of Mercury occurs around the time of its inferior conjunction with the Sun. (3) At that time the planet appears to come rapidly closer to our own, although it is the Earth which actually nears Mercury. (4) During the first or waxing half of the Mercury/Sun cycle, Mercury rises before the Sun as a morning star, and during the second or waning hemicycle it sets after the Sun as an evening star.

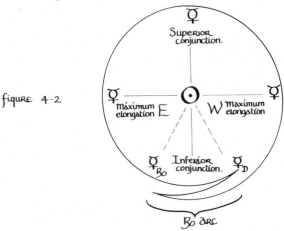

figure 4-2

143

The distinction between Mercury as morning star (waxing) and Mercury as an evening star (waning) is a basic one to make when looking at any particular birth-chart. As morning star, Mercury is behind the Sun in the zodiac. It is either in the sign before the Sun's sign at birth or in earlier degrees of the same zodiacal sign. Diagram 4-3 illustrates such a situation. If we rotate the chart-wheel so that the Sun and Mercury are near the eastern horizon (Ascendant), we will see that Mercury will rise before the Sun, appearing (if it is sufficiently distant from the Sun in longitude) as a morning star before sunrise. When the Sun rises, Mercury will be obscured by the Sun's brilliance.

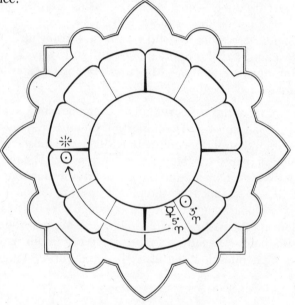

figure 4-3

On the other hand, Mercury as an evening star (waning) is ahead of the Sun in the zodiac. It is either in the sign following the Sun's sign at birth or in later degrees of the same sign as the Sun. If we look at Diagram 4-4 representing a horoscope with the Sun and Mercury in this relationship, and rotate the chart so that they are near the eastern horizon, we see that the Sun will rise before Mercury, and Mercury will be in the sky but invisible throughout the day. If we rotate the chart farther so that the Sun and Mercury are near the western horizon (descendant), we will see that the Sun will set first, leaving Mercury as an evening star over the western horizon.

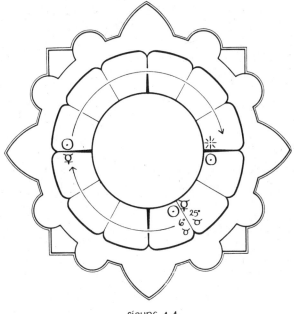

figure 4·4

The meaning of Mercury as either a morning star (waxing) or evening star (waning) can be made clear if we realize that Mercury as morning star heralds a new day, while Mercury as evening star closes an ending day-cycle. This dualism can be significantly correlated with two terms borrowed from Greek mythology: Mercury-*Promethean* (morning star) and Mercury-*Epimethean* (evening star). Prometheus and Epimetheus were two brothers, one who always looked forward, toward the future (*Pro*), the other who, gaze fixed backward, always depended upon precedents and past experience (*Epi*). These two mythological figures can be considered prototypes for what we have come to call the 'progressive' and 'conservative,' for Prometheus was a rebel and reformer, while Epimetheus was the historian, logician and accountant. The terms provide a convenient way of easily differentiating between the two halves of the Mercury/Sun cycle.

Leaving aside for the moment the retrograde period of Mercury, we should stress that its cyclic relationship with the Sun otherwise exhibits the same visual and phase structure as the soli-lunar and interplanetary cycles we have been studying. At the inferior conjunction, Mercury is between the Sun and the Earth, as we have said, a situation similar to what occurs at New Moon when the Moon is between the Sun and the Earth. Mercury in this alignment symbolically focuses most strongly onto the Earth—while it is closest to it—the power of life (the Sun) beginning to differentiate and develop as mind (Mercury). What occurs between the inferior and superior conjunctions (Mercury Promethean) is entirely analogous at the mental level to the already-outlined involutionary or first-hemicycle process spanning Phases 1 through 6 of a twelvefold cycle. What occurs between the superior and inferior conjunctions (Mercury Epithemean) is likewise similar to the second-hemicycle process unfolding during Phases 7 through 12.

From inferior conjunction to superior conjunction, Mercury 'waxes.' It moves away from the Earth, symbolically 'carrying out' the solar impulse imparted to it at conjunction. This is the period during which Mercury as morning star (Promethean) rises ahead of the Sun, heralding the new day. It symbolizes the spontaneous outworking of the mind, often manifesting in persons born with the Sun and Mercury in this relationship as cunning or innate 'know how.' Mental associations are intuitive and analogical rather than logical or analytical, because the mind, having received a new creative impulse or direction from the Sun, cannot rely on an accumulation of past experience in order to draw conclusions. Rather, in order to substantiate the new impulse, it seeks new experience, fresh data, and it does so eagerly. As at the beginning of any cycle, so much is new, fascinating and attractive. Enthusiastically anticipating and experiencing new material, the mind races, as it were, ahead of itself, pausing to 'take counsel' only after the event. It gathers data, sometimes indiscriminately and apparently willy-nilly. Behind this desire for new mental sensations stands the unself-conscious 'wisdom' of instinct and the involutionary process—of the mind operating at the survival-oriented biological level. Also structuring the experience-gathering process is the power of the solar impulse imparted to Mercury at inferior conjunction: the potentiality for eventually integrating fresh data instinctively gathered into a new synthesis, within the framework of more inclusive, better organized mental vistas.

Between the inferior conjunction releasing such a potentiality and the superior conjunction at which it can be fully realized, the mind, thus impelled and drawn on, reaches out toward the future, trying to focus into concrete form today the ideals which should become realities tomorrow. New experiences increasingly point toward and evoke a sense of new possibilities. A major turning point in this first hemicycle of Sun/Mercury relationships occurs when heliocentric Mercury reaches maximum elongation west, its greatest longitudinal distance from the Sun. At this point in the cycle, the Mercury functions are most focally challenged to project a vision in symbols or concrete behavior which will serve as a foundation for the actual fulfillment of solar potential and purpose at superior conjunction. Mercury's maximum elongation in this first hemicycle thus fulfills a building function analogous to the waxing square in the first hemicycle of interplanetary cycles.

As the cycle proceeds, Mercury approaches the superior conjunction with the Sun. The superior conjunction marks the transformation of Mercury morning star (Promethean) into Mercury evening star (Epimethean). At superior conjunction, this change occurs with Mercury in direct motion. After superior conjunction, Mercury no longer waxes; it wanes. From the point of view of the Earth, this superior conjunction is astronomically a 'full Mercury,' since Mercury reflects to us a full disc, and the alignment of Mercury, the Sun and Earth is similar to what occurs among the Sun, Moon and Earth at Full Moon. At superior conjunction, Mercury is as far from the Earth as possible; from the point of view of the Sun it opposes Earth.

This is the symbolic culmination of the Sun/Mercury cycle. The Mercury functions acquire the capacity to achieve a maximum of objectivity or concreteness. As the superior conjunction approaches, the mind becomes laden with unintegrated data and ideals which it must begin to sift through, consider as precedent, order and assimilate. This need and capacity for digestion at the mental level intensifies as the superior conjunction nears. The developing mind, having satiated (or perhaps over-burdened and confused) itself with new experience eagerly sought, is 'directly' challenged to change over from its spontaneous, information-gathering, projective mode to a more deliberate, organized, conservative one. In persons born with the Sun and Mercury in this relation, this may lead to intellectual and analytical clarity and a stress upon the need for mental organization, objectivity and memory.

After the superior conjunction, the purely instinctual activity of the mind allowed play during the first hemicycle (from inferior to superior conjunction) must yield to the development of a deeper understanding, of wisdom. The dual nature of Mercury becomes increasingly apparent as the experiencer becomes objective to and separate from the objects of experience. In contrast to the spontaneous nature of Mercury as morning star (Promethean), Mercury as evening star (Epimethean) symbolizes the need for deliberate and self-conscious application of mental power and systematic reasoning.

Between superior conjunction and Mercury's maximum elongation east, the Sun/Mercury relationship unfolds in much the same way as Phases 7, 8 and 9 in the twelvefold interplanetary pattern we studied in Chapter 2. Maximum elongation again occurs as heliocentric Mercury squares the Earth, but in this second hemicycle of Sun/Mercury relationships, the square is a waning or 'Last Quarter' one. Here the greatest possible stress on applying mental objectivity is made. What had been in the first hemicycle an enthusiastic drive to give vision and form to new ideals settles into a pattern of trying to solve more immediate problems at hand. Mental functioning, if not as innovative as in the first hemicycle, becomes more mature and systematic. The mind is challenged to develop its ability to draw meaning from things which have already happened. In so doing, it turns back upon itself, as it were, and questions the basis on which it had previously operated. This 'Last Quarter' square is again a crisis in consciousness, a parting of the ways at the philosophical or ideological level.

As Mercury has waned, so too has the need for new experience. The mind has been forced to turn pastward, to gain historical perspective for assimilating experience previously gathered, and for providing a context within which to attempt to answer its present questions. After maximum elongation east, the situation is similar to what we encountered at the waning sextile, the beginning of Phase

11 in the twelvefold interplanetary pattern. Mental reorganization must occur, and it can happen either on the basis of a reactionary return to what the mind perceives as the strength and wisdom of tradition—or on the basis of a growing openness to a new creative impulse.

As the cycle closes, then, the question arises as to whether or not the mind has become sufficiently universal in scope to interpret past tradition in a transformed, presently applicable and open-ended way. As if in answer, after maximum elongation east, Mercury begins to move back toward the Sun, toward the coming inferior conjunction. As it does, it slows down, preparing for its station and subsequent retrogradation.

The retrograde period closing the Sun/Mercury cycle spans in time about the last tenth of the entire cycle (an average of about 12 out of 116 days). Most positively, it refers to the final phase of the mind's attachment to the past. But, as Mercury slows and reaches its station, if the mind clings to the past, it can mean the mind coming to a reactionary standstill. This can happen either out of fear, or because past experiences have not been fully assimilated and must again be 'gone over.' The following retrograde period can represent a crystallization at the mental level. It is on this basis, and with the purpose of breaking it up, that the new cycle begins.

On the other hand, Mercury's station and retrogradation can symbolize the mind going over past precedent or re-examining tradition in order to repudiate what of it has become obsolete in light of present questions, problems and future hopes. Mercury-Epimethean/retrograde thus represents a period of *deconditioning* preparatory to the release of a new creative impulse at the inferior conjunction. This period of deconditioning may be confusing or even chaotic, but it is necessary if the developing mind is ever to become sufficiently free of the past to accept to go in a new, future-oriented direction.

In order successfully to pass through such a deconditioning process at the mental level, the mind symbolized by Mercury-Epimethean/retrograde turns inward, away from the taken-for-granted patterns of thinking of family and culture. It must unearth unconscious assumptions and question generalizations habitually made from past experience. Its purpose is to 'return to source,' the power of which will, at the inferior conjunction, fecundate the mind anew, beginning a new cycle of mental development.

The person born with Mercury Epimethean retrograde may be unable to accept the usual patterns of thinking impressed upon his or her nascent mentality by parents, teachers and other traditional authorities. Instead the person may rebel against the past so that new experience can be met more freely than traditional constraints would allow. This may in many instances lead to a more or less prolonged period of confusion, but even this should not be considered absolutely negative. It should be seen as a necessary phase in a developmental process and thereby given a constructive meaning. For Mercury's station and retrogradation lead directly to the inferior conjunction, a new creative impulse and a chance to begin again at a new level.

What actually occurs at any solar conjunction is and remains a mystery. For a few days before and after the exact inferior conjunction, Mercury disappears from view. When it emerges as a morning star on the other side of the Sun, it is nevertheless still retrograde for some 10 to 15 days. A new cycle has begun, and the 'seeds' for a new mind have been implanted—assuming all has gone well at the close of the previous cycle and that there were seeds to be sown. The mind emerging from the solar conjunction is symbolically a mind which has experienced a mystery, an 'initiation' into a new realm of being —however limited or casual this initiation may have been. As a result of this and the previous period of deconditioning, the mind has lost its trust or interest in customary impulses, yet it is not free from them. The cycle has not progressed far enough for the mind to have even a vaguely objective vision of 'where' or to what ultimate purpose mental development is directed. The mind struggles to overcome its own deep subjectivity, as a person who was profoundly asleep struggles to free his mind from strange and wonderful dreamfragments clinging to consciousness as he rises to meet and adjust himself to the morning's brightness. The mind is eager, but with Mercury still retrograde and very near the beginning of the cycle, its activity may be uncertain, its vision perhaps lost and recovered again —or so subjective and idealistic as to be beyond the ken of other, more objective minds. It awakens to the outer world and its realities only slowly, assimilating the inward experience of the new solar impulse, and finding its 'balance' between the two.

In the deepest sense, Mercury-Promethean/retrograde refers to the possibility of a radical transformation at a very deep and basic level of human functioning, for it follows and builds upon the period of cultural deconditioning symbolized by Mercury-Epimethean/ retrograde. Moreover, here, at the beginning of the 'life'-dominated first hemicycle, Mercury travels in a direction opposite to the motion of the Sun, the source of all life-power. As the 'life'-cycle begins, Mercury opposes, as it were, its flow. What this means can be understood when we realize that in animals, and even among less mentally developed or primitive human beings living in jungles (urban, suburban or otherwise) in want and fear, the Mercury-function is entirely subservient to life's needs, immediate requirements and self-preservation, and to unquestioned, deeply ingrained social imperatives and taboos. Then, or after deconditioning has occurred in the lives of modern men and women, intelligence may manifest primarily as rudimentary inventiveness and self-centered cunning in satisfying desires and basic human needs, regardless of the presence, well-being and desires of others.

A time comes in both collective and individual development, however, when people begin to take a more objective and detached view of existence, and eventually begin to think in terms of abstractions, symbols and collective well-being. When this occurs, it means that the mind has become able to dis-identify itself with the urgent and daily needs of the body and lower psychic nature—thus, to stand still, to 'go against' and disassociate itself from more primitive, organic cravings. It looks at these objectively, seeking understanding and generalized knowledge transferrable to other persons, situations as wholes and to the coming generations. All this comes under the category of mind liberated from both the compulsions of culture (Mercury-Epimethean/retrograde) and narrow body-centered desires—a mind working 'against the grain' of the life-force: a mind symbolized by Mercury-Promethean/retrograde.

When Mercury stops again and resumes direct motion, it symbolizes a mind once more polarized toward projecting itself, its new and tentatively focusing vision, into the world, toward experiencing a plethora of new situations and sensations providing material on the basis of which a new level of mental operation can be reached. After the reorientation represented by the entire retrograde period, the new level of understanding to which the mind aspires is no longer centered merely in the urge for self-preservation or a craving for self-aggrandisement. Since the mind has (ideally) left behind the compulsions of both culture and biology, it is therefore free to try to substantiate the new solar impulse in its purity, to try to achieve a new level of integration strictly in terms of *the need* to which what was released at inferior conjunction came in potential answer.

Thus, the entire period of Mercury's retrogradation should be considered a period of reorientation of the mind during which one cycle of activity and development ends and another begins. It is essential that we differentiate between the two types of Mercury retrograde—Epimethean (evening star) retrograde and Promethean (morning star) retrograde, Mercury retrograde at the end of a Mercury/Sun cycle, before inferior conjunction, and Mercury retrograde after the inferior conjunction has occurred. And we must recognize not only the difference, but also the continuity of process between the two.

This difference and continuity becomes more than theoretical, and the pattern we have studied more than abstract or academic, when we realize that since Mercury's entire retrograde period never exceeds about 25 days, any person born with Mercury retrograde will experience by secondary progression* the inferior conjunction, and/or Mercury's station and resumption of direct motion at some time relatively early in life. Even someone born at the very beginning of the retrograde period will experience the inferior conjunction by progression by age 12 or 13, and Mercury will turn direct by progression by the time the person reaches 25.

For persons born with Mercury Epimethean (evening star), Mercury's station and retrogradation may occur by progression at any time between birth and approximately age 65, depending upon how soon after superior conjunction they were born. Persons born with Mercury Promethean (morning star), whether Mercury is

---

*Cf. *The Lunation Process in Astrological Guidance* by Leyla Rael (ASI Publishers, New York: 1979) for a basic explanation of secondary progressions.

direct or retrograde at birth, will experience by progression maximum elongation (if it hasn't occurred before birth) and superior conjunction—possibly maximum elongation after superior conjunction too, depending upon when in the first hemicycle birth occurred and how long the person lives. This 'process by progression' applies as well to practically all natal aspects and configurations, except those involving only very slowly moving planets. What occurs in a person's life and how he or she responds and gives meaning to it when Mercury reaches its station, turns retrograde or direct, reaches maximum elongation or conjoins the the Sun has a particularly deep significance, for it gives direction and 'tone' to the quality of mental development throughout the life. Since Mercury symbolizes functional activities at the core of truly human experience, this process has always basic and far-reaching implications and effects.

The cycle of Venus and the Sun (as seen from the Earth) is entirely similar to the cycle of Mercury and the Sun, although the intervals are longer. While the synodic period (from inferior conjunction to inferior conjunction) between Mercury and the Sun is approximately 116 days, the synodic period of Venus is about 584 days. While Mercury is retrograde for about 19 to 25 days, Venus' retrograde period lasts between 40 and 50 days.

Both ancient mythology and traditional astrology have considered Venus in her dual role as evening and morning star. Venus as morning star, rising ahead of the Sun, is termed Venus Lucifer (literally, "the bearer of light"). Venus as the evening star, appearing in the western sky immediately after sunset and thus following or setting behind the Sun, is called Venus Hesperus (from hesperos, meaning "western").

While Mercury refers to the mind—the 'nervous' functions—Venus represents the inner sense of value, a more 'visceral' type of functions or emotional activities. Venus Lucifer, as morning star rising ahead of the Sun, refers to a type of emotional activity which might be said symbolically to run ahead of the self. It represents a spontaneous quality of feeling reminiscent of adolescence: extroverted, enthusiastic, exuberant. The antennae of the feeling-life are, as it were, extended to the utmost, and the faculty of intuition may develop strongly. The sense of value is attuned futureward; idealism may dominate the inner life, and emotional projection may run high.

Venus as evening star (Hesperus) is by contrast a symbol of a more controlled, reactive feeling-nature. While Venus Lucifer tends to look for correlates to its evolving values, ideals and sense of beauty in the world, Venus Hesperus tends to judge and react to life and events after things have happened, according to a predetermined set of standards. Venus Hesperus can theoretically be characterized as a more mature quality of feeling, for emotionality is not as spontaneous and immediate as when Venus rises ahead of the Sun as morning star. This is not to say that Venus Hesperus represents a passionless or 'cooler' emotional timbre, for it may be just as emotional, perhaps in a more intense, introverted way. Venus as an evening star can also indicate a type of emotional life strongly influenced by traditional or conventional values, or an aesthetic sense dominated by a particular set of standards. It is in that sense essentially conservative and deliberate or calculated.

The same type of reasoning applies to Venus retrograde as to Mercury retrograde. Venus refers to the sense of value, to the functional activity whereby human beings pass judgement upon something's absolute or relative worth: "This is good for me, I love it. This will destroy or irreversibly alter me, and I must run away or protect myself from it." Venus is the 'planet of love' only by extension, for it can just as well be the planet of hate. Its function is to present to us vivid images of what will enhance or degrade our status as human beings. The entire retrograde period of Venus refers to a time when it is necessary and possible to reorient and renew the sense of value. Retrograde Venus in a natal chart indicates that throughout the person's life, he or she will be challenged and has the latent capacity (which must be developed) to transform his or her sense of what is valuable and significant.

The first phase of Venus' retrogradation—Venus Hesperus (evening star) retrograde—refers to a period of recapitulation of past feelings and values. It represents the inner emotional life coming to a stop in order to be once more fecundated by solar will and purpose.

It can involve and require a period of cultural deconditioning, when the feeling-aspect of the inner life must question and emerge from domination by collective, taken-for-granted standards and values.

The inferior conjunction occurs with Venus still retrograde, and it signifies the end of one cycle and the beginning of the next. Venus and the Earth are as close to one another as possible at this time, and the creative impulse symbolically passed from the Sun to Venus at the inferior conjunction, at least symbolically, is most focally transmitted to Earth. Thus, in persons born with Venus and the Sun in close inferior conjunction, the Venus-functions will tend to be unusually active and focused. But since Venus is retrograde, the focalization tends not to be in terms of what we consider 'normal' biological or social effectiveness. It is rather more introverted, for the feeling-nature turns inward for reorientation, and it may find coping with ordinary emotional or social situations comparatively difficult. This is generally true of the entire retrograde period, which can be likened to a shop temporarily closed to customers for inventory and remodelling.

In biologically-dominated human beings, value is related almost exclusively to self-preservation; but as human beings evolve socially and intellectually, self-preservation becomes synonymous with group well-being, both at the physical level and at the level of cultural images and ideals. During Venus' Lucifer retrograde period, higher motives may transform the primary biopsychic sense of value. In the search for such higher values, some men and women turn to asceticism or altruism, sacrificing personal welfare for the sake of great ideals or in the quest for mystical union with God. These are all possibilities represented by Venus Lucifer retrograde, for it symbolizes the feeling-nature seeking its independence from the instinctual nature by opposing it more or less violently. Traditional values may have been called into sharp question (Venus Hesperus retrograde), but the re-nascent feeling-nature is still struggling to free itself from their domination.

When Venus turns direct, the success or relative failure of the struggle begins to become apparent. For Venus as morning star (direct) turns the feeling nature out into the world again. The new vision and purpose 'received' at solar (inferior) conjunction seeks to substantiate itself, and the person born with Venus Lucifer direct is challenged to be a focalizer of such substantiation. Pouring himself or herself into his or her creations, he or she projects his or her values and ideals onto life, seeking to impress the stamp of the new vision upon society. A new phase in the development of the Venus-functions has begun again.

Of course, any characterization given for any single planet, whether retrograde, direct or in any phase of its cyclic relationship with the Sun, is always at least modified, if not 'alchemically' altered by other factors and interrelationships in any particular birth-chart and life-pattern. Single astrological factors can be discussed and evaluated only for the purpose of intellectual analysis and instruction. The essential value of doing so is to reveal the archetypal patterns of processes underlying all astrological symbols, and to train the astrologer's mind to think in terms of them.

When we come to the planets moving outside of the Earth's orbit, the situation is somewhat different from the pattern we studied in relation to Venus and Mercury, planets moving within the orbit of the Earth. While Venus and Mercury turn retrograde as they approach inferior *conjunction* with the Sun—thus while they are between the Sun and the Earth—Mars and the planets beyond it turn retrograde when, from the point of view of Earth, they prepare to *oppose* the Sun. In other words, Mercury and Venus are retrograde during their 'New' phase, when one cycle ends and other begins, while Mars, Jupiter and Saturn, and Uranus, Neptune and Pluto are retrograde during their opposition with the Sun or 'Full' phase; their motion opposes that of the Sun when they also oppose the Sun from the other side of the Earth.

These facts alone are quite significant in understanding the meaning of these planets' retrogradation, especially when we remember that retrograde planets are as close to the Earth as they can be, and that retrogradation is the result of geocentricity—that planets appear to retrograde as a result of the special relationship between the Earth and the rest of the solar system. What actually occurs to create the outer planets' appearance of retrogradation is il-

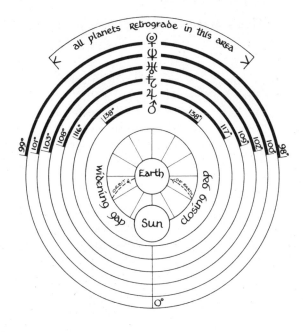

figure 4-5

lustrated in Diagram 4-5. A planet, moving more slowly than the Earth, is heliocentrically moving on the same side of the Sun as the Earth. Geocentrically, the Sun and the other planet are nearing opposition. But the Earth is also moving, more quickly than the other planet. As the Earth comes around the Sun and approaches the other planet, it moves between that planet and the Sun. It passes the slower planet on an inside track—a situation again similar to the illustration of the trains we presented earlier. The situation is almost as if the Earth, here representing concrete reality and the need in answer to which all planetary cycles proceed, *intervenes* in the developing relationship between the planet and the Sun, just before that relationship reaches its culmination. The Earth is to the other planet a 'reminder' of the original need the cycle was meant to fulfill. The other planet, about to be confronted with the concrete reality of what has been accomplished thus far (symbolized by its opposition with the Sun) stops, goes over territory it has most recently covered, and, so to speak, asks: "Have I forgotten anything? Is there something that needs to be adjusted or redone before the cycle is fulfilled and things become set? Are there any loose ends to be tied up? Any mistakes to be rectified?"

While Venus and Mercury orbit within the Earth's orbit and therefore represent two aspects of the inner life—mind and feelings —planets from Mars outward refer to the realm of outer activity. Planetary functions referring to the inner life undergo deconditioning and reorientation at the most inward, subjective phase of their cycle with the Sun, for what is most needed for a new cycle to begin is inner renewal and redirection. Planets referring to more objective activities back up for retrogradation just as their cycle with the Sun is about to culminate in outer manifestation—for what is required to bring something to the kind of objective realization and successful culmination possible and necessary at the opposition is perspective, clarity and deliberate, focused action. In all cases, when a planet has the opportunity to operate most focally in terms of its own type of activities, the Earth intervenes, as it were, and the planet backs up, goes over territory it had previously traversed, makes a major aspect with the Sun to change its hemicycle relation to it and, finally, resumes direct motion into new territory.

The deeper meaning of the retrogradation of the planets from Mars outwards becomes apparent when we realize that what is possible and necessary for successful culmination at the opposition—the above-mentioned qualities of objectivity, perspective and clarity—is also the foundation upon which the second hemicycle develops in its evolutionary mode. For the opposition not only ends the first hemicycle of activity; it begins the second. Retrogradation at the solar/planetary opposition is thus an opportunity for repairing whatever must be healed or redone in order to bring the cycle to successful culmination. It is also, perhaps more importantly, a preparation for a possible repolarization or change of gears, the success or relative failure of which will determine the quality of experience and challenge —evolutionary or devolutionary—during the remainder of the cyclic process. Retrogradation is therefore an opportunity for radical transformation and reorientation, for breaking the hold of 'life,' the sway of the involutionary/devolutionary process, over the nascent consciousness, so that a new realm—the realm of 'mind' and the evolution of consciousness—can be entered and a new level of functioning developed later on.

Like the retrograde periods of Mercury and Venus, the retrograde periods of Mars, Jupiter, Saturn, etc. must be divided into two phases—one before the opposition to the Sun, one after it. But the sequence of what must be done and the issues that must be met are in the case of the planets outside the Earth's orbit the reverse of what has to happen in the cases of Venus and Mercury. These planets within the Earth's orbit turn retrograde at the close of their *second* hemicycle with the Sun. Their retrogradation therefore refers to a deconditioning process, first, at the mental and cultural level, then to a process of repolarization at the level of 'life' and biopsychic compulsion. Since the retrograde periods of Mars, Jupiter and Saturn (and Uranus, Neptune and Pluto) occur at the end of the *first* or involutionary hemicycle with the Sun, deconditioning at the biological level must occur first. Biopsychic compulsions must be met and brought under conscious control before whatever will be seen or realized at the opposition can be made to serve a progressive purpose at the mental-cultural level afterward.

Retrogradation prior to the solar/planetary opposition thus symbolizes the planetary function coming to a stop, preparing the prenascent consciousness to receive the objective illumination of the opposition. It allows sufficient time for the planetary function to retrace the final, culminating steps in its involutionary development, and for the process of biopsychic deconditioning to occur. If the latter is successful, the opposition symbolizes birth in objective consciousness. The following second hemicycle of the overall process then stresses evolutionary development rather than devolutionary disintegration.

After the opposition, the planet remains retrograde for a time equal to its retrograde period before the opposition. This second phase in the retrograde process is necessary as a period of transition during which the change-over from one hemicycle and level of activity and development to the next can be assimilated. The process of biopsychic deconditioning occurring before the solar/planetary opposition may have operated in what seemed at first a seriously disturbing or cathartic manner. The retrograde period following the planetary/solar opposition also requires the kind of social and interpersonal interaction we saw operating during Phases 7 and 8 of the twelvefold planetary pattern we studied earlier. This leads to the planet's station and resumption of direct motion, which ends the entire reorientation process. The second hemicycle proceeds on the basis of what has been accomplished—for better or for worse—since the planet first turned retrograde.

When Mars initially goes retrograde, some kind of brakes or self-induced obstacles to its usual outward-directed activity tend to appear. Spontaneity often becomes prey to inner conflicts or self-doubt. Something in the capacity to mobilize energy and act—either for self-preservation according to the values represented by Venus or within the set of social and religious imperatives and taboos represented by Jupiter and Saturn—has become problematic and needs to be re-examined. Rather than proceed in its habital manner, Mars may, so to speak, timidly check back with Venus: "Are you sure this is what you really want?" Or it may double-check with Jupiter or Saturn: "Are you sure this is permissible and really OK?" In this way, the capacity to act (Mars) is purged of obsolete directives or taboos, strengthened or repaired if necessary. Sexuality, aggression or ambition may become particularly focal issues up for re-evaluation.

After the opposition, understanding of past mistakes should grow. Action may still not be as spontaneous as when Mars is direct, but it is not as unthinking either, having acquired a more deliberate character, wary, as it were, of repeating past transgressions or of falling into compulsive, biologically-dominated patterns. The capacity for action should now be redirected toward accomplishing chosen ends, perhaps within a wider than merely personal sphere of influence. As Mars approaches its second station and then resumes direct motion, the capacity to mobilize one's resources may again assume a spontaneous character, but by now it should have become definitely reoriented, having a different set of values upon which to act, a different set of goals toward which to aspire.

Mars is retrograde for only a relatively short time—about one tenth of its two-year cycle. With the planets beyond Mars, the lengths of the retrograde periods increase and span approximately the arc between the waxing and waning trines of each planet and the Sun.

Jupiter turning retrograde refers to the need to reorient and perhaps heal or repair the sense of social participation and/or religious activities. In a birth-chart, retrograde Jupiter may refer to some kind of social or religious maladjustment—that is, to an inability or unwillingness to participate in traditional social or religious patterns and rituals in the usual, expected way. This is because a person born with Jupiter retrograde is challenged to bring to fulfillment in life a new level of social participation and religious feeling. The new level of consciousness and activity should satisfy the personal or meta-personal need which called forth the creative impulse released at the prenatal Sun/Jupiter conjunction. For this reason, when interpreting a significant aspect or retrograde planet in a birth-chart, it is often quite revealing to go back to the prenatal conjunction beginning the cycle. The zodiacal sign, and especially the meaning of the Sabian Symbol for the degree on which the conjunction before birth occurred can be invaluably instructive.

During the first half of Jupiter's retrograde period, before the Jupiter/Sun opposition, the urge for purely personal expansion (so aggrandized in our socity) may slow and reverse itself. The quest for power or outward accomplishment may become an inner questioning, a search for a new set of ideals or spiritual meanings. The religious sense may turn inward, toward direct experience and away from the patterns of any particular church. After Jupiter's opposition to the Sun, a new kind of co-operative spirit may develop. An individual may feel pressure to integrate expansive urges with the efforts of others sharing similar ideals. A need and capacity may develop to formulate or express in words, actions or other forms what has been seen or objectively realized at the solar opposition. The need to understand past social or religious patterns may also surface, and an objective grasp of historical processes may develop to deepen the mind and give a broader meaning to social participation and religious striving.

As Saturn turns retrograde, all social and traditional boundaries may come to be questioned. A person born with Saturn retrograde cannot rely solely upon external agents—father, society, cultural assumptions—for self-definition and stabilization. The person must become self-reliant and develop his or her own resources. Fulfillment in stable personality must come from within, born of individual experience and self-conscious introspection. During the first half of Saturn's retrograde period, consolidation is required, and dependence upon external structures must lessen.

This is why in the lives of many people born with Saturn retrograde the father is absent (physically or psychologically) or otherwise unable to fulfill the child's Father-Image in a constructive, satisfying way. Such a situation can lead to one kind or another of father-complex—one in which the Father-Image becomes overly idealized or distorted (because contact with a real, loving *and* fallible father is lacking), or one in which persists a longing for someone, sometimes anyone, to fulfill the father-role. In either case, the Father-Image, such that it is, dominates the consciousness and life-pattern.

The way in which such a situation is usually worked out is for some substitute for the structuring power of the father to be found. This may be a husband, mentor or guru—or a compelling archetype, whether of a historical or mythological figure, or a set of philosophical or spiritual principles. On the one hand, such a solution may not be any real solution at all. For a dependency pattern may merely perpetuate itself. On the other hand, the mentor—human or otherwise—may embody for the growing person something which has not been developed in the family lineage, something which may be not only impersonal but transpersonal. In identifying with the Figure, the youth may activate something previously lacking within and become self-reliant and independent. He or she may also be challenged to move to a greater-than-merely-personal level of activity and consciousness. In such a case, the challenge of retrograde Saturn has been met at the highest level, for the involutionary process of growth and development gives way to a truly evolutionary process of self-actualization. Thus the initial father-complex can be and often has been a steppingstone to greater personal integration and significant accomplishment.

Since the father is the symbol of the structuring power of the culture, and gives to the family its defining socio-economic and class status, a person born with Saturn retrograde after its opposition with the Sun is also required by circumstance or inner need to achieve these outer markers of stability, definition, and social standing for himself. One may be unwilling or temperamentally unable to accept inherited strictures on one's social standing, and such a situation may be in the long run a blessing rather than a curse. For the key to creative self-actualization is always the way in which a person responds, the meaning given, to the circumstances of birth and life. No birth-chart alone can ever tell an astrologer whether a person will use seemingly difficult aspects and life-circumstances as a productive springboard to greater integration, accomplishment or transformation—or if he or she will become a hopeless neurotic paralyzed by insecurity, fear and the complexities of defense mechanisms. Retrograde planets in general pose such a challenge. A person born with Saturn retrograde after its opposition with the Sun is especially challenged to discover and tap inner resources of courage and conviction.

The retrograde periods of Uranus, Neptune and Pluto follow the same essential pattern as those of Mars, Jupiter and Saturn. But the periods when these outermost planets are retrograde increase in length with the planets's distance from the Sun. Because they move so slowly in relation to the Sun, the retrogradation of Uranus, Neptune and Pluto occurs at the same season each year as the Sun moves through the zodiacal signs between roughly 120° and 240° away from the relatively stationary planet. This seasonal retrogradation advances through the zodiac at the same rate the planet does.

Due to the transpersonal, transformative nature of what these planets symbolize, and to the present stage of human consciousness in its development, we may not be able significantly to define and distinguish the retrograde periods of these planets from the periods in their cycles with the Sun when they are direct. The idea of a 'reorientation of functions of reorientation and transformation' is not only grammatically redundant but obscure, and it also seems a distinction too fine for us to make at the present time.

When we deal with planets at the level of transits, we can, however, differentiate between direct and retrograde motion. A transiting planet often passes over a natal planet or an angle of a horoscope three times because of retrogradation. The first transit is direct, the second retrograde, and the third direct again. When a three-pass transit ocurs, it can be thought of as a threefold process in which

(1) a need is felt or a situation is presented (first direct transit)

(2) a solution is inwardly conceived or outwardly presented (second, retrograde transit)—and

(3) the new idea or form is worked out or developed (third, direct transit).

When the transiting planet is Uranus, Neptune or Pluto, phase (1) presents a challenge to transformation which is either assented to or fought against during phase (2). The results of the transit—whether or not the transformative process has been allowed to operate successfully—begin to become clear at (3). Such a process sometimes repeats itself in its entirety, especially when Neptune or Pluto is moving very slowly. An entire threefold process can thus span a year or more, and a repeated, sixfold process two years or longer.

A more detailed analysis of a planet's retrogradation can be made according to Diagram 4-6, in which the entire process of retrogradation is broken down into six basic stages or turning points. Such a loop can be drawn and interpreted any time a process of retrogradation becomes pertinent, either in terms of progressions or transits, of the time it spans or in relation to natal factors it traverses. Linking into a process what occurs in life at the times of the six turning points should enable the astrologer to understand the underlying meaning of the process. Knowing the turning points of the retrogradation process and what happened in the client's life in relation to them should reveal to the astrologer the meaning of the events in the client's development. The meanings of the Sabian degrees on which the turning points occur should lend qualitative understanding and luminosity to the interpretation.

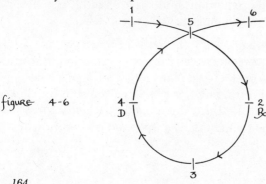

figure 4-6

1. The date and degree of a planet's entrance to the arc over which it will pass three times
2. The date the planet becomes stationary, the degree at which it begins to retrograde
3. The date and degree of the planet's aspect to the Sun (inferior conjunction for Mercury and Venus, opposition for all the others)
4. The date and degree of the planet's second station and resumption of direct motion (this will be the same degree as in #1 above).
5. It is sometimes interesting to note the date a planet re-traverses the degree in which it previously opposed or conjoined the Sun.
6. The degree (the same as in #2 above) and date on which the planet leaves the arc over which it has passed three times and enters upon new, previously untraversed territory.

5.
Rectangular and Triangular Formations in Horoscopes

Only in astrological textbooks are planetary aspects separated from one another. Their natural habitat is rather in complex interrelatedness to one another—in birth-charts integrating a myriad of aspects into more or less complex patterns. In fact, single aspects can never be fully understood out of the context of all the other aspects in a horoscope.

For example, we have seen that an opposition refers to the phase midway in a cyclic process when a change of gears has to take place, when one must 'wake up' and consciously participate in the rest of the process. As awareness develops, one becomes able to use, and responsible for how one uses, the activities or biopsychic functions represented by the opposing planets. The nature of the planets involved in the opposition; the zodiacal signs, Sabian degrees and houses of the horoscope in which they are found; and even the salient points about the prenatal conjunction beginning the cycle of which the opposition is the culmination: all these indications give the astrologer valuable clues about what the conflict leading to birth in consciousness may involve.

The opposition itself, however, does not tell us anything about the best way to use or integrate into the overall life-pattern the growing awareness and objectivity, once awakened; it does not help us to understand the full significance and dynamic interrelationship between the opposition-symbolized factors and other facets of our lives and processes of unfoldment. The aspects linking the opposition into the rest of the chart—that is, the aspects the two planets at either end of it make to other planets—as well as the aspects linking the two hemispheres of the chart divided by the opposition: these are the keys to what can and most naturally should be done with or about the awareness, capacity or development symbolized by the opposition.

In order to begin to be able to interpret the complex and dynamic interrelationships between aspects, one of the first things the astrologer should do is to try to determine whether specific group patterns of planets and aspects exist in a particular chart. Groupings of aspects were not unknown in traditional astrology, but they were almost entirely limited to sequences of one kind of aspect. Of the latter, only the trine and square were used in practice. Thus, when two planets in trine to one another were also trine a third planet, three mutual trines or a 'grand trine' was the result. When four planets formed a series of squares, a 'cosmic' or 'perfect' cross was mentioned.

The main reason for considering these sequences of the same kind of aspects significant was that the grand trine emphasized one of the four elements (fire, earth, air or water), because the three planets were placed in zodiacal signs of the same element. While to most astrologers, a grand trine linking three planets is a very 'good' indication, there are astrologers who do not consider it too favorable, for they feel it tends to over-emphasize one of the four elements; it may also stress a rather dream-like approach to life lacking in dynamism and concreteness. Likewise, the perfect or 'grand' cross stressed one of the quadruplicities of zodiacal signs—cardinal, fixed or mutable. Such a repetition of squares is usually considered very 'difficult,' yet some astrologers saw in it a sign of remarkable strength and capacity for action. Overall what was mainly considered important about these configurations—the grand trine and perfect cross—was the factor of the zodiac, not the strictly structural element, i.e., the geometrical pattern made by the planets regardless of the zodiacal signs, elements or qualities in which they were located, nor the dynamic element of their aspect interrelationship.

The meaning attributed to the familiar T-square (or T-cross) reflects this preoccupation with zodiacal factors and repeated aspects. The configuration was named for its two squares, not its opposition. And it is interpreted as a perfect cross from which one of the four factors is missing. The 'empty' factor is therefore seen as a zone of release for the energies produced by the combination of three planets in two squares including three of the four zodiacal elements.

What usually is not emphasized in interpreting the two kinds of crosses, 'perfect' and 'T'—and which is really a key to understanding all types of complex aspect patterns—is the fact that these configurations are really combinations of *two* kinds of aspects, opposition *and* square, while the grand trine is composed of only *one* kind of aspect, the trine. The grand trine is thus unique. There is no other configuration (except a stellium, which does not fit into the same category of patterns as those we are discussing here) composed of only one kind of aspect. Once the linking of different kinds of aspects is recognized as significant, the possibility of giving specific meanings to combinations of them according to the particular aspects involved should become evident.

The three basic features of a primary planetary pattern are:

(1) that combinations of two or more kinds of aspects display a clear-cut kind of symmetry,

(2) the configuration of aspects should be closed and complete, spanning 360°, and

(3) it should be a regular polygon capable of being inscribed in a circle.*

This last-mentioned criterion results from the fact that in astrology every moving factor is related to and given meaning in relation to a whole circumference or cycle, whether the 360° of the zodiac, or of the wheel of houses, or the 360° span from conjunction to conjunction between planetary pairs.

Patterns meeting the above criteria can be divided into two basic categories: four-sided and three-sided figures, i.e., rectangles

---

*One can, of course, consider significant and interpret aspect configurations spanning fewer than 360°—for example, a trine, bisected into two sextiles, an opposition divided by a semi-square and sesquiquadrate. We would rather, however, consider these secondary, not primary, configurations. Nevertheless, in particular charts, especially those of an overall hemispheric type, such secondary patterns may form the basic structure of the horoscope.

and triangles, the square or perfect cross being only one specific case of rectangle, and the grand trine being only one particular instance of triangle. In the following, we will cover the basic figures, but especially if non-regular polygons covering the whole 360° (such as trapezoids) are considered, the variations are practically endless.

RECTANGULAR PATTERNS

Because the perfect square includes both square and opposition aspects, it can be seen as the foundation of all regular, closed configurations in which two or more types of aspects are interwoven. Indeed, geometrically speaking, as already mentioned, the square figure is only a special kind of rectangle—a rectangle whose four sides are equal and whose diagonals cut each other at 90° angles.

The accompanying figure shows how, if we keep the vertical line (theoretically the meridian of the birth-chart—or the line of the solstices) as a basis, we can draw any number of rectangular patterns. In the square, the four sides and four angles are equal. As we decrease the length of one side, the length of the complementary side increases until, at the limit, the rectangle becomes concentrated, as it were, into the vertical line.

We are thus dealing with a *series* of rectangular patterns, the two extreme possibilities of which are the square and the line—astrologically, the grand cross and the opposition (or multiple opposition). In between these two cases, we find a theoretically infinite number of possibilities for rectangular patterns. The grand cross becomes a kind of ideal or archetypal rectangle. Actually, only those rectangles which link aspects should be considered in astrology, and six basic kinds can be distinguished.

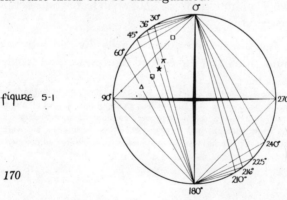

figure 5-1

This series of rectangles can be established very simply by considering this angular relationship between the two diagonals or oppositions. In the perfect square, the diagonals make two equal angles of 90° each. The relation is thus 1:1. When, the oppositions are connected by trines and sextiles, the diagonals form angles of 120° and 60° to one another; the two angles are in 1:2 relation. A relation 1:3 is found in a rectangle linking semi-squares (45°) and sesquiquadrates (135°). A relation 1:4 occurs when semiquintiles or deciles (36°) and bi-quintiles (144°) are related. When the angular distance between the two diagonals or oppositions are 30° and 150°, we find aspects of semi-sextile and quincunx, and the ratio between the two oppositions is 1:5. We can also add a rectangle in which the aspects between the two diagonals are quintiles (72°) and tri-deciles or sesqui-quintiles (108°); the ratio between two such related diagonals would be expressed as 2:3.

The series of four rectangles 1:2, 1:3, 1:4, 1:5 (not counting the square or 1:1 ratio and the quintile or 2:3 ratio) parallels the series of rectangles upon which the shapes used in Greek design and architecture were based, according to the principle of 'dynamic symmetry' rediscovered some years ago by the American scholar J. Hambidge. Indeed, since the days of Pythagoras, the rectangle was the very symbol and signature of Greek philosophy and culture—the symbolic key to the mysteries of Man and the universe.

The fundamental factor which all astrological rectangles have in common is the presence of two oppositions as diagonals. It is this factor which must be stressed in interpreting all rectangles, including the grand cross or perfect square. What changes and gives each specific type of rectangle its particular meaning and significance is *the relationship between the two diagonals*, the aspects integrating the four ends of the two oppositions. In fact, whenever two oppositions are found, what the astrologer should find out and consider immediately is the way in which they are related to one another. The nature of the aspects linking the four planets involved in the two oppositions of a rectangle indicate what a person must meet and pass through in order to achieve the kind of awareness and objectivity represented by the oppositions, and how that awareness and ability to function, once it is awakened and made manifest, can and must be integrated into the person's life and the life of the community.

In more psychological terms, the opposition refers to a polarization of two biopsychic functions and to the awareness and ability to consciously participate in further developmental processes that can and should be actualized on the basis of the tension of the polarization. An opposition or multiple opposition *alone* is a theoretical possibility never net in practice. It is in some ways reminiscent of what happened to Burden's ass—the donkey who, standing equidistant from two equal bales of hay, starved to death because there was no reason to go toward one pile rather than the other. This is a situation in the abstract (for both the donkey and the astrologer) because in practice one never encounters only an opposition or multiple opposition; other factors are always involved. The opposition poses a challenge to develop awareness, to break free of unconscious compulsion. How—in relation to what other activities and functions besides the two opposing ones—that awareness most naturally develops, what spurs it, what can or should be done with or about it once it blossoms, can best be seen in other aspects. In terms of rectangular patterns, these are represented by the aspects linking the four ends of the diagonal oppositions.

At the opposite end of the rectangle-spectrum from the theoretical multiple opposition is the grand cross. The simplest way to approach a study of it is to consider the case of the zodiacal pattern constituted by the line of the two equinoxes (Aries 1° and Libra 1°) and solstices (Cancer 1° and Capricorn 1°). This is what we might call the archetype of all perfect squares or grand crosses, the basic illustration of all quadrature.

Such a quadrature rests on the pattern of the seasons, which in human experience is the origin of man's structured sense of time in relation to all life processes. The daily flow of life-experiences would have no definiteness, no larger pattern, no frame of reference if it were not for seasonal changes. Through contrasts and well-defined changes, the flow of life begins to assume a form, a rhythm, a sequential meaning and character of order. As a result, human beings sense that there are laws of change, that time has a periodical structure—that, therefore, predictability is possible. All this makes civilization, science, philosophy—and, underlying them all, astrology—possible. The square figure is indeed the symbol of all foundations of concrete, masterful living.

Traditional astrology has unfortunately over-stressed the destructive meaning of both the opposition and the square. Thus, oppositions are popularly supposed to refer only to dilemmas, conflicts between opposite points of view and the breaking asunder of opposing factors. Squares are thought of as aspects of violence related to the shattering of things, to tragedy, etc. These meanings are only partly correct—which is to say that they are also partly wrong, for they are accurate only insofar as the negative expression of planetary relationships is concerned.

As we have seen from several points of view, the opposition, positively speaking, signifies the need and ability to be objective to happenings and experiences. It is the basic symbol of consciousness or awareness, and it need not, especially when linked with other aspects, refer to the kind of situation in which Burden's donkey found himself. As to the destruction associated with squares, it is directed toward obsolete structures—be they behavior patterns, dependencies or crystallized dogmas, ramshackle tenements or outmoded social institutions—which no longer serve healthy functions, or toward objects and situations which must be removed and cleared away before greater things can take place.

A perfect square configuration in a birth-chart represents a tight linking of two kinds of consciousness-building processes (oppositions) which produces four 90° aspects (squares) and leads to a very thorough and exhaustive type of clearing-up activity. What is actually meant by this 'linking of two kinds of consciousness-building processes'?

In the seasonal cross of the year, spring activities symbolically oppose fall activities—that is, the birth (or rebirth) of living organisms is seen to be in dynamic contrast to organic disintegration and death. Out of this contrast, human beings come to gain a consciousness of the impermanence of all that lives, a consciousness of change. In the opposition between the summer solstice and the winter solstice, human beings learn, on the contrary, to deal with the relatively permanent factors in life: family, a home, a personality—community, a state, a civilization.

These two kinds of consciousness taken together—the consciousness of the inevitable periodicity of life and death and the

consciousness of the possibility of building long-lasting structures—refer to the very foundation of all human realizations and
endeavors, the very basis of human reality. By integrating these two
kinds of awareness, man functions as a civilized, morally responsible, cooperative being.

Therefore, the essential meaning of the grand cross configuration is the need and capacity to develop a type of integration of
awareness (opposition) and activity (square) which is only possible *if*
there is also the readiness to give up all lesser allegiances and the attachment to whatever each planet at the four corners of the perfect
square represents. The type of integration possible with a perfect
square depends almost entirely upon whether the individual is able,
at crucial turning points, to let go of whatever he or she is attached
to. If the person does not let go, the perfect square can become the
kind of wheel of torture on which medieval criminals were quar-
tered. If one becomes objective to and free of the separative pulls and
unconscious compulsions of the opposing planets (i.e., of the bio-
psychological functions and drives they represent), then one can be a
deeply and powerfully integrated person. The key will inevitably be
knowing when to forge ahead and when to detach.

The character of the squares involved, whether they are 'waxing' or 'waning', involutionary or evolutionary, can give significant
clues to the kind of challenge of action and/or letting go that has to
be met and the best way to meet it. Whether the configuration falls
in angular, succeedent or cadent houses also points to the life-areas
through which the consciousness-raising process and subsequent integration through action is most likely to take place. Of course,
whether the cross is found in cardinal, fixed or mutable signs is of
signal importance.

A grand cross in angular houses and fixed signs is found in the
horoscope of Albert Schweitzer. The oppositions are between
fourth-house Pluto and tenth-house Mars; first-house Saturn and
seventh-house Uranus. There is an additional opposition between a
third-house Moon/Neptune conjunction and ninth-house Jupiter,
and it forms a T-square to the first-house Sun/Mercury conjunction.
While we are primarily interested in the grand cross, it is practically
impossible to ignore these other aspects of the chart.

The grand cross itself primarily refers to the need for radical transformation on two levels: the level of Mars (personal desire and capacity to mobilize energy and act) and the tenth house (public life, 'vocation' or calling); and the level of Saturn (the sense of form or structure, authority, one's relation to one's ancestral tradition and culture) and the first house (individual selfhood). With Pluto in the fourth house, the deepest, most fundamental 'tone' urging transformation welled up from Schweitzer's deepest roots: his ancestral Christian-European tradition. Since Saturn is in the first house, all the issues of this ancestral tradition became focused, for Schweitzer, in his own individuality.

This was made very clear by Schweitzer himself when, at a great turning point in his life he realized that he had not the

> inward right to take as a matter of course my happy youth, my good health, and my power of work. Out of the depths of my feeling of happiness there grew up gradually with me an understanding of the saying of Jesus that we must not treat our lives as being for ourselves alone. Whoever is spared personal pain must feel himself called to help in diminishing the pain of others. We must all carry our share of the misery which lies upon the world.*

Thus, the Pluto/Mars opposition challenged a complete impersonalization of the level at which passions, desires and the search for well-being and achievement operate. True to its fulfillment, and the fulfillment of the Saturn/Uranus opposition, Schweitzer broke away from his ancestral culture by going to Africa, to live among and heal the natives there. He did not merely break away in hateful rebellion; he infused the best of his ancestral tradition with luminous meaning by taking the atonement of its sins upon himself. Since the Saturn/Uranus opposition spans the first and seventh houses, it also presumably refers to Schweitzer's marriage to a Jewish woman—a definite departure from normal Christian-European patterns at the time, and another indication of his 'marriage' to those historically dispossessed and persecuted in the name of Christianity.

My Life and Thought, pp. 81-82.

The seeming serenity of Schweitzer's later years is, however, belied by the picture of him his birth-chart presents: a man with tremendous conflicts and a Saturnian sense of form, but also with passionate intensity (Mars in Scorpio) and explosive energies swayed by deep and even dark Images (Pluto in the fourth house). Schweitzer's peace had tragic roots indeed, and it was not easily won. He believed that every man's personality is a mystery that no other person should seek to probe or intrude upon. Indeed, his own words suggest that this mystery may not even be a thing for the individual to fathom himself. True to the grand-square (and T-square, a total of six squares) in his chart, the mystery should be acted out rather than passively known or observed. For Schweitzer, only in action does the mysterious whole of personality reveal itself and become conscious in affirmations of life and emanations of spiritual light.

The pressures of such high expectations of oneself could have been too great for a lesser man to bear. Yet Schweitzer bore—and fulfilled—them heroically. His great love for all life, the stability of his formalistic mind sustained by the majestic, ordered music of Bach (of which he was acknowledged the greatest interpreter) made him overcome within himself what he had felt as the sins and foreseen as the disintegration of his European culture. His way of overcoming was to heal the sick and, in fulfillment of the highest symbolism of any Cross, to atone as an individual for the sins of the many. Such an interpretation of Schweitzer's life and chart becomes the more inspiring and accessible for each of us when we realize that from a process-oriented point of view, his grand cross formed when the faster-moving Mars and Saturn came around to oppose and square the relatively slower-moving, historically significant Pluto/Uranus square.

While the life of Albert Schweitzer certainly points to the socially and spiritually constructive possibilities of a grand square, the case of the Russian dancer, Nijinsky, had a less happy outcome. In his chart the two oppositions at right angles to one another are in angular houses and mutable signs. Mercury at the nadir opposes retrograde Saturn at the Midheaven. A rising, separating Moon/Mars conjunction opposes to exteriorize the historically most significant, forming Neptune/Pluto conjunction in the seventh house.

Despite his great renown and artistic ability, emotional confusion and tragedies in unorthodox interpersonal relationships led to mental instability and ultimate institutionalization.

If instead of a perfect square, we consider the other rectangle configurations, we also find two lines of opposition, but their relationship is of a different order. Between these two lines there is not the sharp contrast as between the diagonals of the perfect square. A rectangle points in a certain direction—the more so, the greater difference between the lengths of the sides. It does not challenge, like the perfect square, a general, complete kind of actional integration —a challenge which, if not successfully met, often leads to a general confusion or tragic sense of failure or frustration. It presents a challenge for a particular kind of integration.

This is why the rectangular shape has been used in many temples and chambers of initiation. These buildings were built to symbolize the process of transition from one stage of personal-spiritual unfoldment to the next—the fulfillment of a great goal. Seen in the vertical plane, a rectangle becomes *a door*, something to pass through, to enter a new realm. Practically speaking, in a birth-chart, its orientation in relation to the angles and other horoscopic axes is most significant. Most fundamentally, the two oppositions of a rectangle pose the 'problem'; the aspects relating the four ends of the diagonals of the rectangle indicate the best manner in which what is represented by the oppositions can be integrated and the overall life-task met.

Actually, what occurs in practice is that a client comes to an astrologer with a basic life-situation or problem. When looking at the birth-chart, the astrologer identifies the basis of the problem with one or both of the oppositions. This lets the astrologer know what underlies the problem in the client's life. The aspects linking the two oppositions reveal the best way the client can meet and integrate the situation into his or her overall development.

One of the most practically constructive and spiritually harmonious possibilities of any rectangle is indicated when the two oppositions are linked by sextiles and trines.* Where fully active, this 'harmonic rectangle' points to the potential development of a character strongly organized in an attempt to take an important step in personal growth and/or spiritual development. The configuration tends to bring the polarized elements symbolized by the opposing planets into a unity because a strong sense of organization (sextile) and a cohesive, purposeful vision (trine) are potential in the personality. Whatever tensions arise in the life or personality that are symbolized by the opposing planets do not necessarily 'go away.' But they can be 'laid on the altar,' as it were, or channeled toward the concrete completion of a significant life-task.

Examples of 'harmonic' or 'mystic' rectangles abound. A most significant case is that of Dag Hammarskjold, the late Nobel prize-winning Secretary-General of the United Nations. The two diagonals of the rectangle are formed by oppositions between Mercury and Saturn, and a Moon/Neptune conjunction opposing Uranus. They are integrated by sextiles between Mercury and Moon/Neptune, and between Saturn and Uranus, while Saturn and Moon/Neptune are trine, as are Mercury and Uranus. To reach integrations of often violently clashing opposites in the field of international interests was the pattern-setting Secretary-General's purpose and, often, ability. In active practice, his vision (trine) of global integration was tested and brought down, as it were, to the level of practical, political organization (sextile).

---

*I believe that I was the first astrologer to study and interpret this configuration. It is mentioned in my book *The Astrology of Personality* (1934-35). At first I called it a 'mystic rectangle' because its shape seems to have been used in initiation chambers and temples of older civilizations; altars in these structures had also been constructed on its proportions. Later on I realized the inadequacy of the term, that it was confusing, especially considering the way it has been used and abused of late. I then began to call it a 'harmonic rectangle.'

Some astrologers, perhaps not agreeing with my claim that such a rectangle had an integrative or harmonic character, have spoken of it, years later, as the X-configuration. This, is, of course, in line with such terms as perfect cross and T-square—and we shall see in a moment that some astrologers have also spoken of a Y-configuration, which I consider as a species of triangle. The question here—besides the fact that all such 'X's' are not integrated by sextiles and trines—is perhaps whether you like the alphabet better than geometry, but it may go deeper. In speaking of rectangles and triangles, I am envisioning shapes in which dynamic centers (the planets) constantly interact. What is important is the interaction between these centers, and the geometrical concept expresses this fact better than the alphabetic formulation—especially since letters such as T, X and Y are not found in all languages. Today one should think universally, not in terms of national cultures and alphabets!—DR

Stressing the more 'mystic' aspect of the configuration is the chart of Paul Foster Case, the occultist especially regarded for his work and still-in-print book on the Tarot. In his chart, Mars/Neptune and Mercury/Moon oppositions structure the rectangle. The sextiles are between Mercury (which is also conjunct Uranus) and Mars, and the Moon and Neptune. The trines are between Mercury and Neptune, and the Moon and Mars. The total integration evokes the potentiality for developing an innovative mind which is mystically inclined and open to inspiration from 'higher levels.' The involvement of Mars suggests also the capacity to mobilize resources and act to fulfill the higher vision.

Another kind of powerful integration is shown in the horoscope of the late Director (some would say despot) of the F.B.I., J. Edgar Hoover. Here Mars opposes Saturn, while Mercury opposes Jupiter, making the personal level of operation (Mars and Mercury) the conduit for sociocultural images and imperatives (Jupiter and Saturn). The sextiles are between Mercury and Saturn (a clear, well-structured yet conservative mind) and Mars and Jupiter (the ability to organize a power-base and expand it). Jupiter and Saturn, and Mercury and Mars are trine. Hoover knew where he stood in relation to social issues, and he knew how to impress his vision on his surroundings. A formidable combination indeed!

The complex chart of Henry Ford again presents a fitting example. Born at the time of a Full Moon, his natal soli-lunar opposition is linked by sextile and trine to the longer-lasting opposition between Saturn and Neptune, a fitting symbol of the dissolution of social structures at the threshold of the industrial era which Ford, the inventor of assembly-line manufacture, helped usher in.

When two oppositions are linked by semi-squares and sesquiquadrates, a particularly dynamic potentiality results. To our knowledge, this figure has never been named, but it could be called an 'octilinear rectangle' since it is based on division of the circle by Eight. Here, in a concentrated form, arise all the issues we discussed in relation to the semi-square and sesquiquadrate. Through meeting them, whatever is polarized by the two oppositions can become integrated and manifest as a workable way of life or world-view. Whatever is started in life should bring about very focused and concrete results, particularly if the sesquiquadrate operates in its positive aspect as an enthusiastic 'outreaching' (square + semi-square) and the challenge of the semi-square (dissemination of one's vision in order to fulfill the needs of the public one serves) is fulfilled.

An octilinear rectangle is found in the horoscope of Ram Das, in which the Venus/Neptune opposition and the Saturn/Pluto opposition are integrated by semi-squares between Pluto and Neptune, and Venus and Saturn. Venus and Pluto, and Saturn and Neptune, are thus sesquiquadrate. The need to break down and regenerate ossified social structures, authority images, etc. is stirred into operation by the use of value-transforming psychedelic drugs and mystical experiences or spiritual discipleship. The surrender of self, or at least the radical transformation of one's sense of self-worth, is also challenged by the Venus/Neptune opposition. Neptune is made the more focal in this configuration, since it is at the 'point' of what we have called a "Finger of the World"—a triangle whose base is a square, the two ends of which are both sesquisquare a third planet. The square is between an almost exact conjunction of Sun and Uranus, and Saturn. Since Neptune is in the third house, the challenge is indeed to transform and transcend a culture- and religion-conditioned sense of everyday reality—and to deepen the mind by, at least at first, unfocusing its 'hold' on such a taken-for-granted sense of what is 'real.' Jupiter, the planet of social participation and religious images, rises (septile the focal Neptune and conjunct Pluto—which is semi-square Neptune), and the Sun/Uranus conjunction is in the eleventh house of social transformation—all told, a powerful challenge to lead and participate in transformative processes as a result of personal experience.

In general, the rectangle linking two oppositions by semi-squares and sesquiquadrates can be particularly productive of effective integration if the individual is thorough and persistent enough to actually put across and carry out the vision, uncompromisingly and at the same time trying to take into account the needs of the biospheric, psychological and social environment. Much, of course, depends on the actual planets involved and whether the semi-squares and sesquiquadrates between them are 'waxing' or 'waning,' thus involutionary or evolutionary. If this type of rectangle links planets like Mars, Uranus, Pluto and/or the Sun, the dynamic intensity of the configuration would be particularly stressed.

While neither the semi-square nor the sesquiquadrate is part of the arithmetically derived involutionary series, after we have understood the principles underlying the three interwoven aspects of all cyclic processes (involution, devolution, evolution), we can *place* these aspects in the waxing half of a cycle. The semi-square falls at the middle of phase 2 between the semi-sextile and sextile; the sesquisquare falls at the midpoint of phase 5 between the trine and the quincunx. Each of these aspects, when waxing, can be understood to be the point at which the process of the particular phase in which it is found reaches its culmination and maximum intensity. In the sense of cycles-within-cycles, as midpoints of phases these aspects are analogous to oppositions (or division by Two) of the phases in which they are found. They thus refer to a possible point of release or objectification of what needs to occur during that phase.

The figure joining two oppositions by semi-sextiles and inconjuncts or quincunxes has no name. It indicates that what the oppositions represent can best become integrated through everyday work and close, personal bi-polar relationships, possibly in which self-improvement and serving the needs of one's partner would be stressed. Zodiacally, what is emphasized in such a configuration is usually the relationship between succeeding 'masculine' and 'feminine' signs— although if the opposition aspects are not exact, the semi-sextiles may link the ends and beginnings of the same signs. Only small orbs should be allowed when one considers such a rectangle. The orbs can be a little larger in the case of harmonic rectangles, but not larger than six degrees in most cases.

An example of a rectangle involving semi-sextiles and inconjuncts is found in the horoscope of George Sand, the flamboyant 19th-century romantic novelist and feminist prototype. The oppositions are between second-house Mars and Neptune in the eighth house of sexual relationships, and between the first-house Moon and Jupiter in the seventh house. The rectangle is thus concentrated in the houses referring to personal expression and interpersonal relationships and marriage. Sand's romances, scandalous for her time, were well-publicized, especially her liaison with the composer Chopin. Through them and through meeting the personal crises they engendered, she was able to transcend the cultural imperatives and taboos of her day. In the process, and through her ardent dedication to her craft, she set an example of independence admired and emulated even by contemporary women.

Other rectangles based on the quintile occur when the ends of two oppositions are related by semi-quintiles or deciles (36°) and bi-quintiles (144°), or when the oppositions occur at 72° intervals (quintile) and the other sides of the rectangle are 1½ quintiles or 108° (tri-decile or sesqui-quintile) in length. These rectangles of the quintile variety stress the potentiality of creativity in one form or another. But we should recognize that creativity may manifest in many more ways than those we usually consider, for example, in the arts. In an expanded sense, creativity refers to the capacity of an individual to transform the environment in some manner, material or social, so that the person leaves an individual mark upon it. Creativity can thus refer to any activity through which an individual effectively projects upon any kind of material at hand or upon the way of life of his or her community the manner of thinking, the vision or ideal, the typical form of behavior which expresses his or her individuality.

An example of a rectangle structured by semi-quintiles and bi-quintiles is found in the horoscope of Krishamurti. Here, Venus and the Moon are in opposition, as are the Sun and Uranus. The Moon and Uranus are semi-quintile, as are the Sun and Venus; and the Sun and Moon—and Venus and Uranus—are therefore bi-quintile.

In concluding this necessarily abridged study of rectangular configurations, we should note some important general points. First, some rectangles may not fall into the categories we have described, but may nevertheless seem significant on their own merits. For example, the chart of Clyde Barrow—of Bonnie and Clyde fame —displays the integration of two oppositions (Mercury and Jupiter —and Uranus and Neptune) by septiles (Mercury/Uranus and Jupiter/Neptune) and trines (Mercury/Neptune and Jupiter/ Uranus). A similar configuration is found in the chart of the 19th-century occultist and author of the *Secret Doctrine*, H.P. Blavatsky. In her horoscope, the Moon (fourth-house) opposes Pluto (tenth-house) and the sun opposes Jupiter (which is conjunct Uranus). The septiles are between the second-house Sun and the Moon, and between the eighth-house Jupiter and Pluto. The Sun and Pluto are trine, as are the Moon and the Jupiter/Uranus conjunction. Another atypical case is the birth-chart of India's Prime Minister Indira Gandhi, in which two oppositions are integrated by a variety of aspects. Here, two oppositions (Saturn/Uranus and Venus/Pluto) are linked by a 153° quincunx (Venus/Saturn), a 35° semi-quintile (Venus/Uranus), a sesquiquadrate (Pluto/Uranus) and a novile (Pluto/Saturn). Required in fulfilling all such patterns is a highly original integration of what is presented by the oppositions, and it must include the essential meanings of all the aspects in evidence.

The generalization underlying the interpretation of all types of rectangles is therefore that the way in which the oppositions are related is the key. While in order to qualify as a 'classifiable' rectangle, aspects should be standard, recognized ones, not too far 'out of orb,' other non-symmetrical patterns linking a variety of aspects must also be recognized to exist as subsets of classifiable configurations. The purpose for classifying astrological phenomena resides not so much in creating pigeon-holes into which subsequent examples can be made to fit, as in creating in the student's mind a sense of pattern—a sense of a continuum of patterns having not only identifiable categories, but underlying principles of formation as well. Once the basic principles are grasped, the student should be able to generalize his or her experience to creatively interpret patterns falling 'in the cracks' between established categories.

TRIANGULAR CONFIGURATIONS

Geometrically speaking, the equilateral triangle is the most stable of all forms. The astrological grand trine normally links the three aspects of each of the four elements. It presents every mode of existence in its essentially threefold nature. It is unique in all astrological configurations in that it is composed of only one kind of aspect—and just as the grand cross is the archetype of all rectangular patterns in astrology, the grand trine occupies the same position in relation to triangular configurations.

The equilateral triangle symbolizes in most religions perfection of being—i.e., God as the supreme foundation of all existence. In that sense, it is the symbol of both a static and transcendent condition. It contains no opposition aspect; therefore, it is essentially subjective. It simply *is*, without conflicts, what it *is*. However, if an expansive planet like Jupiter dominates a grand trine, this 'what it is' may keep enlarging itself until some internal pressure or external boundary causes it to explode or to become objectively manifest within a form—which may produce conflicts or tension. In a particular chart, not only are the actual planets joined by the grand trine significant; what may be as important is the way in which the grand trine is integrated (by what other aspects) into the overall pattern of the chart. Since a grand trine refers to a fullness of vision, or something complete as an ideal at the level of ideas or archetypes, when it is integrated into the chart via an opposition, what is complete at the level of ideas has a more obvious or pointed possibility or necessity for concretization in the world or in the life and personality of the individual.

When one point of a grand trine is involved in an opposition, the opposition's other end almost inevitably falls at the midpoint of one of the trines, forming sextiles to the other two planets in the trine: a 'kite' formation. In such a pattern, vision or understanding and purpose (trines) find the possibility of outward manifestation in objective form (oppositions and sextiles) through organizational genius and the capacity for planning and enlightened management in which needs and answers to needs are brought together. The functional activities represented by the planet at the midpoint of the bisected trine should be those through which is focused and released what the entire configuration represents.

There are other symmetrical triangular configurations spanning the complete 360° of the circle which have not the stability of the grand trine because they are triangles one side of which is smaller than the other two, which are of equal size. The planet forming the apex of the triangle is at the inverse midpoint of two planets in aspect forming the triangle's base. This is also the case in the grand trine, but multiplied and entirely mutual, as each planet is at the inverse midpoint of the arc connecting the other two. On one hand, this contributes to the cohesiveness of the grand trine, but it also serves to keep its focus more or less diffuse and unmanifest (unless, of course, it is involved in a kite or with other focalized aspects integrating it into the overall pattern of a particular chart). The planet at the apex of the non-equilateral triangle can act as a kind of dynamic release or 'seeding' point for whatever is represented by the planets and aspect forming the triangle's base. The most important aspects in the configuration, however, are not necessarily the two pointing toward the apex. Depending upon the overall Gestalt of a particular chart, the foundation-aspect—the base of the triangle (no matter in which direction the pattern points)—could be considered the most significant operation which is 'trying,' as it were, to manifest through the other two equal aspects in one way or another.

One of the these types of triangular configurations has been studied by some astrologers and variously called the 'Y-configuration' or 'Yod' or 'Finger of God.' This configuration is produced when two planets in sextile to one another each form quincunxes to a third planet at the inverse midpoint of the sextile. To single out such a pattern as particularly important, however, without taking into consideration the others of the series of which it is part—and the principles according to which all acquire significance—seems to lack a basic understanding of astrological procedure as well as common sense. For another triangle is formed when a quintile and two bi-quintiles are similarly linked as in the so-called Y-configuration, and we have already mentioned the instance of a square linking two sesquiquadrates.

Granted such aspects as quintiles, bi-quintiles and sesquiquadrates are more difficult to spot in charts drawn in terms of zodiacal longitude, but that should not be sufficient reason for failing to recognize the principles of organization underlying major configurations in which such unfamiliar aspects may be found. At the limit of the series of symmetrical triangular configurations we find the so-called T-square, which is really a triangle in that it links three planets, one at the inverse midpoint of the aspect formed by the other two. In this case, the base of the triangle is the opposition, while the equal sides are composed of squares. The triangle whose base is an opposition is not a very 'tall' triangle, but it nevertheless fulfills the criteria of triangularity fulfilled by the other three.

All these symmetrical triangular configurations in which the three related planets are not equidistant—i.e., not constituting a grand trine—have one thing in common. They refer to a state of dynamic equilibrium which is calling for some sort of resolution. On the one hand, the planet at the apex of the triangle can in many cases be interpreted to provide a possible outlet to release and relieve whatever tension is involved in the relationship between the two planets forming the triangle's base. But release and relief are not the same as resolution. For all these triangular configurations represent a dynamic trend toward a fourth point which is not necessarily occupied by a physical planet (although in a particular chart it may be). The 'empty point,' as it were, pulls to itself the combined biopsychic energy of whatever is represented by the three planets in triangular configuration. This point is the point in opposition to the apex of the triangle. When aspects are not exact, this point may or may not coincide exactly with the midpoint of the aspect forming the base of the triangle. In such a case, an area rather than a point may be considered. In either case, the accompanying figure illustrates the 'direction' of each of the configurations toward what we will call the 'tension point.'

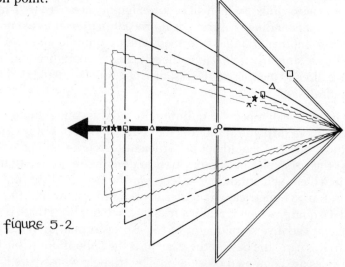

fiqure 5-2

In the so-called 'Yod' configuration (which, of course, can be upside-down, horizontal or diagonal in a chart), the 'tension point' is opposite the planet to which the quincunxes point—thus at the midpoint of the triangle's sextile base. The same principle applies to the so-called T-square. The 'tension point' is the zodiacal degree which, if occupied by a fourth planet, would transform the T-square into a perfect or grand cross. This is why the T-square acts like and is indeed a triangular, rather than rectangular configuration.

To avoid confusion, we shall repeat here that the grand trine stands apart because it is completely unique, balanced and self-sufficient. In and of itself, it is a configuration devoid of tension. It does not indicate any drive toward anything. It simply is what it is in fullness of being, and for this reason symbolizes spirit or divine perfection. In all other triangular configurations, the fact that one planet, the apex, is equidistant from two other planets in significant relationship to one another indicates a certain amount of tension between the apex-planet and the base-planets. The nature of the tension and the way it seeks resolution (and not merely relief!) varies, of course, with the nature of the particular aspects involved. Needless to say, perhaps, the house positions of the planets, and the zodiacal signs in which they are found, are also of the utmost significance.

Perhaps the best way of interpreting this triangular situation in general is to say that in the so-called Y-configuration—whether it involves quincunxes, bi-quintiles, sesquiquadrates or squares—one planet is related to two others by equidistant paths. Thus, symbolically speaking, a possible choice is shown to exist between two ways of life, two approaches to a definite situation symbolized by the planets and aspect forming the triangle's base. We could clarify the matter and refer it to zodiacal symbolism by saying that at the inverse midpoint of two planets in sextile in, say, Virgo and Scorpio, a third planet is quincunx them both in Aries. This can be interpreted to mean that, while Aries seeks its complement in Libra (the empty point at the midpoint of the sextile), it can seek it in two ways: the Virgo way or the Scorpio way. This configuration involving Aries-Virgo-Scorpio has, as it were, Libra as its goal; it is in a state of tension toward Libra. But there are two possible approaches toward resolving the tension: the Virgo approach (purity, discipleship, work, service or retraining) or the Scorpio approach (union through feelings, cooperation or commerce, root-identification, sexuality, etc.). We could go further and say that the whole configuration is poised, so to speak, toward relationship and relatedness—release or relief may be found in Aries (self-motivation or self-centeredness), but not necessarily resolution of the whole question of relationship implied in the configuration in its entirety.

Again, the houses of the birth-chart and the actual planets involved—as well as the way in which a triangular pattern is oriented in terms of the cross of horizon and meridian, and linked to other elements of the chart and the chart's overall Gestalt—are of the utmost significance.

Examples of significant triangular patterns abound, both in general practice and in horoscopes we have already used as examples. We can look again at the birth-charts of Mohandas Gandhi, Albert Einstein, Albert Schweitzer, Werner Erhard and Ram Das, and find significant T-squares or triangles whose bases are oppositions. Gandhi's horoscope in particular shows the T-square as a species of triangle, for in it both a T-square and a grand trine 'point to' or 'hang off' the tenth-house Moon. Both the Saturn/Neptune trine and the Venus/Mars vs. Jupiter/Pluto opposition seek release through the Moon and the field of Gandhi's public life. A vision of transformed social structures (Saturn trine Neptune) illumines, as it were, the Mahatma's struggle with sexuality and marriage at the personal level, and both seek expression through the charismatic persona represented by the tenth-house Leo Moon. Resolution of both configurations thus coincides in the horoscope's fourth house—the field of experience related to a person's ancestral 'roots' and the kind of in-depth personality integration that can occur when their sustaining power is effectively and appropriately tapped.

Einstein's ninth-house Jupiter/third-house Uranus opposition is bisected by Pluto in the twelfth house—a fitting symbol of the socially transformative, Plutonian catharsis released through Einstein's work. But the configuration's 'direction of resolution' points toward the sixth house, the area from about 25° Scorpio to 2° Sagittarius. In terms we presented earlier, while Taurus (Pluto) seeks its complement in Scorpio, it can seek it in two ways: the Aquarius (Jupiter) way or, specifically in Einstein's chart, the Virgo (Uranus) way.

The Jupiter/Aquarius 'path' presumably refers in Einstein's life to his international (ninth house) and social fame and involvement, as well as to the development of his humanitarian sense and relationship to his ancestral Jewish religion. Since Jupiter is in waning square to Pluto, Einstein was challenged to let go of inherited, obsolete structures determining the level at which he operated in these areas. He was born a German Jew, gave up his German citizenship at an early age to become a neutral and, to him, more humanistic, less militaristic Swiss; and while he was asked to become President of the State of Israel after Chaim Weitzman's death, he also had to arrive at his own, more open and universal attitude to his Jewish tradition and consequent status as a Jew.

On the other hand, Uranus is seen in 'waxing' square to Pluto, thus challenging Einstein to become a definite vehicle for establishing through his life what was released as a transforming, universalizing impulse at the Pluto/Uranus conjunction before his birth (in the last two degrees of Aries in 1850-51). The Virgo (Uranus) path thus refers to what was released through Einstein's innovative mind (third house Uranus) and to his utter dedication to the difficult, and thankless, task he undertook after he had already made his reputation as a 'genius.' Along this path he had to meet many deep personal crises (Virgo and the sixth house), not the least of which was facing what he termed the "biggest mistake" of his life: signing a letter to President Roosevelt urging the U.S. to commit a considerable amount of its already-taxed-by-wartime resources to the development of an atomic bomb before, it was feared, the Germans did.

Although the configuration's point of resolution lies in Einstein's sixth house, Einstein never truly resolved or satisfactorily answered the great philosophical questions engendered by his early work in relativity. While younger physicists readily adopted the statistical, probability-based world-view of quantum mechanics, Einstein nevertheless determinedly maintained that "God does not play dice with the universe." He sought an encompassing alternative to quantum mechanics to no avail throughout the remainder of his life. He never adapted to the role of a public figure, either, and in true twelfth house fashion increasingly withdrew to his study at home and at Princeton University.

In Werner Erhard's chart, the Sun opposes a retrograde (naturally!) Saturn in the tenth house, and both are squared by the seventh house Moon. This is a configuration involving the most basic of factors, challenging individualization and independent emergence through marriage and close personal relationship conditioned by a strong Mother-Image—all conditioned by what must have been a difficult or in some way lacking father-son relationship. But here marriage *releases* the psychic tension involved in the 'wake up and individualize' Sun/Saturn opposition. *Resolution* comes only through first-house personal integration and being, through perhaps undergoing a 'test of isolation'* by separating oneself from the taken-for-granted patterns of one's time, adopting and maintaining an unpopular stance.

The T-square in Ram Das's chart also involves the Moon at the 'short end.' The Moon is in the sixth house of retraining, spritual discipleship and personal crises of readjustment, while the bisected opposition is between tenth-house Venus and third-house Neptune. Public life is again involved, but resolution comes through the twelfth house—through the universalization, indeed ritual-like illumination, of all day-to-day activities, and by carrying the self-sacrificing burden of participating in and leading a large-scale social movement.

The T-square in Albert Schweitzer's chart is between Jupiter and Neptune (in opposition to one another) and Mercury (square to both). The Jupiter/Neptune opposition points to to the need to transform and make entirely inclusive the sense of social participation. Moreover, it symbolizes the necessity of making religion more than a merely cultural, taken-for-granted activity. The challenge is to make religion a truly spiritual pursuit, whose great Images live in and through one's open and transformed being. Mercury (in Capricorn and in superior conjunction with the Sun)—Schweitzer's formalistic mind—potentially provides an outlet for expressing what is symbolized by this Jupiter/Neptune opposition. Both Mercury and the Sun are on a degree symbolizing a "total commitment to a transcendent goal." Yet the configuration's resolution points toward Cancer and the seventh house, toward "the focalization of complex inner potentialities in harmonic and concrete relationship" (Cancer 24°). Schweitzer apparently had such a relationship, not only with his wife, but also with his original and highly focused image of the person of Jesus, who became for Schweitzer a living presence and true exemplar.

Another triangle, a grand trine, is also present in Schweitzer's chart. It links Venus, the Moon and Uranus. Since Saturn is opposite

---

*Cf. *An Astrological Triptych: The Way Through,* "Twelve basic challenges and tests of individual existence," by Dane Rudhyar (ASI Publishers, New York: 1978).

Uranus, and is therefore at the 'resolution point' of the trine between Venus and the Moon, a 'kite' formation results. The integrative 'vision' symbolized by the grand trine can thus be exteriorized via Saturn's power of organization.

Grand trines are also found in the horoscopes of Jimmy Carter, Herman Melville (cf. Chapter 2), and the two charts in which two grand trines interpenetrated to form Stars of David. Carter's grand trine involves ninth-house Pluto, fifth-house Uranus and first-house Moon—a perhaps 'fateful' personal involvement in expressing a vision of large-scale, cathartic social processes. In Carter's case, however, Saturn rises before the Moon, and the Moon is just separating from its prenatal conjunction with Saturn. Expression of the Pluto/ Uranus trine (rooted in the same Pluto/Uranus conjunction as Einstein's Pluto/Uranus square) is therefore heavily influenced by Saturn—i.e., by the Father-Image and conservative, perhaps taken-for-granted or dogmatic social imperatives and taboos.

We have already found triangles formed by a square and two sesquiquadrates—what we have called a "Finger of the World"— and we point again to the horoscopes of Werner Erhard and Ram Das, and also to the chart of Henry Ford. Erhard's Moon/Saturn square points with two sesquiquadrates to second-house Pluto, which is also conjunct the Moon's South Node. The great question posed by any focal second-house indication is always how best to use one's resources, whatever they may be. Here, an amassing of wealth or public renown can be seen as a way of releasing the biopsychic tension involved in the Moon/Saturn square. The resolution of the configuration points, however, to the eighth house, the field in which an individual's resources are shared with others.

A similar house-situation is found in the birth-chart of Henry Ford, whose sesquiquadrate triangle 'points' to the Moon in the second house (at the cusp of the third). The square is a waxing one between Venus and Uranus—a challenge to transform one's sense of values and one's capacity to give form to one's ideas. Ford's industrial innovations and the automobiles they mass-produced surely brought him much in the way of monetary gain, and helped to make of him an autocratic empire-builder. While the configuration's resolution points to Leo and the eighth-house/ninth-house cusp, Ford's

Sun is there (he was born at Full Moon) and whatever resolution there may have been seems rather to have fueled the already fully formed Leonine ego. Nevertheless, Ford, in true Full Moon fashion, stood as a real-life exemplar—in his case, of the Horatio Alger 'myth' of a man who, through his own initiative (and perhaps ruthlessness) managed to go from (almost) rags to riches, accomplishing much of social significance along the way.

The triangle in Ram Das's chart links the square between eighth-house Saturn and eleventh-house Sun/Uranus to the third-house Neptune. The use of drugs or a yearning for unorthodox or mystical experiences can be interpreted as a release from the biopsychic tensions of an overly rigid, traditional background restricting satisfying and transformative interpersonal and social relationships. The resolution of the configuration points to the place occupied by tenth-house Venus. The Sabian Symbol for Venus's degree (coincidentally the same degree as Werner Erhard's Saturn) pictures a large cross *"illumined by a shaft of light. . . lies on rocks surrounded by sea mist."* The degree challenges focused individualization (the cross) out of the undifferentiated psychic and collective 'sea,' and indicates that a *"spiritual blessing"* (the shaft of light) will strengthen those *"who, happen what may, stand uncompromisingly for their own truth."*

A triangle involving two quincunxes and a sextile is found in the horoscope of George Sand. Saturn and Neptune in the seventh and eighth houses are sextile, and both are quincunx the first-house Moon. The Saturn/Neptune sextile is waning, beginning in the Saturn/Neptune cycle the final phases of a process symbolically transforming the Father-Image and heralding the acceptance of broader social archetypes. A new integration, on the basis of transformed relationships, is possible and challenged here. The midpoint of the sextile (the point opposite the Moon) coincides with Jupiter at 27° Libra. While the symbolic references to relationships are obvious here, Jupiter's Sabian degree emphasizes the ability to *"transcend the conflicts and pressures of the personal life."* Ms. Sand's personal life—especially where relationships were concerned—was indeed subject to conflicts and pressures, both inner and outer. She was indeed forced, and at least partially able, to become objective to and transcend them.

Another triangle involving a sextile and two quincunxes appears in the chart of Werner Erhard. As in the case of George Sand, a waning sextile between Saturn and Uranus forms the configuration's base. Mercury in Libra in the 5th house opposes the midpoint of the 10th/12th house sextile. Release of the sextile challenging reorganization at the level of the Father-Image and of social archetypes is through creative mental activity and communication (5th house Mercury) and interpersonal relationships (Libra). With Saturn and Uranus in such a relationship, it is interesting to note the eclectic nature of the est training and particularly how much of the American New Thought movement from earlier this century has been incorporated into it. The configuration's resolution, however, is symbolized by the early degrees of Aries in the 11th house—a challenge to pioneering social transformation. Since the 11th house follows the 10th, it also poses the question, What will a successful individual do with or about his success, and as well with the rebellious attitude or feeling of deep discontent that made him act as a reformer or revolutionary to begin with?

Such concepts could be developed much further and a whole book written about rectangular and triangular aspect patterns. But enough may have been said to indicate how the basic ideas might be extended and applied to particular situations. We have interspersed what we hope will be useful examples throughout the text, but if they are to prove valuable, they should be studied in depth along with complete biographical information for the persons whose charts have been used.

The study of simple rectangular and triangular configurations is only a basic step toward the visualization and interpretation of the whole pattern made by all ten planets of a birth-chart. As a foundation, it does help to develop one's mind to see and think in terms of the whole chart, rather than according to the merely analytical procedure, which is satisfied to list aspects and planetary positions as separate factors and somehow to see what they might add up to. Both methods are nevertheless valid when used together—as they always should be—the former to present a whole view of the individual person and his or her potentialities, the latter to clarify the many detailed features of the personality in everyday life.

6.
Interpretation and Intuition: On Putting It All Together and "Howto"

In the traditional approach to chart-interpretation, each of the many factors in a horoscope is considered separately. The astrologer, having memorized a myriad of definitions and keywords (or stocked his or her library well with a variety of tabulated texts), applies these, one by one, to the positions of planets in houses and zodiacal signs, and to the aspects each planet—as 'ruler' of a definite category of things, characteristics or events—makes singly to other factors in the chart. Then he or she tries to synthesize them all—an often difficult task because so much data has been generated, and many of the definitions contradict one another.

Various more or less mechanical or mathematical procedures have been devised to solve this problem of synthesis. Some astrologers advocate set formulas for interpretation—for example, Sun sign first, then Ascendant, then the Moon. Others start by interpreting the Ascendant and first house, then work their way around the wheel of houses, including in their interpretation of each separate area of life the planets in the houses and the zodiacal signs on the cusps. Still others advocate beginning an interpretation from the house with Aries on its cusp and following the zodiac around from there. Variations on such themes are practically endless. More mathematically-minded practitioners have devised quantitative ways of ascertaining the relative importance and strengths of all the components of a chart.

Only very recently has a new approach to astrology and chart interpretation begun to emphasize the element of *Gestalt*—the overall pattern of a horoscope. Such a point of view becomes increasingly significant and necessary when we look at a birth-chart in the spirit in which we presented it in Chapter 1, as a message from the whole Sky (or universe or cosmos) to the growing, developing whole person.

This trend toward Gestalt in astrology has developed during the last fifty years, paralleling a similar approach in philosophy and psychology. The astrologer following it looks at the birth-chart as a whole and tries to grasp the meaning of the total pattern which planets, house cusps, aspects, etc. make. The first astrologer to deal with overall horoscopic patterns was Marc Edmund Jones, who classified basic chart shapes into seven categories.* When one truly follows a Gestalt approach, however, pigeon-holing an overall planetary pattern into one of several categories is not enough. If the old approach of adding essentially separate and perhaps contradictory factors together is still followed, the Gestalt classification of any particular horoscope becomes one more piece of data to be somehow fitted together with a myriad of others. True Gestalt awareness means that the astrologer must look at the birth-chart as a whole first, and start the entire interpretation from there. It is an esthetical approach— that is to say, the astrologer must look at the chart as a lover of art would look at a beautiful painting, seeking to understand the integrity and the meaning of the whole without paying exclusive attention to its separate parts.† A truly Gestalt-based interpretation allows the meaning of the chart to flow from a sense of pattern or form, from the way a particular chart is structured, according to the principles underlying its unique make-up.

This is because only a birth-chart's Gestalt—its particular overall pattern as a whole—is unique. No single factor in a birth-chart is unique, not even the exact degree on the Ascendant. Any one placement, position or aspect has happened before, and it will happen again in the relatively near or distant future. What is unique and integral about a birth-chart—as about the person for whom it stands

---

*Cf. his book *The Guide to Horoscope Interpretation* (McKay: 1941).
†The esthetical nature of such an approach was developed for, I believe, the first time in my book *The Astrology of Personality* (1934-35).—DR

as a symbol of seed-potentialities—is the total interrelatedness of all its components.

What is required to see and understand a birth-chart's unique Gestalt is a holistic ability we exercise daily, but because it is so much a part of our common experience we don't question it or realize its significance. When we meet a person, we do not meet a nose, two eyes, two arms, etc. Unless something is obviously missing or blatantly over-emphasized, we never think of running down a check-list to investigate all the basic 'parts.' Neither do we meet and interact with a set of character traits or psychological categories of behavior. We are not normally aware of any separateness of anatomical or personality 'parts' as distinct from the whole person. What characterizes an individual person is not a number of separate elements, but the structure and dynamic operation of interrelated physiological and psychological factors which in their togetherness constitute what we call his or her appearance, character or personality.

Nevertheless, within this pattern of wholeness, one or two factors among the many which impinge upon our senses and minds may stand out as being stronger than the others. The sheer strength of one factor considered separately is not what matters most. It is the way in which the strong factor is integrated into the operation of the total person. To the astrologer or psychologist, what should be most important is not merely the fact that one aspect of a person's nature is stronger than others. The concern should be the way in which the dominant factor is or can be integrated into the others and in turn is affected by them.

A similar truth is found when we consider a man or woman living in a community. Modern psychology has given up the romantic notion that an individual can be understood in a kind of splendid isolation regardless of where the person comes from or lives. A person can only be understood in relation to his or her environment and times—i.e., in relation to family, social group, culture and the complex pressures of the period. The entire constellation of these factors at one's birth and throughout life, together with the meaning one gives to them and therefore the way in which one responds to them, is what makes up the significance, integrity and uniqueness of one's life.

All of the above applies equally to factors in a horoscope. When we approach a chart, we should not (at least not at first) be solely aware of *a* Mars, *a* Venus, *a* fifth house, etc. as separate, definitely defined entities. Neither should we be aware primarily of *a* square, *an* opposition, or even *a* T-square or a particular kind of rectangle. We should rather perceive first the whole constellation—a pattern which is always greater than the sum of its parts. The nature of the whole and the relationships of all its parts, not only to one another but to the whole itself, is what gives to the parts their specific qualities and meanings. Only within the whole is each part related to all other parts. Only in total interrelatedness with one another and with the whole do all the parts, specific relationships and groups of relationships between them acquire their full significance.

Such alchemical transformations of meanings are multiplied many-fold in the total interrelatedness of a horoscope's overall pattern. Any planet, placement or aspect is thus one factor within a group of factors, the birth-chart's whole pattern—i.e., the state reached by the solar system as a whole at the time of a person's birth. Every planet operates, whether or not it forms exact aspects with any other planet. (Indeed the very fact that a planet makes *no* aspect whatsoever—a rare occurrence if we use the full spectrum of arithmetical and geometrical aspects as well as proper orbs and a sense of process—is an important factor to consider in itself.) Every aspect also operates in some way. But its specific operation, which of its many possible meanings is called into play in a particular chart (and at a particular time in a person's life), how the actualization of its potentialities can be involved in the actualization of all other possibilities in the chart and vice versa: all this depends upon the way a particular aspect is woven into the overall pattern of the chart and upon the operation of every other aspect.

It is not easy, initially, to see birth-charts as wholes in which all component parts are at once meaningfully related to one another and to the whole. It requires a rather special faculty which operates among artists contemplating a work of art and responding to what it radiates as a whole, and in some scientists and mathematicians who, confronted with or contemplating a complex pattern, are able to 'feel' what kind of solution to a problem will be found. Then they carefully work out a detailed demonstration, step by step, arriving at approximately the same result they had anticipated.

What is it that allows a scientist or mathematician to 'feel' an elegant solution before its logical deduction? What enables a person to achieve mental synthesis without prior intellectual analysis?

On the one hand, practice and training geared toward the perception of definite structural patterns within complex wholes. On other other hand, one cannot detect, let alone resonate to the meaning of "definite structural patterns" unless one thoroughly understands the principles according to which such patterns are built and acquire meaning. We are speaking here of acquiring what in Chapter 1 we called "back of the neck knowledge"—knowledge which is so much a part of the knower that the person forgets about knowing it. It is effective knowledge because it is unself-conscious and therefore always spontaneously and appropriately available when 'tickled' in the right way.

Such knowledge becomes in practice intuition. It does not develop from mere memorization or intellectual self-programming, although these are steps or phases in the process of activating and developing the intuitive faculty. Active intuition requires as a foundation a deeply felt understanding (literally, to stand under) of principles. As basic principles are truly understood, they form a new foundation (what one stands on) for one's thinking, future studies and application of what one has learned. The principles one learns thus help to organize the mind and thinking of the learner. When one truly learns basic principles and builds what they signify into one's consciousness and being, the learning—both in terms of its content and the process of learning itself—*transforms the learner.* To the degree that the principles one learns are 'cosmic' or universal in scope, to the same degree will the mind be structured along universal lines. To the degree universal principles organize one's mind and thinking, to the same degree will one be able to perceive what is universal and whole in every particularity—be it an astrological chart, a person's life-story and destiny, or an algebraic equation.

For the scientist or mathematician, the principles of scientific methodology, number, logic and mathematical operations form the foundation of operative intuition. Over the course of his training, they become so ingrained in him, so much a part of his being and consciousness that he 'forgets' he knows them. He does not need to consult a textbook of possible solutions or try to solve a problem by a process of eliminating operations which will not work. Instead, he thinks in terms of all the principles and operations he has ever learned —or rather, they act through him; his thinking is structured by them. All the years of his education and experience are present and focused in him as he contemplates a problem.

In order to fully activate intuition, so too must a would-be astrologer become thoroughly and unself-consciously familiar with the 'tools of the trade'—i.e., planets, houses, aspects, signs, progressions, transits, etc. But this familiarity must not be willy-nilly, without structure or form. Each basic tool must be understood in a consistent, coherent way according to what it symbolizes at its own level. This means that the astrologer must also understand the principles of cycle, process, number and symbolism according to which basic astrological tools acquire meaning. In this sense, learning astrology is actually a process of learning a variety of consistent, even compelling and exciting 'stories'—the story of the planets, the story of the houses, the story of the signs, etc.

In this book, we have told, consistently and interestingly, we hope, the story of astrological aspects. The stories of other astrological factors are told in other books, and an annotated reading list is supplied in Appendix II. The homework of the would-be astrologer, before he or she ever faces a horoscope and a client, is to learn and think through these various astrological 'stories.' There is no 'howto' apply them directly to birth-charts *and* achieve the kind of mental synthesis which does not follow purely intellectual analysis. There are no short-cut techniques of fitting keywords into sentences that can substitute for an astrologer's active intuition. One can proceed, however, through a structured process of learning and assimilating astrological and psychological principles, and on the basis of such a process one can activate and develop intuition.

For example, there are many ways to approach and consider the zodiac. One can begin the 'story' of the signs starting from the vernal equinox and the sign Aries, or with Capricorn and the winter solstice. One can take the signs in successive pairs (zyzygies), or in terms of a threefold dialectic moving from a cardinal, to a fixed, to a mutable sign. Similarly, one can tell the 'story' of the houses beginning at the Nadir or at the Ascendant. Houses can also be given meaning in terms of the way we usually number them, counterclockwise, or in terms of the Sun's passage through the sky during the day—clockwise. The planets, too, can be considered and given meaning in a number of ways—heliocentrically, geocentrically, in various pairings, etc. Like the signs in relation to the zodiac, and the houses in relation to the complete diurnal circle, planets also acquire meaning only in the context of the whole solar system. They represent dynamic centers of activities and functions, and each planet reveals a different facet of its nature when considered in relation to each other planet. A different sort of picture emerges each time one tells a 'story' from a different point of view; and each 'story' is valid at its own level *if* one is careful to be consistent and flexible in one's interpretation. Each 'story' of a whole symbol thus reveals its parts in a new light.

While telling and retelling these astrological 'stories,' it is not important to be able to apply them directly to particular birthcharts. The process of learning astrology in this story-telling spirit should be approached as an adventure—to borrow a phrase, an "adventure in consciousness." Its purpose is to allow the universal principles behind astrological symbols to permeate and restructure the student's mind and thinking. Granted, such a process takes a relatively long time, several years at least. But in a culture in which the training of a physician requires almost twelve years beyond standard elementary and secondary schooling, and of a psychologist nearly seven, why should we expect the training of an astrologer to be appreciably shorter?

In addition to being well-versed in all the nuances of astrology *per se*, the astropsychologist has also to deal with human nature in all its aspects and manifestations—individual and collective, structural, developmental, relational, cultural, historical, etc. Any counselor must be objective to—and be able to state for potential clients —his or her general philosophy of life and approach to psychology. A counselor must have an understanding of the deeper social and cultural issues behind the types of problems clients face, and a sense of what is necessary, practical and possible in human development among contemporaries. These disciplines too, like astrological symbols, can be treated as 'stories' to be told, retold from a variety of points of view, and thought about in depth.

One of the best ways for an astrologer to sharpen technical skills and develop holistic vision is to read biographies. A horoscope, timed or solar if necessary, the whole life of progressions and major transits can be drawn up for study along with a particular person's biography or memoirs. More than any other technique, studies of whole lives can provide the kind of insight on which a deep and intuitive understanding of human nature develops.* Such understanding is crucial for an astrologer, because it is one thing to be able to deduce problems or diagnose psychological difficulties from a horoscope; it is quite another to have the kind of deep understanding of human functioning necessary truly to counsel a client, to help give the most constructive meaning possible to life-circumstances, and to understand the best, most 'growthful' and *dharmic* way to face and deal with whatever problems or difficulties the client meets in life.

When on the basis of such in-depth preparation, an astrologer contemplates a birth-chart, focused in the practitioner's very being is a fully assimilated synthesis of astrological and, in the broadest sense of the term, psychological principles, *and* the mental structures built during the process of learning about them. Having become thoroughly familiar with all the basic astrological tools, the astrologer is able to notice everything in a chart all at once. The act of contemplating the birth-chart becomes a single gesture in which the astrologer embraces the entire horoscope with his or her eyes and total mental being—and not merely with an intellect laden with memorized, disparate definitions and keywords.

Since the various 'stories' behind basic astrological tools have also become second nature to the astrologer, they can begin to *retell*

---

*The serious student is urged to study the lives of persons whose birth-charts we have used as examples throughout this book. Only within such a context can the full impact of what we have pointed out be seen, for it has been with such studies as a background that we have written. While a full presentation of our examples' broadest implications has been beyond the scope of this book, the student who follows up our presentation with his or her own researches will be amply rewarded. Not only what we have written, but also what we have only been able to hint at will become clearer.

themselves in terms of their particular interrelatedness in the horo-scope. The astrologer who thoroughly knows, for example, the 'Mars story,' the 'Saturn story,' etc., instantly knows what these two sym-bolic centers of activities would have to do with one another when in a particular aspect. Since the astrologer also knows all the 'aspect stories,' he or she also knows what squares have to do with opposi-tions or trines, how what is required by each aspect interrelates with what is required by all the others. The practitioner approaches the chart as a unique whole first, allowing the total Gestalt—the princi-ples on which it is based—to tell him or her what is most basic in the chart, and therefore where and how to begin an interpretation. The chart *interprets itself*, so to speak, through the astrologer who has learned to think in its own language—*astrologese*—and who thereby allows the chart to reveal what in it, as a unique whole, is significant.

Then, when the astrologer sits with a client, the same kind of single-gesture, open-ended mental embrace can also apply to the cli-ent's life-pattern. It too is a 'story,' a process unfolding step by step throughout the client's life. Astrologers should become as adept as psychologists and social workers in eliciting from clients a brief, but basic history covering the salient facts of the client's background. With this as preparation, what had previously been chart interpre-tation on the part of the astrologer alone can become with a client's active co-operation a truly deep and meaningful *life* interpretation. By applying the symbolic indications of the birth-chart, progressions and major transits to the facts of the client's history and life-pattern, the perceptive and intuitive astrologer can allow the light of mean-ing to shine through the opacity of particular events in the client's life. These become more than mere happenstance or the result of a cause-and-effect progression—whether this would be considered purely in terms of the outward momentum of events or the inner mechanics of psychological patterns.

What astrological symbols should do to the events of a client's life is to reveal their deepest significance—that is, to show how and for what purpose events have occurred as particular manifestations of phases in the client's process of overall development. This occurs when the practitioner is able to superimpose universal principles of process on the facts of the client's life, when the astrologer is able to recognize that a sequence of events in a client's life is typical of what happens in a certain astrological 'story.' On such a basis, the astrologer can extrapolate from the events not only what the next phase in the process is likely to entail, but also the events' meaning: what they were and are meant to accomplish in the client's life.

On the basis of a client's history, an experienced and intuitive psychotherapist can often predict with what seems uncanny accuracy future developments in the client's life. This is because the therapist has seen and understood so many complete human 'stories' that he or she can anticipate how a particular variation will probably progress. It is necessary to say 'probably,' however, becuase the psychologist sees primarily only the mechanics—the psychological 'how'—operating behind sequences of events and circumstances. While the psychologist sees a good deal of what is 'normal' and expectable in terms of human *reaction*, he or she has no way of seeing an overall picture of what is possible for a particular person in terms of conscious *response* or *dharma*. The psychologist, unlike the astrologer, has no birth-chart from which to intuitively deduce the potentialities inherent in a client's birth. The psychologist therefore has no way of knowing what the client's problems or life-circumstances *are for*, i.e., what they are meant to actualize in the process of the client's overall development.

Thus, the usual type of counselor can only operate on the equivalent of the old astrological dictum "Character is destiny," and its therapeutic correlate, "Change character, change destiny"—or on a more modern, but essentially little-changed restatement of these: "We create our own reality." From the point of view of a truly process-oriented astrology, both of these statements are only partially true. It is obvious that a person with a chip on his shoulder creates his own reality by inviting angry or defensive others to knock it off. His 'character' does indeed to a great extent shape his 'destiny' and a picture that he lives in an explosive, unstable world from which he must further insulate himself. But even such a person did not create the society and the family into which he was born and to whose pressures he was forced to react.

The fact is that all of us are born into situations conditioned by circumstances long antedating our birth. We *react* to their pressures mostly unconsciously through our youth and formative years, primarily in terms of our innate temperaments and in ways that are mirror complements of the pressures themselves. Having no control over the form the pressures take, we essentially have no control over our complementary reactions to them: we are like molten metal assuming the negative shape of the positive, pre-cast mold into which it is poured.

As vessels are formed to certain aesthetic dimensions and utilitarian shapes depending upon the function they are ultimately meant to perform, we can only assume that there is an underlying purpose for the shape of the particular mold into which we are 'poured.' Yet the process of creating a 'negative' to a mold's 'positive' is only one step in the process of sculpting a vessel. It is analogous in human development to the period of youth and adolescent rebellion, when a person reacts against the pressures of family and society. If the process continues in its usual way, another 'pouring' will be made, and eventually a vessel resembling its initial parent mold will be produced. This is essentially what happens to people, particularly in their late 20's and 30's, if the basic tone of their life has been primarily a reaction against the pressures of their youth. Such a person first reacts to the pressures, then reacts against the reaction, ultimately becoming like what he first reacted against.

On the other hand, after the rebellion of adolescence—which today often extends up through the mid-20's or later—a person has the possibility of becoming objective both to the nature of the pressures against which he or she is reacting, and to the reactions themselves. It then becomes possible for the person to give meaning to the pressures and reactions—primarily by seeing them as phases of larger processes. According to the meaning given them, the person becomes able not merely to react, but to respond deliberately to the circumstances of life—which by then have already been set up and have acquired, if not a life of their own, at least a momentum in a general direction.

Did the person create the reality of these life-circumstances among and because of which he or she 'awakens'? Before even attempting to answer this question, we should realize that the attempt should not be taken lightly. This is a question which has, in one form or another and sometimes literally, bedevilled human beings since time immemorial. Its simplicity is deceptive, for interwoven into such a query are all the great and deep issues facing mankind throughout the ages: What is the nature and purpose of human existence? Of the universe itself? The writers of the Book of Job phrased it: Why does evil manifest in the life of a seemingly righteous man?

Most fundamentally, the answer we give to the question "Do we create our own reality?" depends upon the meaning we give to the word 'I.' If by 'I' we mean our experience of being 'I, myself—Paul or Jane,' we actually refer to the ego (which literally means merely 'I')—that is, to the outcome of a process begun with the birth of a human organism at a particular time and place. The organism has an innate temperament and genetic make-up—variations on the general theme of being human and parallel at the biological level to the social and cultural inheritance a person 'comes into' at birth—and the organism as a whole reacts in characteristic ways to the pressures of its early environment. These reactions are referred, first, to a diffuse sense of organic wholeness, and later to the centralizing ego, itself structured around the name the child is called and learns to identify itself by.

When we answer the question "What is 'I' " in such a way, we must answer our original question about creating our own reality in the negative. For how can an 'I' whose process of becoming focused and concrete begins at birth have shaped or be responsible for what antedated its birth and later impinged upon its nascent senses and consciousness, enabling it to become, not only what it is, but conscious of itself? Such an 'I' creates its own reality only in a limited and purely personal way, according to how it reacts to the pressures of its environment. It reacts in good measure according to the body's innate temperament, but how could an 'I' developing out of the experiences of a particular organism with a certain temperament have 'created' the organism's temperament?

Such questions can be and often are answered by including in the concept of 'I' the notion of a transcendent soul which chooses for reasons of 'learning lessons' or 'soul evolution' its future temperament, birth-environment, parents, time and place of birth—and therefore the horoscope under which it was born. If we define 'I' in such a way, we can indeed answer our original question about creating our own reality in the affirmative. But to so identify 'I' as or with such a soul seems to us a basic semantic, metaphysical and psychological fallacy. Certainly, the concept of 'soul' is to the 'I' who thinks about it merely that: a concept not grounded in experience or observation. Moreover, it is a concept formulated long before the person's birth. It is part of the cultural inheritance he or she 'comes into' at birth, part of what shapes his reactions to life. Nevertheless, there may be something like a soul in some way *associated with* the particular person who claims it.* But saying that the person *is* a soul, when what the person experiences as himself or herself and can to some extent control, is what should best be called the ego, makes little sense and is ultimately confusing. If something transcendent to what we normally identify as 'I, myself' has at least a significant part in shaping our reality, we should acknowledge it for what it is—which is actually rather mysterious, complex, and probably our personalization of greater forces and processes operating in the universe. We have previously referred to these as *karma* and *dharma*, as the residua of past actions and the necessity of compensating for or furthering what they have produced.

Thus the alternative we feel we must pose to the popular dictum "We create our own reality" is that we *respond* to the reality with which we are confronted. *Collectively*, and over many generations, human beings as a species operating in a variety of cultures have created a more or less common reality. Within that collective context we do not create our personal reality any more than a seed creates the rain and warm sunshine to which it responds by germinating or remaining quiescent in the spring. We are responsible for our responses to the life-circumstances into which we awaken as would-be individuals and adults. Yet, in all humility and not in evasive pride, we must also acknowledge the greater collective and universal forces and processes having shaped these circumstances focused into our particular lives and personalities.

From a process-oriented point of view, our birth-charts reveal the highest of our potentialities—that is, the 'story' in seed of what we may face in order to take what kind of evolutionary, i.e., karmic

---

*Cf. *The Planetarization of Consciousness*, by Dane Rudhyar (ASI Publishers, New York: 1977), Chapter 7: "Soul-Field, Mind and Reincarnation."

and dharmic 'next steps.' Whether we created our reality matters only if we desire forcibly to change it. If, on the other hand, we desire to fulfill its highest potentialities, we must illumine it with meaning.

We are prepared to do so astrologically when we have done our astrological, psychological and philosophical 'homework'; when we are able to approach a birth-chart as a unique whole and allow our interpretation of it to unfold according to the way the chart itself is structured, according to the principles underlying its particular make-up; when we are able to pierce through the opacity of a client's life pattern and allow it to become translucent to the light of its own meaning, to the glow of the life-pattern's own special purpose and process, which shines through what could previously only be perceived as events or psychological patterns.

In conclusion—and perhaps as a new beginning for some readers—all of the preceding takes on a more definite and inspiring meaning if we consider what an astrology student thinks a study of astrology *is for*. If he or she aspires to learn astrology in order quickly to delineate birth-charts, to collect fees and impress clients by stating a few more or less spectacular possibilities or events, the process-oriented approach we have presented here may not be what is wanted. The would-be astrologer who is ready and willing to devote some years of his or her life to preparation and study may not want to do so unless the student feels that such work will be able to give real help to clients, and also give a new dimension to the astrologer's own mind. What is to be most deeply and meaningfully gained by dedicating at least part of one's life to the study of astrology is a profound expansion and deepening of one's consciousness, and of the way in which one meets life and all its crises and opportunities.

C.G. Jung said that any analysis which does not transform both the analysand and the analyst is not wholly successful; the purpose of astrology is not merely to counsel others. It is also, as important, to enable the astrologer to better understand his or her own life-process, to see it as a phase in the larger, universal process of which it is a meaningful, dynamic expression.

Appendix I

Example Horoscopes

Neils Bohr
Oct. 7, 1885
Solar Chart

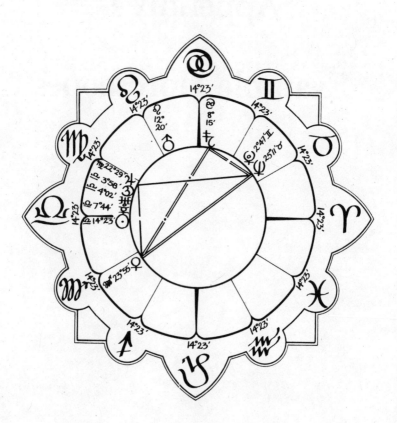

Jerry Brown
Apr. 7, 1938
34N03   118W15
20:00 U.T.

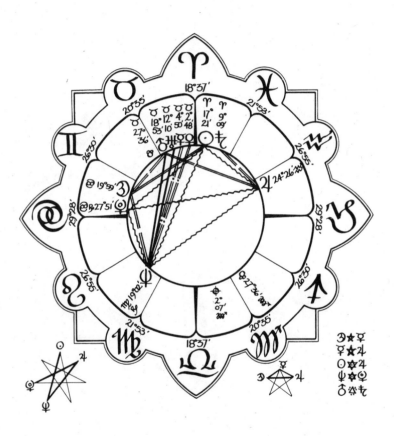

Andrew Carnegie
Nov. 25, 1835
56N04   3W28
6:14 U.T.

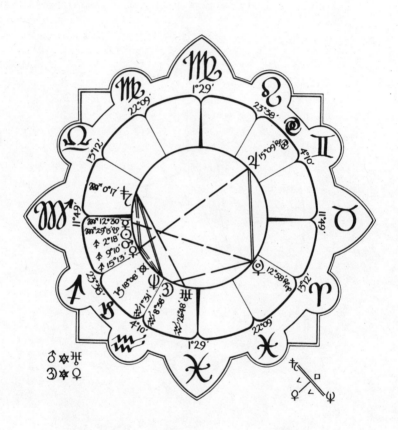

Jimmy Carter
Oct. 1, 1924
32N02   84W24
13:00 U.T.

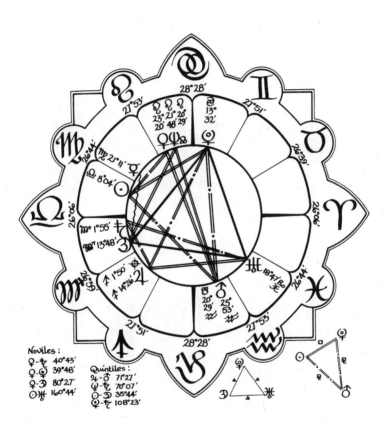

Paul Case
Oct. 3, 1844
43N06   77W27
11:00 U.T.

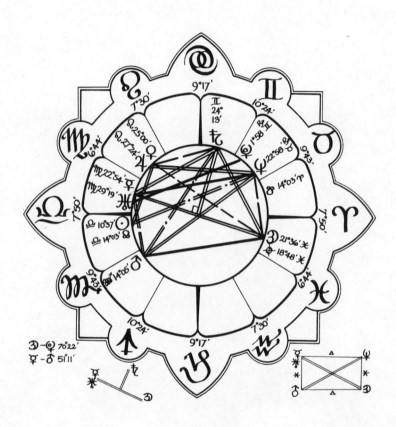

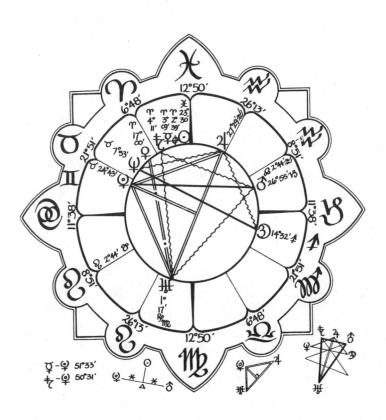

215

Werner Erhard
Sept. 5, 1935
39N57   75W10
27:25 U.T.

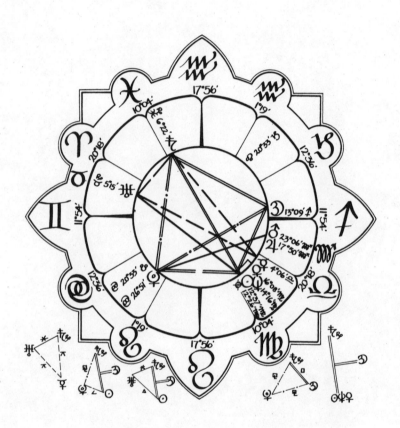

Henry Ford
July 30, 1863
42N18   83W15
19:55 U.T.

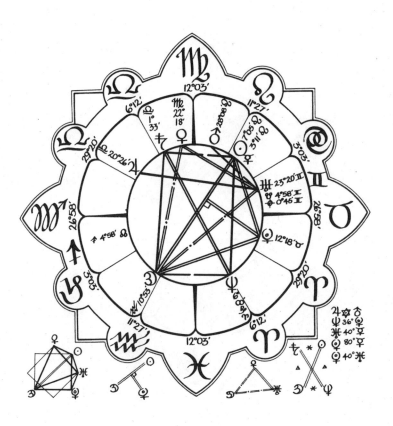

Mohandas Gandhi
Oct. 2, 1869
21N30   70E00
2:53 U.T.

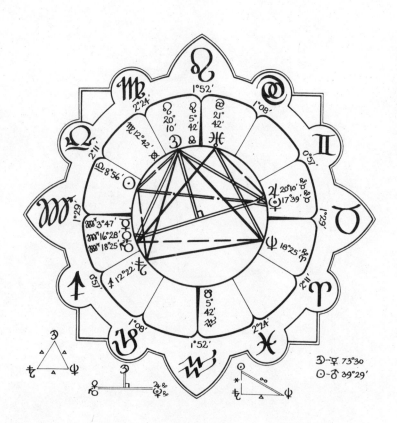

Dag Hammarskjold
July 29, 1905
Solar Chart

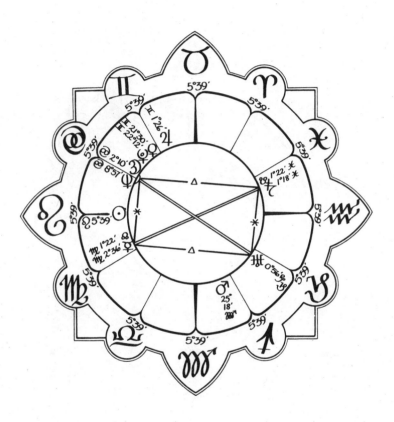

219

J. Edgar Hoover
Jan. 1, 1895
Solar Chart

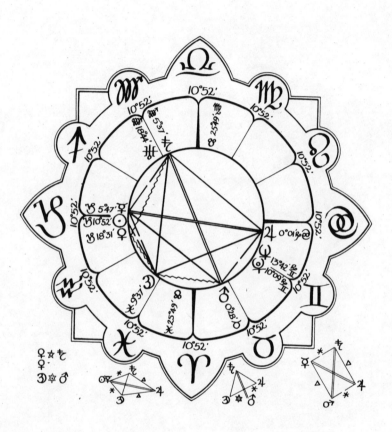

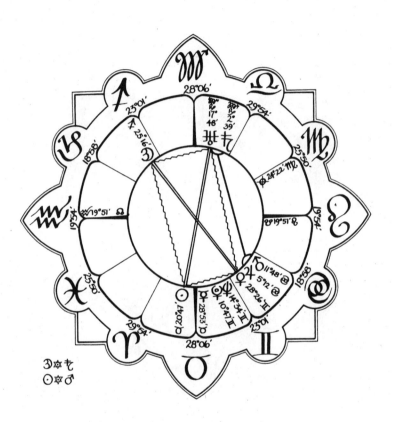

Herman Melville
Aug. 1, 1819
40N45   73W57
Solar Chart

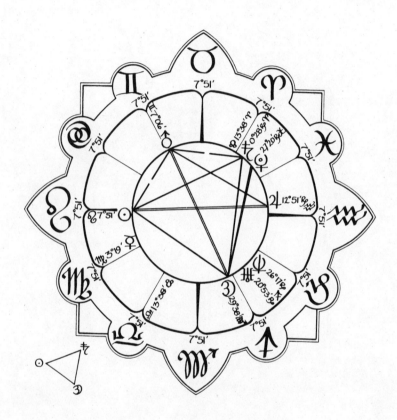

V. Nijinsky
Mar. 12, 1890
50N27   30E32
20:29 U.T.

Ram Das
Apr. 6, 1931
42N22 71W04
14:20 U.T.

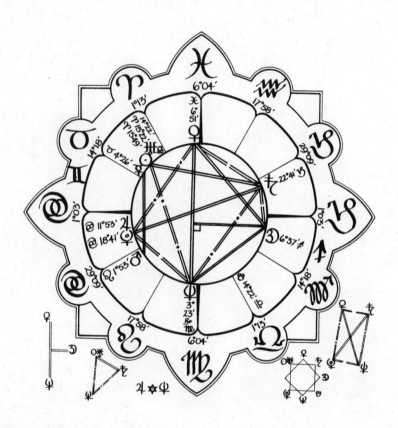

Franklin D. Roosevelt
Jan. 30, 1882
41N48   73W56
25:15 U.T.

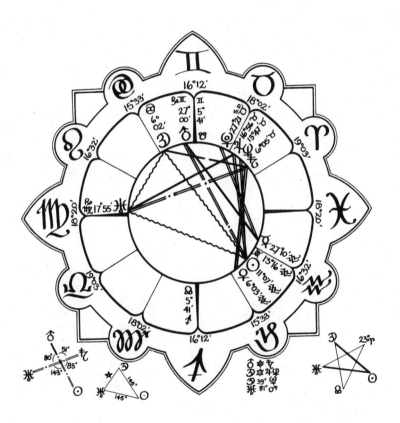

225

George Sand
July 1, 1804
48N50   2E20
22:06 U.T.

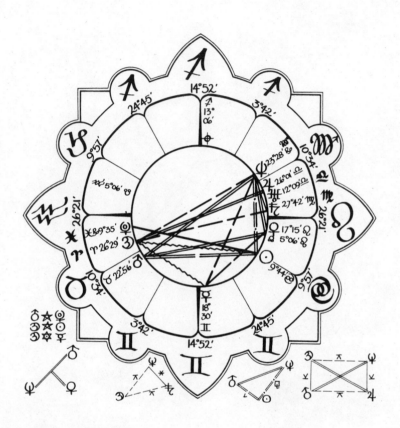

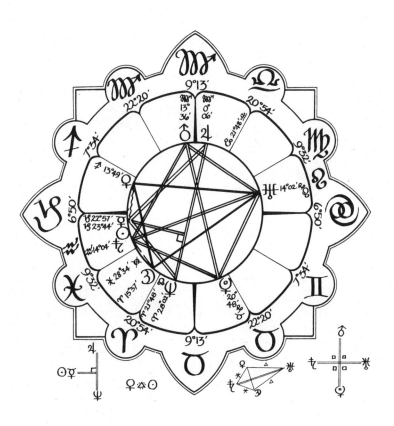

George Bernard Shaw
July 26, 1856
53N20   6W15
1:05 U.T.

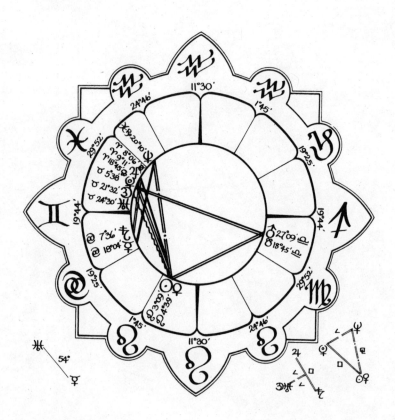

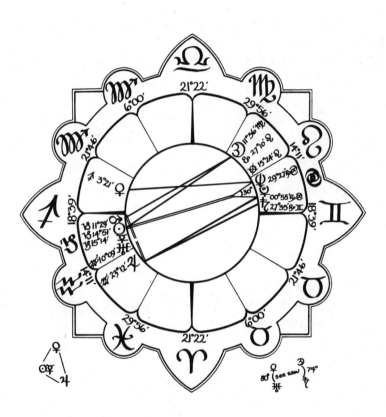

All example horoscopes have been recalculated with Campanus cusps on a DR-70 astrological computer. With the exception of the following, all birth-information was taken from *The Circle Book of Charts* (Revised Edition, 1979):

Edmund G. Brown, Jr.
April 7, 1938
43N03   118W15
20:00 U.T.
Original birth-data from
Brown by Orville Schell (New
York, Random House: 1978)
Rectification by A.L. Milner

Jimmy Carter
Oct. 1, 1924
32N02   84W24
13:00 U.T.
Chart in common usage

Werner Erhard
Sept. 5, 1935
39N57   75W10
27:25 U.T.
Werner Erhard by William
Warren Bartley (New York,
Crown Publishers: 1978)

Franklin Delano Roosevelt
Jan. 30, 1882
41N48   73W56
25:16 U.T.
Dane Rudhyar, *American
Astrology*, September, 1942

Albert Schweitzer
Jan. 14, 1875
48N45   8E00
6:22 U.T.
Dane Rudhyar, *Horoscope*,
March, 1949

Alan Watts
Jan. 6, 1915
51N25   0W00
6:20 U.T.
Autobiography,
In My Own Way

Appendix II

Suggested Reading By Subject

INTRODUCTORY STORIES:

The Practice of Astrology
    The First Step: To Understand the Nature and Purpose of
                             What One is About to Study
    The Second Step: To Assume Personal Responsibility for the
                             Use of One's Knowledge
    The Third Step: To Establish a Clear Procedure of Work

Person-Centered Astrology
    Astrology for New Minds; The Astrology of Self-Actualization

The Astrology of Personality
    Preface to the Third Edition
    First Section: 1. Astrology Faces Modern Thought
                     2. Astrology and Analytical Psychology
                     3. Individual, Collective, Creative and the
                        Cyclic Process
                     4. A Key to Astrological Symbolism
                     5. A Classification of Astrological Viewpoints

From Humanistic to Transpersonal Astrology

THE STORY OF ASTROLOGY'S DEVELOPMENT:

The Practice of Astrology
    The First Step: To Understand the Nature and Purpose of
                             What One is About to Study

Person-Centered Astrology
    Astrology for New Minds

The Astrological Houses: The Spectrum of Individual Experience
    Part One

The Astrology of Personality
    Prologue; First Section

From Humanistic to Transpersonal Astrology

The Galactic Dimension of Astrology (The Sun is Also a Star)
    Chapter 1.   Introduction to the Galactic Level of Con-
                     sciousness
    Chapter 2.   When the Sun is Seen as a Star
    Chapter 9.   The Challenge of Galacticity in Humanistic
                     Astrology

Fixed Stars:
  Astrological Timing: The Transition to the New Age
                    IV. Stars, Constellations and the Signs of
                        the Zodiac
  The Galactic Dimension of Astrology (The Sun is Also a Star)
                    Chapter 9

Horary Astrology and Oracular Techniques:
  The Practice of Astrology: The Twelfth Step
  An Astrological Mandala: Part Four

Sabian Degree Symbols:
  The Astrology of Personality: Chapter 10
  *An Astrological Mandala: The cycle of transformations and its
  360 symbolic phases*

This reading list is not meant to be exhaustive. All books listed have
been written by Dane Rudhyar unless otherwise noted. If not available at your local bookstore, they may be purchased by mail from
the New York Astrology Center, 127 Madison Avenue, New York,
NY 10016.

AURORA PRESS

Aurora Press is devoted to pioneering books that catalyze personal growth, balance and transformation. Aurora makes available in a digestible format, an innovative synthesis of ancient wisdom with twentieth century resources, integrating esoteric knowledge and daily life.

Recent titles include:

COMING HOME
Deborah Duda

CRYSTAL ENLIGHTENMENT
Katrina Raphaell

CRYSTAL HEALING
Katrina Raphaell

SILVER DENTAL FILLINGS • THE TOXIC TIMEBOMB
Sam Ziff

AWAKEN HEALING ENERGY THROUGH THE TAO
Mantak Chia

TAOIST SECRETS OF LOVE
Mantak Chia

THE LUNATION CYCLE
Dane Rudhyar

SELF HEALING, YOGA AND DESTINY
Elisabeth Haich

For a complete catalog write:

AURORA PRESS
P.O. BOX 573
SANTA FE NEW MEXICO 87504
(505) 989-9804

INDEX